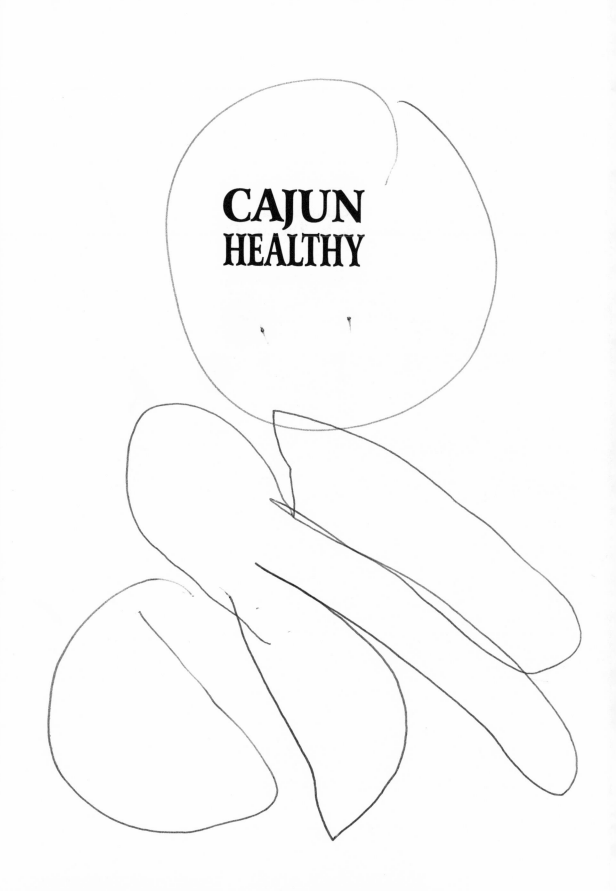

CAJUN
HEALTHY

**Other books
by Jude W. Theriot, CCP**

Cajun Quick (1992)
New American Light Cuisine (1988)
La Cuisine Cajun (1990)
La Meilleure de la Louisiane (1980)

CAJUN HEALTHY

Jude Theriot

PELICAN PUBLISHING COMPANY
Gretna 1995

First printing, September 1994
Second printing, June 1995

Library of Congress Cataloging-in-Publication Data

Theriot, Jude W.
    Cajun healthy / Jude W. Theriot.
        p.   cm.
    Includes index.
    ISBN 1-56554-085-9
        1. Cookery, American—Louisiana style.   2. Cookery, Cajun.   3. Low
-fat diet—Recipes.   I. Title.
    TX715.2.L68T47   1994
    641.59763—dc20   94-18499
                                                              CIP

Illustrations by Joyce Haynes

Manufactured in the United States of America

Published by Pelican Publishing Company, Inc.
1101 Monroe Street, Gretna, Louisiana 70053

To Madolyn McCoy, my personal secretary for over twelve years: I will always appreciate your dedication, loyalty, and friendship. I could not have found a more valuable and competent individual anywhere on earth. Thanks for all you do for me.

To Virginia Rue, a good friend, who kept pushing me to write this book: You told me that with all the weight I was losing and all the good food I was eating, I'd make a million on this book. You kept telling me the world needed this book. You even started taking advance orders! I appreciate your enthusiasm and friendship.

To Rose Manuel LeBlanc and Carroll Patrick LeBlanc, my parents-in-law, for their support through the tough times and for parenting my wife of over twenty-one years. I appreciate your caring and your friendship.

Contents

Introduction

Why did I write a no-fat/low-fat cookbook? I wrote it for the same reason I wrote all my cookbooks: me! That's right. I wrote this book because I needed a healthy cookbook for me. Those who know me know that I started to pick up a few pounds (awe heck, not a few pounds, many pounds). In fact, the word *tons* comes to mind. Seriously, I got *big*!

I have to credit a few people for helping me decide to embark on a healthy lifestyle and a serious change in my eating patterns. First, I owe the National Heart Attack Risk Study of St. Patrick's hospital kudos for starting me thinking about my weight and the increased risk of heart disease. This is a national study that has a branch at St. Patrick's hospital. They come in twice a year and take your blood pressure, weight, cholesterol, etc. They also bring with them certified staff nurses who talk to you about your potential risk of heart disease, changing your eating habits, and exercise. After a few visits, the seed was planted. This group doesn't use scare tactics; they provide information. That information concerned me enough to start thinking about my weight and lack of physical exercise.

Next on my list of people to thank is my doctor, Norman Davidson. Norman definitely got me thinking in his deadpan way. He told me something like this at my last physical: "I am really surprised that you don't appear to show any signs of coronary heart disease." He said that he almost hoped I had shown some signs, so he could convince me to start losing weight. Boy, did that start me thinking. Basically, he was saying that it was just a matter of time before I would start to have problems. At least, that's what I thought he was saying. He just spoke so softly and smiled and asked questions about my knowledge of food and why I had not put it to use. I mumbled something like I was a great teacher and great at telling others how to improve, but not really that good at following my own advice.

Anthony Robbins, a dynamic self-help instructor, helped me to realize that I have the power within myself to change my life. All I needed was the commitment! I listened to tape after tape, viewed a few of his videos, and one day, decided that I would change my direction and course of life. I did! That day, I decided that I would take the knowledge of food that I have been blessed with and use it to lose weight and keep it off.

My wife, Debbie, was another person who played a major role in my decision to make the lifestyle change. I guess it was when she finally gave up trying to get me to lose weight, that I decided I had to make a significant change. I realized that if she finally gave up and resigned herself to the fact that I would not, could not, and did not lose weight; I never would. Then I knew it was time for me to make a change.

Let me say that none of the people listed here know the extent of their impact on my way of thinking! I think it is important to say what I've said because perhaps you will be able to relate to this story. I'm not writing this only as a book to use to lose weight, even though I know firsthand that a low or very low-fat diet combined with consistent light exercise will cause you to lose weight. I am really just putting down recipes that I know are good—at least to me—and I am encouraging anyone who needs good and tasty food that is low in fat to look at this book and perhaps use the recipes.

The time commitment required to change your eating habits is not that significant when you consider that doing so will allow you more time to live. I needed this book not to increase the *quantity* of my life, but rather to make a significant impact on the *quality* of my life. I can honestly say, after losing seventy-nine pounds and multiple inches, that the quality of my life has dramatically improved. I've lost weight before, but never before have I felt that I would succeed. I've always been giving up things on diets, but now I am not dieting! I am eating my way to weight loss. I eat around three thousand calories most days. I am eating snacks all day long. I eat until I am full.

I need to quickly tell you that diet alone won't do it. You will have to do some kind of exercise. I decided to walk. When I started walking at the start of this lifestyle change, I could not walk a half mile, and it took me more than thirty minutes to try. I now am walking two and a half miles in about 40 to 45 minutes, depending on the day and where I am walking. I make a little better time walking on an outdoor high school track than I do on an indoor track that takes 13 laps to make a mile.

Exercise is not just a nice thing to do; it is vital and necessary. It helps to maintain your *lean muscle mass*. Why is lean muscle mass important? All my life I've been told that I had to raise my metabolism and that exercise would help do that. I always wondered just where my metabolism was located. Well guess what? Lean muscle mass is where your metabolism is—or at least where it is controlled. It is lean muscle that burns calories. If we diet and lose lean muscle mass in the process, we lower our metabolism. Now it begins to make sense. That's why I lost weight, but had less energy. As I dieted, my body needed less food because it was going to "sleep!" Add to that the fact that muscle weighs about five times what fat weighs. Another way of saying the same thing is that fat has five times the volume of muscle. No wonder I could lose so much weight. I was losing muscle. This time, I lost inches first. My clothes started to fit and actually started to get baggy. I have a belt that I was wearing when I started. It is kind of my marker. It is old, but I am still wearing it because it is an accurate marker of where I am going and where I have been. I am down ten inches on that belt in just over six months. I intend to wear that belt until I reach my goal, then I'm going to save it forever. It is my trophy. I want it to be a reminder of where I was and, more importantly, where I will not return. Like Tony Robbins says, I have changed who I am and how I view myself. That is the key!

Now I am using my knowledge of food and how the body metabolizes that food to ensure my success. If you need to share in that success, if you want to share in that success, or if you can simply use some delicious and easy-to-prepare no-fat/low-fat recipes, then this book is for you. But remember, I wrote this book for myself! That is not any different than any of my cookbooks. I always write for myself! I recommend that you make the recipes just like I make them the first time. There are wide margins on each page for a purpose. Make notes; write in the book: "I like this recipe!" or "This is a great recipe, but I really don't like the mushrooms, so cut the mushrooms and add more carrots and onions," or "Too hot, cut the red pepper," or "This recipe needs more . . ." A cookbook is a guidebook. It is intended to give you ideas and guidance. I expect you to really like some of my recipes, and I expect that you won't like some. We all have different tastes, likes, and dislikes. I write for me. If your tastes are similar to mine, you'll like most of my dishes. Where we differ, you may not care for a recipe. That's what makes life fun. We are all different! I don't view that as a weakness, but rather as a strength. Take my book and make it your book. Nothing would please me more than for you to tell me that you enjoy my book and that you have marked all over it and changed the things you wanted to change. I also like to hear from people on their individual likes and dislikes. It just might be that your way would taste better to me as well. Enjoy using this book, and I wish you a long, *Cajun Healthy*, and happy life.

A word of caution: Be sure to see your doctor before you start on any exercise program or change in your eating style. We all have specific needs and wants. Your doctor has to be consulted for your health's sake. You should have a team approach if you want to be successful. You need to talk to your physician and work out a plan that will work for you. Your doctor can help you with specifics on an exercise and eating plan.

Lagniappe

Lagniappe is a Cajun French word that means "a little something extra" or "a little something for nothing." In the olden days, whenever a Cajun would shop at a store or at a roadside stand, the proprietor would always throw in a little something with the purchase, just as a gesture of good will. It is somewhat similar to the "baker's dozen."

Today, the word has remained with its meaning, but alas, the custom is mostly gone. However, because I give you my *lagniappe* with each recipe, you get to experience just what the practice was like. These *lagniappe* sections are filled with hints, suggestions, ideas, cooking techniques, and things that will make using the recipe easier. They might also contain general cooking tips, bits of humor (at least as I see it), and little insights from my years of cooking. Additionally, you will find a complete list of nutritional values per serving with every recipe. There are occasional hints on freezing and refrigerating and bringing the food back to life for a "second showing."

When I travel around the country to teach my classes, my students tell me over and over again that they like this addition to my cookbooks. In fact, they tell me to put more of myself into the sections. I hope I've done that in this book. The *lagniappe* sections are somewhat expanded. I have also learned in my traveling around this great land that there are many people out there who really enjoy reading cookbooks just as some people enjoy reading novels. In fact, I heard from one such individual who was on a car trip with her husband. She was reading my last cookbook and just "laughing up a storm." Her husband looked over and said, "I thought you were reading a cookbook!" Now, I don't want to let you think that I am writing a book of comedy, but I do want you to enjoy my writing, especially in the *lagniappe* sections. I readily admit that I use the this section to step out and just talk to you.

I honestly hope that you enjoy the *lagniappe* section as much as you enjoy the recipes, and I hope that you take full advantage of them. I really believe that the *lagniappes* will make the overall experience of *Cajun Healthy* more rewarding, informative, engaging, and delectable!

NOTE: For all recipes, carbohydrate, fat, and protein values are given in grams; cholesterol and sodium values are given in milligrams. "Trace" indicates a negligible amount of that item. The values are for one serving or one tablespoon, unless otherwise indicated.

A food is considered to be nonfat when it has less than one gram of fat and when that small amount of fat does not impact on the overall caloric content of that food.

CAJUN
HEALTHY

Appetizers

GARDEN DIP

2 cups no-fat sour cream
1 .9-oz. packet vegetable
soup mix

1/2 tsp. Tabasco® Sauce
1/2 tsp. onion powder
1/4 tsp. garlic powder

Combine all the ingredients in a mixing bowl and mix together well. Return the mixture to the sour cream container, and refrigerate for at least two hours. Stir well. Serve as you would any dip, with nonfat crackers or chips or any vegetable for dipping. Serves 10.

Lagniappe: This dip will help you stick to a nonfat routine. One of the things people miss when they diet is regular food. This is as close to regular food as you can get. It has all of the taste and none of the guilt! Eat it with nonfat crackers, and eat to your heart's content.

This dip serves as a wonderful snack when you are craving something fattening, and your body and mind won't know you didn't really give in. I'm talking about when you come home from work and you are starving, but you haven't thought about what you are going to cook. This dip will do it! You will stop eating it sooner than you think. It is good, and it turns your appetite off for enough time to think about preparing dinner. Try it; you'll be amazed.

Calories—82; Fat—.4 g; Protein—6.9 g; Carbohydrates—19.7 g; Cholesterol—0 mg; Fiber—trace; Sodium—469 mg

3.4 of the 82 calories are from fat.
4% of the calories come from fat.

BLACK-EYED PEA DIP

Butter-flavored nonstick
  vegetable oil spray
1 medium onion, finely
  chopped
1/2 medium bell pepper,
  finely diced
1/4 cup minced celery
4 cloves garlic, crushed
  then minced
2 (15 to 16-oz.) cans
  black-eyed peas (nonfat
  peas)
1 tsp. Cajun Spice Mix (see
  page 274)

1 tsp. sweet basil
1/2 tsp. cumin powder
1/2 tsp. cayenne pepper
1/2 tsp. Tabasco® Sauce
2 tbsp. Worcestershire
  sauce
1/4 cup medium hot
  jalapeños, finely chopped
1 tbsp. red wine vinegar
1/2 cup cilantro, finely
  minced
1/4 cup green onion tops,
  finely minced
1/2 cup no-fat sour cream

In a large, heavy nonstick skillet, spray the butter-flavored vegetable oil. Heat the skillet over medium heat until hot, then add the onion, bell pepper, celery, and garlic. Sauté, stirring constantly, for 5 minutes, then add all the remaining ingredients except for the cilantro, green onions, and sour cream. Cook, stirring often for 15 minutes. Use a slotted spoon to crush the peas as you stir them. You should be able to mash most but not all of the peas. Add the three remaining ingredients, reduce the heat to low, and cook, stirring constantly for 5 more minutes. Remove from the heat and serve hot, or refrigerate and serve chilled. Serve with low-fat tortilla chips or nonfat crackers. Makes about 4 cups of dip.

Lagniappe: My mother always made me eat black-eyed peas on New Year's Day for good luck and wealth. I always hated them when I was growing up, but eating black-eyed peas once a year wasn't that bad. I don't know when it was that I actually started liking them, but I did. I like them so much now that I decided to put them in this dip. Now you can have good luck and wealth all year long—or at least a super dip! Given the choice—especially when you are hungry—I'm sure you'll choose the dip any day.

You can make this dip in advance and refrigerate it. I keep it tightly covered in the refrigerator for up to one week, if it lasts that long. It's great to have around as an instant filler snack. I also like it as a spread on French bread. I spread it on and put it under the broiler for a few minutes as sort of an open-face pea sandwich.

Per 1/4 cup serving:
Calories—61; Fat—.4 g; Protein—2.3 g; Carbohydrates—11.2 g;
Cholesterol—0 mg; Fiber—.6 g; Sodium—281 mg

4 of the 61 calories are from fat.
7% of the calories come from fat.

BOILED SHRIMP PICKLES

2 lb. Boiled Shrimp (see page 108), peeled and deveined
1 medium red bell pepper, cut into strips
1 medium onion, cut into circles
1 medium purple onion, cut into circles
3 cloves garlic, crushed and minced
1/4 cup celery, finely chopped
2 tsp. Cajun Spice Mix (see page 274)

1/3 cup sugar
1/4 cup light brown sugar
1 cup red wine vinegar
2 tsp. fresh basil, finely chopped
1/2 cup distilled white vinegar
1 tsp. Tabasco® Sauce
2 tbsp. white wine Worcestershire sauce
4 whole cloves
4 whole allspice
1 tsp. celery seeds

Place 1/3 of the shrimp in a layer on the bottom of a plastic container (or glass container) that has a tight-fitting lid. Cover with 1/3 of the red bell pepper strips, onion circles, purple onion circles, garlic and celery. Repeat the process two more times using 1/3 of each of the above each time. In a medium mixing bowl, mix all the remaining ingredients together and stir until most of the sugar is dissolved. Pour this mixture over the shrimp and vegetables, then tightly cover and refrigerate for at least 8 hours. Shake the container a few times during the refrigeration time to be sure all the flavors have blended. When you are ready to serve, just remove the lid and serve with toothpicks or dish shrimp onto a bed of shredded lettuce. Serve chilled. Serves 6.

Lagniappe: A great recipe for a covered dish. You can make it up to 24 hours in advance, then tightly cover and refrigerate it until you are ready to serve. This also makes a wonderful low-fat shrimp salad dressing; just make your salad and toss with the shrimp and enough of the liquid and pickled vegetables to coat the salad greens well. The flavor of the shrimp will create a wonderful dressing with practically no fat at all. I also like to bring this appetizer to a covered dish supper, especially when I know that there will be many high-fat dishes calling out my name! Eating shrimp takes the edge off of not being able to sample all the goodies that may be present. This is an example of the small changes and choices you have to make if you are going to be serious about eating low-fat foods. You have to plan for the things you can eat, but never plan to suffer. There are so many foods you can choose to help you stay healthy.

Calories—270; Fat—.5 g; Protein—31.8 g; Carbohydrates—30.3 g; Cholesterol—29 mg; Fiber—.4 g; Sodium—802 mg

5 of the 270 calories are from fat.
2% of the calories come from fat.

CAJUN WHITE BEAN DIP

Butter-flavored nonstick
  vegetable oil spray
1 medium onion, finely
  chopped
1/2 medium bell pepper,
  finely diced
1/4 cup finely minced celery
3 cloves garlic, crushed and
  finely minced
2 (15 to 16-oz.) cans white
  beans (great northern or
  navy beans)
1 tsp. Cajun Spice Mix (see
  page 274)
1 tsp. chili powder
1/2 tsp. cayenne pepper
1/2 tsp. Tabasco® Sauce
1 tbsp. white wine
  Worcestershire sauce
1/4 cup medium picante
  sauce
1/4 cup cilantro, finely
  minced
1/4 cup finely minced green
  onion tops
1/2 cup no-fat sour cream

Spray a large, heavy nonstick skillet with the butter-flavored vegetable oil. Heat the skillet over medium heat until hot, then add the onion, bell pepper, celery, and garlic. Sauté, stirring constantly, for 5 minutes; then add all the remaining ingredients, except for the cilantro, green onions, and sour cream. Cook, stirring often, for 15 minutes. Use a slotted spoon to crush the beans as you stir them. You should be able to mash most, but not all of the beans. Add the three remaining ingredients, reduce the heat to low, and cook, stirring constantly, for 5 more minutes. Remove from the heat and serve hot, or refrigerate and serve chilled. Serve with low-fat tortilla chips or nonfat crackers. Makes about 4 cups of bean dip.

Lagniappe: In the area of the state where I grew up, we didn't really start eating red kidney beans until I got out of high school. When you think of red beans, you are thinking of New Orleans. In Cajun country, most often the bean of choice was the white bean—either great northern beans or navy beans. I can remember many a bean, sausage, and rice meal growing up. It was always a white bean. Today, as Louisiana cultures have blended Cajun and Creole, North and South, city and country, things have changed. Today, I eat red beans at least as often as white beans.

With this recipe, I wanted to use the bean that I ate in my youth. It makes a delightful low-fat dip. You can refrigerate it, then just pull it out cold or pop it in the microwave for a quick warming. I like this dip as an appetite killer. Just a few dips will help take the edge off of starvation and help get you to the dinner table without passing out. It is an excellent choice of a low-fat snack that not only tastes good, but is really quite good for you.

Per 1/4 cup serving:
Calories—85; Fat—.2 g; Protein—5.4 g; Carbohydrates—15.5 g; Cholesterol—0 mg; Fiber—1.7 g; Sodium—297 mg

2 of the 85 calories are from fat.
2% of the calories come from fat.

OYSTERS DE LAC CHARLES

1/3 cup chili sauce	**24 large oysters in shells**
1/3 cup catsup	**(about 6 1/2 to 7 lb.)**
2 tsp. horseradish	**3 lb. rock salt**
1 tsp. Tabasco® Sauce	**4 strips bacon (2 oz.)**
1 medium shallot, minced	**Finely chopped green onion**
2 cloves garlic, minced	**tops, for garnish**

Preheat the oven to 425 degrees. In a medium-sized bowl, stir together the chili sauce, catsup, horseradish, Tabasco® Sauce, shallots, and garlic. Spread a 1/2-inch layer of rock salt in a rimmed baking sheet or 4 pie plates.

To shuck oysters: Scrub them well, then place an oyster, rounded side down, on the work surface. Grip the oyster with a towel to protect your hand, leaving the hinged end exposed. Force the tip of an oyster knife into the hinge. Twist the blade to pry the shells apart. Slide the knife along the inside of the upper shell, severing the muscle. Discard the upper shell. Slide the blade under the oyster to loosen it from the lower shell. Set the shell on the bed of rock salt. Repeat with the remaining oysters.

Spoon about 1 teaspoon of the cocktail sauce over each oyster. Bake the oysters in their rock salt beds in the preheated oven for 15 to 20 minutes, or until the edges curl.

Meanwhile, heat a medium-sized skillet over medium heat. Add the bacon and cook until it is crisp. Drain the bacon on a white paper towel, then crumble. Sprinkle bacon bits and green onion tops over the baked oysters before serving. Serves 8.

Lagniappe: Oysters are angelic just by themselves. Saucing and baking them makes them divine. This is a recipe in which I used to wrap each oyster with a whole slice of bacon, then broil it. I have found that the bacon taste still comes through quite nicely when I just use the crumbles; it no longer overwhelms the zesty flavor of the fresh oysters. You can mix the cocktail sauce ahead of time and store in the refrigerator, covered, for up to 2 days. Be sure to throw the used oyster shells away after they are served. It is too hard to sanitize them after use.

I keep my oysters in the shell in the coldest part of my refrigerator until I'm ready to use them, but I never leave them for more than a day or two. If you don't want to use fresh oyster shells, you can also serve this dish in ramekins. Just place about 3 oysters in each ramekin, serving 2 ramekins to each person. Spoon 3 teaspoons of cocktail sauce into each ramekin and bake as above.

Calories—100; Fat—5 g; Protein—6 g; Carbohydrates—7 g; Cholesterol—32 mg; Fiber—trace; Sodium—424 mg
44 of the 100 calories are from fat.
44% of the calories come from fat.

Note: This recipe exceeds the recommendation of the American Heart Association in that over 30 percent of the calories come from fat. While it is an excellent recipe, I want to make sure you realize it exceeds the 30 percent recommendation.

OYSTERS JOSEPHINE

1 tbsp. unsalted butter
1 lb. shrimp, peeled and
   deveined
3 cloves garlic, crushed and
   minced
1/4 cup finely chopped
   celery
6 large fresh mushrooms,
   sliced
1/2 cup all-purpose flour
1/2 tsp. thyme
1/2 tsp. sweet basil
2 whole bay leaves

1/4 cup evaporated skim
   milk
1/4 cup no-fat sour cream
1/4 cup dry sherry
1/2 tsp. Tabasco® Sauce
1/2 tsp. salt
1 tbsp. white wine
   Worcestershire sauce
2/3 cup catsup
24 oysters with their liquid
1/4 cup finely minced fresh
   parsley

Preheat the oven to 375 degrees. Heat a large nonstick skillet over low-medium heat until it is hot. Add the butter, and sauté the shrimp, onions, garlic, celery, and mushrooms together in the butter for 3 minutes over the low-medium heat. Add the flour, thyme, basil, and bay leaf; cook for 3 more minutes. Add the skim milk, sour cream, sherry, Tabasco® Sauce, salt, Worcestershire sauce, and catsup. Blend together until the sauce is smooth and thick.

In a medium-sized saucepan, poach the oysters in their liquid until they curl around the edges, about 4 minutes. Remove the oysters from the pan and drain them on white paper towels. Place the drained oysters in a 2-quart casserole or in individual au gratin dishes, cover them with the sauce, and sprinkle with the parsley. Bake at 375 degrees for about 17 minutes. Serve at once. Serves 4 as an appetizer.

Lagniappe: This is a unique and tasty oyster dish that is different from the usual oyster casserole. You can make the dish in advance, bake it, then refrigerate it for later use. I don't like to freeze this dish; I don't like the quality after it has defrosted.

Calories—370; Fat—7.5 g; Protein—8 g; Carbohydrates—37.6 g; Cholesterol—8 mg; Fiber—.3 g; Sodium—585 mg

68 of the 371 calories are from fat.
18% of the calories come from fat.

OYSTERS REBECCA

1 bunch curly fresh parsley
2 tbsp. fresh basil
3 cloves garlic
1 tsp. chopped shallots
8 large fresh mushrooms
1 cup chopped green
  onions
1 8-oz. pkg. fat-free cream
  cheese
1/3 cup unsweetened
  applesauce
1/2 tsp. Tabasco® Sauce

2 tbsp. Worcestershire
  sauce
1/2 tsp. fresh ground black
  pepper
1/2 tsp. salt
1/4 tsp. allspice
1 tsp. onion powder
1 cup fat-free cracker
  crumbs
24 fresh oysters, parboiled
Paprika to garnish

Preheat the oven to 450 degrees. In a food processor at high speed, chop the parsley, basil, garlic, shallots, mushrooms, and green onions until finely chopped. Add the cream cheese, applesauce, Tabasco® Sauce, Worcestershire sauce, black pepper, salt, allspice, and onion powder; blend until smooth. Add the cracker crumbs and blend together until they are blended into the sauce. Dry the oysters on white paper towels and place 3 parboiled oysters in each of 8 individual 6-ounce ramekins. Cover the oysters with generous amounts of the cream cheese sauce mixture, dust with paprika, and place in the preheated 450-degree oven until the sauce begins to bubble and becomes lightly browned, about 12 minutes. Serve hot. Serves 8.

Lagniappe: Oysters are always divine in a sauce. Unfortunately, sauces generally are high in fat and loaded with calories. This recipe gives you the taste of fancy oysters without the fat. The dish is made in minutes and can be completely mixed in the food processor. Parboiling the oysters is simple. Just pour the oysters and their liquor into a medium saucepan; then heat over low heat until the oysters become white and puffy and curl around the edges. Remove the oysters from the saucepan and place them on white paper towels to dry most of their juices. This is an extraordinary dish.

Calories—130; Fat—1.2 g; Protein—15.2 g; Carbohydrates—20.2 g; Cholesterol—22 mg; Fiber—1.5 g; Sodium—440 mg

11 of the 130 calories are from fat.
8% of the calories come from fat.

OYSTERS ROCKEFELLER

2 10-oz. pkg. frozen
　spinach, partially thawed
1 10-oz. pkg. frozen mus-
　tard greens, partially
　thawed
1 bunch green onions,
　chopped
1 stalk celery, broken into
　pieces
1 bunch parsley
1/2 head red tip lettuce
Liquid from 1 qt. oysters
2 1/2-oz. packets Butter
　Buds

1/2 cup Pernod liqueur
1/4 cup Worcestershire
　sauce
1 tsp. Tabasco® Sauce
1 tsp. Cajun Spice Mix (see
　page 274)
1/4 tsp. salt
3/4 cup bread crumbs
1 qt. oysters
10 lb. rock salt
8 pie pans
48 large oyster shell halves,
　scrubbed clean

Preheat the oven to 450 degrees. In a food processor, purée the spinach, mustard greens, green onions, celery, parsley, and red tip lettuce until very well blended. If you need a little liquid to blend, use some of the oyster liquid. Mix the puréed vegetables with the oyster liquid, Butter Buds, Pernod liqueur, Worcestershire sauce, Tabasco® Sauce, salt, and bread crumbs; blend together well. Pat the oysters dry on white paper towels. Fill the bottom of the pie pans with rock salt. Place an oyster on each of the half oyster shells, then cover it thickly with the Rockefeller sauce and place the shell in the rock salt. Put six stuffed shells in each pie pan. Bake at 450 degrees for 18 to 20 minutes, or until lightly browned. Serve hot with plenty of fresh French bread. Serves 8.

Lagniappe: This is a phenomenal copy of the rich Rockefeller sauce. Don't tell anyone this is a low-fat recipe; they won't be able to tell. The flavor and taste are so close to the real thing that you will be amazed.

A word of caution about using real oyster shells: Use shells that you have shucked yourself and keep them very cold until you are ready to use them. I usually shuck the number I need, then scrub the shells well and freeze them until I'm ready to use them. They will keep in the freezer for up to three months. I just defrost them and keep them on ice right up to the time I stuff them. Why do you need to take such care? Bacteria will grow on the shell if this care is not taken. Remember to throw the shells away after you use them once. Do not try to reuse them! After making this low-fat recipe once, you may never make the butter-loaded version again.

Calories—200; Fat—3 g; Protein—12.5 g; Carbohydrates—28.9 g; Cholesterol—48 mg; Fiber—2.6 g; Sodium—950 mg
27 of the 200 calories are from fat.
13% of the calories come from fat.

SAUTEED CRABMEAT

**Butter-flavored nonstick
  vegetable oil spray**
1 clove garlic, finely minced
**1/2 cup finely minced green
  onions**
1 tbsp. finely minced celery
1/2 cup dry white wine
**1 1/2-oz. packet Butter
  Buds**

1/4 tsp. Tabasco® Sauce
**1/4 cup finely minced fresh
  parsley**
1/2 lb. lump crabmeat
1/4 tsp. salt
**1/2 tsp. fresh ground black
  pepper**
1 tbsp. fresh lemon juice

Heat a nonstick skillet over medium heat until hot, then lightly spray it with the butter-flavored nonstick vegetable oil spray. Return to the heat and sauté the garlic, green onions, and celery for 2 minutes, stirring constantly. Add the wine, Butter Buds, and Tabasco® Sauce; then blend together well. Cook until the sauce thickens, then reduce the heat to a simmer. Cook until the liquid is reduced by about one-third. Add the parsley, crabmeat, salt, and black pepper. Shake the pan often, cook for 3 more minutes, then add the fresh lemon juice. Cook, shaking the pan, for 1 more minute. Serve at once, either on pasta or bread or as a topping for other seafood or meats. Serves 4.

Lagniappe: It really helps to use a nonstick skillet, because it allows you to use just the one spray of butter-flavored vegetable oil spray. We start out with a very light sauté, then move the dish to a butter-flavored braise. Try to only shake the pan which will help prevent tearing the crabmeat apart. If I serve this with pasta, I like to toss the pasta with the crabmeat and sauce or add it to the skillet and shake it around until the pasta is lightly coated. Use this sautéed crabmeat on top of pork loin or veal for another delightful treat. Do not make this in advance. The crabmeat is so delicate that it needs to be cooked just before you are ready to serve.

Calories—101; Fat—1 g; Protein—11 g; Carbohydrates—6.7 g; Cholesterol—45 mg; Fiber—.2 g; Sodium—360 mg

9 of the 101 calories are from fat.
9% of the calories come from fat.

SCAMPI BOREL

1 tbsp. extra virgin olive oil	1/2 tsp. Tabasco® Sauce
2 lb. shrimp (21-25 size), peeled and deveined	1/2 tsp. fresh ground black pepper
4 cloves garlic, crushed and minced	1/2 tsp. cayenne pepper
1 tsp. fresh rosemary (or 1/2 tsp. dried)	1/2 cup dry vermouth
	3 tbsp. fresh lime juice
2/3 tsp. salt	1/2 cup finely chopped fresh parsley

Heat a large skillet over medium-high heat until it is hot. Add the olive oil and heat it until it begins to smoke. Add the shrimp and sauté them in the oil until they are browned, about 4 minutes. Add the garlic and rosemary; cook for 2 minutes. Add the salt, Tabasco® Sauce, black pepper, and cayenne pepper and blend it in well. Deglaze the pan with the vermouth and lime juice, then reduce the heat to medium and cook until about half of the liquid is gone. Add the fresh parsley and cook for 1 more minute. Serve with plenty of hot fresh French bread. Serves 6.

Lagniappe: This is a low-fat version of a recipe that my Aunt Agnes Borel (Auntie) used to serve. It retains the wonderful flavors of the dish she served without the volumes of fat. I also altered the spices to increase and enhance the variety of flavors in order to fill the void created by the missing fat.

Calories—206; Fat—5 g; Protein—31.6 g; Carbohydrates—4.6 g; Cholesterol—231 mg; Fiber—.1 g; Sodium—499 mg

45 of the 206 calories are from fat.
22% of the calories come from fat.

SHRIMP LE CHAMPIGNON

Butter-flavored nonstick
  vegetable oil spray
1 bunch green onions,
  finely chopped
3 cloves garlic, crushed and
  finely minced
2 stalks celery, finely
  chopped
1/2 large red bell pepper,
  finely diced
1 qt. low sodium chicken
  broth (1 g fat per cup)

2 bay leaves
1 cup Pickapeppa sauce
2 tbsp. dry vermouth
1 tsp. Tabasco® Sauce
1 lb. large shrimp (24 per
  lb.), peeled and deveined
1 tsp. Cajun Spice Mix (see
  page 274)
1 lb. large fresh
  mushrooms, sliced

Lightly spray a medium-sized skillet with the butter-flavored nonstick vegetable oil, then place the skillet over medium heat. When it is hot, add the green onions, garlic, celery, and bell pepper and sauté for 3 minutes. Add the chicken broth and bay leaves, and bring the mixture to a boil. Let it boil for 5 minutes, stirring occasionally. Add the Pickapeppa sauce, vermouth, and Tabasco® Sauce and reduce the heat to low; simmer the sauce for 30 minutes, stirring occasionally.

When the sauce is just about through, spray another skillet with the butter-flavored spray and place over medium heat. Split the shrimp about halfway through from head to tail and season them with the Cajun Spice Mix. Brown the shrimp in the skillet, cooking all sides. They should split open and be nicely browned around the edges, about 3 minutes. Add the mushrooms and sauté with the shrimp, stirring often for 2 more minutes. Cover the shrimp and mushrooms with the sauce from the other skillet and let the shrimp and mushrooms simmer for 15 minutes. The sauce should thicken nicely. Serve hot with plenty of hot fresh French bread. Serves 4 as an appetizer.

Lagniappe: The key to this dish is the Pickapeppa sauce. You will find it near the Tabasco® Sauce and the Worcestershire sauce in the supermarket. It is available nationwide and has been around for quite a long time. It is a Jamaican sauce made with tomatoes, onions, sugar, and cane vinegar, and it is delicious. I like to sprinkle this sauce over fat-free cream cheese and spread it on a fat-free cracker. The combination is a real zinger! Just writing about it makes me hungry. Enjoy this great appetizer with the goodness of shrimp and wonderful fresh mushrooms. The mushrooms add an earthy quality that is most distinctive.

Calories—274; Fat—4 g; Protein—29.5 g; Carbohydrates—29.4 g; Cholesterol—174 mg; Fiber—1.3 g; Sodium—1436 mg

36 of the 274 calories are from fat.
13% of the calories come from fat.

SHRIMP MOUSSE

Olive oil-flavored nonstick
  spray
1 envelope plain unflavored
  gelatin
3 tbsp. evaporated skim
  milk
2 tbsp. cream sherry
1 8-oz. pkg. fat-free cream
  cheese
1 cup nonfat plain yogurt
2 cups Spicy Boiled
  Shrimp, chopped (see
  page 108)
1 cup minced celery

1/2 cup minced green
  onions
1/2 tsp. Tabasco® Sauce
1 tbsp. fresh lemon juice
1 tbsp. Worcestershire
  sauce
1/2 tsp. fresh ground black
  pepper
1/4 tsp. white pepper
1 tsp. onion powder
1/2 tsp. salt
1/4 cup minced fresh
  parsley
2 tsp. prepared horseradish

Spray the bottom of a four-cup mold with the vegetable oil spray; set aside. Sprinkle the gelatin over the milk and the sherry in a medium-sized saucepan. Let it stand for 3 minutes. Add the cream cheese to the pot and place over medium heat until the cheese melts, stirring often. Add all the remaining ingredients, except for the last two. Cook, stirring constantly, for 4 minutes. Add the parsley and horseradish; blend together well. Pour the mixture into the four-cup mold, cover with plastic wrap, and refrigerate until the mixture is firm. To serve, unmold onto a nice serving plate and serve with nonfat crackers or fresh vegetables. Makes about 4 cups of shrimp mousse. Serves 12.

Lagniappe: Shrimp mousse is a Louisiana favorite. You will scarcely notice the difference between this excellent alternative and the regular type. This mousse is outstanding for parties or for entertaining, but it is also wonderful just to keep handy for when you get a severe case of the nibbles! I like to keep something like this in the refrigerator because it looks and tastes like real food. A few crackers covered with this delicious mousse will kill your appetite and make you think you are eating rich and elegant food. I do like to use a mold that has a seafood look to it. It doesn't really improve the taste, but it makes you think it does.

Calories—90; Fat—.8 g; Protein—12.8 g; Carbohydrates—6.4 g; Cholesterol—68 mg; Fiber—.1 g; Sodium—299 mg

7 of the 90 calories are from fat.
8% of the calories come from fat.

STUFFED ARTICHOKE HEARTS

1 tbsp. olive oil
1 bunch green onions, finely chopped
6 cloves garlic, finely minced
1 tsp. finely minced shallots
1/4 cup finely minced celery
1/4 cup finely minced red bell pepper
6 slices fat-free whole wheat bread, diced
1/2 cup dry white wine

1/2 cup chicken broth
1/2 cup Italian seasoned bread crumbs
1/2 cup nonfat parmesan cheese
2 tbsp. romano cheese
1/2 tsp. Tabasco® Sauce
1 tbsp. white wine Worcestershire sauce
1 tsp. dried basil
1/2 tsp. dried oregano
1 8.5-oz. can artichoke hearts

Preheat the oven to 375 degrees. Heat the olive oil in a medium-sized saucepan over medium heat until hot. Sauté the green onions, garlic, shallots, celery, and red bell pepper in the olive oil for 5 minutes, or until the vegetables are limp and begin to brown. Add the bread, and sauté for 1 minute. Add the white wine and chicken broth, and heat for 2 minutes over medium heat. Add the Italian seasoned bread crumbs, nonfat parmesan cheese, Romano cheese, Tabasco® Sauce, Worcestershire sauce, basil, and oregano. Blend together well.

Cut each artichoke heart into four pieces. Make a round ball with the stuffing mix and form into the artichoke heart quarters. Press the stuffing well into the heart. Bake at 375 degrees until golden brown, about 15 minutes. Serve hot. Serves 6.

Lagniappe: You can make this dish well in advance and refrigerate or freeze it until you are ready to use. If you are going to freeze or refrigerate, do so before baking. I like to freeze these on a flat sheet. Place the stuffed hearts on the sheet and cover the sheet with plastic wrap. Freeze until the hearts are hard (at least overnight). Remove the tray, place the hearts in a zip-lock freezer bag, label and date the contents, and freeze for later use. It is very important to date and label anything you freeze. You should try to use frozen food soon after freezing for best results. I like to use frozen food within two months of freezing.

Calories—182; Fat—3.5 g; Protein—7.4 g; Carbohydrates—33.6 g; Cholesterol—3 mg; Fiber—3.5 g; Sodium—667 mg

32 of the 182 calories are from fat.
18% of the calories come from fat.

STUFFED JALAPENOS

1 8-oz. can seeded mild
  jalapeños
Ice water to cover
1 8-oz. container fat-free
  cream cheese
1/4 cup sharp cheddar
  cheese, finely grated

2 tbsp. onion, finely minced
2 tbsp. finely minced red
  bell pepper
3 tbsp. no-fat sour cream
1/4 tsp. Tabasco® Sauce
1 tsp. Worcestershire sauce

Wash the jalapeños with cold water and cut them in half lengthwise. Place the cut jalapeños in a small bowl and cover with ice water, then set aside for later use. In another mixing bowl, cream the fat-free cream cheese, cheddar cheese, onion, red bell pepper, sour cream, Tabasco® Sauce, and Worcestershire sauce with an electric mixer until well blended and smooth. Remove the jalapeños from the ice water and drain them on paper towels. Stuff each of the halves with the cheese mixture, then cover with plastic wrap and refrigerate until ready to serve. Serves 6 as an appetizer.

Lagniappe: I use the mild jalapeños because there are so many people who can't take the heat of the hot ones. Interestingly enough, this stuffing helps to cool your mouth right after it gets hot! The cream cheese and sour cream have a calming effect on the capsaicin oil, which makes the pepper hot, so it's like taking a hot and cold shower at once. It's invigorating or foolish, depending on how you look at it! Don't let the ease of this recipe deter you, it is scrumptious.

Calories—68; Fat—1.7 g; Protein—7.3 g; Carbohydrates—4.4 g; Cholesterol—12 mg; Fiber—.3 g; Sodium—608 mg

15 of the 68 calories are from fat.
23% of the calories come from fat.

STUFFED MUSHROOMS KATHLEEN

3 lb. large mushrooms (with large caps)
Butter-flavored nonstick vegetable oil spray
2 tbsp. extra virgin olive oil
1 medium onion, finely chopped
1/2 cup finely diced bell pepper
3 cloves garlic, minced
1 cup chicken broth or chicken stock
1 cup dry white wine
2 tsp. Cajun Spice Mix (see page 274)

1 lb. small shrimp, peeled, deveined, and finely chopped
1/2 tsp. Tabasco® Sauce
1/2 cup nonfat parmesan cheese
3/4 cup seasoned bread crumbs
1 1/2-oz. packet Butter Buds
1 lb. lump crabmeat
1/2 cup minced green onions
1/4 cup minced fresh parsley

Preheat the oven to 375 degrees. Separate the stems from the mushroom caps carefully so the caps don't break. Set the caps aside, finely chop the stems, and set aside for later use. Spray the mushroom caps with the butter-flavored nonstick vegetable oil spray and place them in the oven for 10 minutes. Remove and let them cool for later use.

Heat a large nonstick skillet over medium heat until hot, then add the olive oil and heat until it begins to smoke. Add the onions, bell pepper, garlic, and the finely chopped mushroom stems; sauté for 5 minutes, stirring often. Add the chicken broth, dry white wine, Cajun Spice Mix, shrimp, and Tabasco® Sauce. Simmer for 10 more minutes over medium heat, stirring constantly. Remove the skillet from the heat and stir in the parmesan cheese, bread crumbs, Butter Buds, crabmeat, green onions, and parsley. The mixture should be warm enough to blend together thoroughly stirring with a large spoon. Stuff the cooled caps with the stuffing mix, then place on a baking sheet. Bake at 375 degrees for 15 minutes. Serve at once. Serves 8.

Lagniappe: This is a spectacular appetizer! It is also good enough to serve as an entree. If you have a food processor, you can chop all your vegetables very finely in the processor. Depending on the size of the caps, you may have some dressing mix left; if you do, it makes great stuffing for just about anything. I like to use it to stuff tomato halves or squash halves. When I stuff tomatoes, I bake them at 425 degrees for about 20 minutes. Before I stuff squash halves, I scrape a little of the squash meat out to make enough room to hold the stuffing, then I bake the squash at 350 degrees for 30 minutes. All three uses of the stuffing mix are mouth-watering. Enjoy!

Calories—291; Fat—6.5 g; Protein—29.2 g; Carbohydrates—26.2 g; Cholesterol—132 mg; Fiber—1.4 g; Sodium—835 mg

59 of the 291 calories are from fat.
20% of the calories come from fat.

STUFFED MUSHROOMS CHAD THOMAS

16 large fresh mushrooms
1/2 cup minced green onions
1/2 cup grated nonfat mozzarella cheese
1/4 cup minced fresh parsley

2 cloves garlic, finely minced
1/3 cup nonfat Italian dressing
2 tbsp. Italian seasoned bread crumbs

Wash and clean the mushrooms, then drain on paper towels. Remove all the mushroom stems and finely chop them. Place the chopped mushroom stems in a large bowl. Add the remaining ingredients, except for the vegetable oil spray, and stir together well. Allow the mixture to stand in the refrigerator for 2 hours, covered. Spoon the mixture into each mushroom cap, heaping the mixture on. Lightly spray the bottom of a baking sheet and place the stuffed mushroom caps on the sheet. Lightly spray with the vegetable oil spray. Bake at 375 degrees for 15 minutes, or until golden brown and the cheese has melted. Serves 4 and makes 16 stuffed caps.

Lagniappe: I know that I always tell you never to wash mushrooms, but every rule has its exceptions. In this case, *never* means *never unless I say so!* Actually, I want these mushrooms washed so the water that is absorbed will help to steam and tenderize the mushroom caps. This is simple, elegant, and easy. Don't let it fool you; it is great tasting and low in both fat and calories. Enjoy!

Calories—79; Fat—.6 g; Protein—7.5 g; Carbohydrates—11.8 g; Cholesterol—4 mg; Fiber—1.5 g; Sodium—484 mg

5 of the 79 calories are from fat.
6% of the calories come from fat.

Soups and Gumbos

BEAN AND PASTA SOUP

2 14.5-oz. cans beef broth
1 can water
8 oz. dry non-egg pasta
1/2 tsp. salt
1 tsp. Tabasco® Sauce
1 1/2 tsp. onion powder
1/2 tsp. garlic powder
1 tsp. sweet basil
1/2 tsp. oregano leaves

1 8-oz. can stewed
  tomatoes
1 17-oz. can whole kernel
  corn, drained
1 15.5-oz. can great
  northern beans and liquid
1 15-oz. can light red
  kidney beans

In a large saucepan over medium-high heat, bring the beef broth and water to a hard boil. When at a full boil, add the pasta, salt, Tabasco® Sauce, onion powder, garlic powder, basil, and oregano; cook for 5 minutes, stirring to prevent sticking. Add the stewed tomatoes and corn. Cook for 2 more minutes, then add both cans of beans with their liquid. Cook for 3 more minutes. Serve hot. Serves 6.

Lagniappe: This is a wonderfully easy soup that is filled with flavor and is very filling. Complete with complex carbohydrates, protein, and a wholesome taste, it is sure to please. This is down for a serving of six, but it is so low in fat that you can have two servings if you like. You'll feel like you've eaten a complete meal and, for that matter, you have. It only takes a few minutes to make and you have a dish that will satisfy you. This soup is great for lunch or an evening meal. You can make it in advance, but it has more liquid just after it is made. If given the chance, all the pasta and beans have a tendency to absorb the liquid and make the soup thicker. The flavor intensifies, but the liquid significantly decreases. All in all, this is the soup that helped me through the tough days when I was starving and needed to eat something quickly. It is ready in a jiffy and good to the last bite.

Calories—316; Fat—2.5 g; Protein—15.3 g; Carbohydrates—61 g; Cholesterol—0 mg; Fiber—8 g; Sodium—1458 mg

22 of the 316 calories are from fat.
7% of the calories come from fat.

BOUILLABAISSE CAJUN

1 tbsp. olive oil
1 large onion, sliced
2 stalks celery, julienned
1 leek, julienned
3 large carrots, julienned
4 cloves garlic, crushed and
   minced
3 large tomatoes, peeled
   and diced
2 tbsp. tomato paste
2 cups Sauterne wine
3 qt. low sodium chicken
   broth
1/8 tsp. saffron
3 whole bay leaves
1 tsp. Tabasco Sauce
1/2 tsp. black pepper
1/2 tsp. cayenne pepper
1 tsp. salt

1 whole lobster tail (16
   oz.), cut into 8 pieces
   (shell on)
1 lb. large shrimp, with the
   shells on
1 lb. sea scallops
16 medium clams, washed
   and scrubbed clean
16 medium mussels,
   washed and scrubbed
   clean
1 lb. red snapper, cut into
   bite-size pieces
1 cup Herbsaint or Pernod
   liqueur
1 cup finely chopped green
   onions
1/2 cup finely minced fresh
   parsley

Heat a large soup pot or gumbo pot over medium heat until hot, then add the olive oil and heat until it is hot. Add the onion, celery, leeks, and carrots and sauté for 5 minutes. Add the garlic, diced tomatoes, and tomato paste. Let it cook for 5 minutes. Add the white wine, chicken broth, saffron, bay leaves, Tabasco Sauce, black pepper, cayenne, and salt and simmer for 15 minutes. Add the lobster, shrimp, sea scallops, clams, and mussels . Bring back to a boil, then reduce the heat to low and let the seafood simmer in the bouillabaisse for 20 minutes. Add the red snapper and cook for 10 more minutes. Adjust seasonings, add the Herbsaint or Pernod, green onions, and parsley. Simmer for 2 more minutes, then serve at once with plenty of hot fresh French bread. Serves 8.

Lagniappe: Bouillabaisse, with all it's incredible ingredients, can now be made just about anywhere in the country. We have such wonderful seafood readily available all over. This soup brings together the bounty of the sea in a Cajun spicy dish. It is a very impressive-looking soup with a variety of tastes. Be sure to scrub the clam and mussel shells well.

They should be tightly closed until you put them in the hot liquid. Be sure to check the shells after they are cooked; they should be open. If they don't open, discard them and don't eat them. There is a good chance that they are bad or were improperly handled from the time they were fished from their beds. Some people don't like to use the shells, but it definitely improves the taste of the soup as well as the eye appeal. I strongly recommend the use of the clean, fresh shells.

Calories—408; Fat—7.3 g; Protein—50 g; Carbohydrates—19.6 g; Cholesterol—155 mg; Fiber—1.3 g; Sodium—1797 mg

66 of the 408 calories are from fat.
16% of the calories come from fat.

CATFISH COUBILLION

2 tbsp. peanut oil
1/3 cup all-purpose flour
2 medium onions, chopped
1 large bell pepper, chopped
2 stalks celery, chopped
3 cloves garlic, finely minced
1 10-oz. can RoTel diced tomatoes and green chilies
2 15-oz. cans tomato sauce
2 cups water
2 tsp. Cajun Spice Mix (see page 274)

1 tsp. paprika
1/2 tsp. cayenne pepper
2 whole bay leaves
1/2 tsp. Tabasco® Sauce
3 lb. catfish fillets, cut into thirds
1 cup chopped green onions, chopped
1/2 cup minced fresh parsley
6 cups cooked long grain white rice

In a large gumbo pot over medium heat, heat the peanut oil until hot. Add the flour and cook to make a brown roux by stirring constantly until the golden dark brown color is reached. When the color is reached, add the onions, bell pepper, celery, and garlic and sauté in the roux for 4 minutes. Add the RoTel tomatoes and the tomato sauce, then cook for 12 minutes, stirring often. Add the water, Cajun Spice Mix, paprika, cayenne pepper, bay leaves, and Tabasco Sauce; reduce the heat to low and let the coubillion simmer for 35 minutes. Add the catfish, raise the heat to medium, and cook, stirring occasionally, for 12 minutes. Add the green onions and parsley, stir them in well, and cook for 5 more minutes. Serve hot over cooked white rice. Serves 8.

Lagniappe: This is an old Cajun favorite. Use the kind of fish you have. While it is great with catfish because the farm-raised meat is so sweet and cooks fast, it is also great with whatever fish you happen to have. Just adjust the cooking time according to the type of fish you add. This is a Cajun take-off on the French court bouillon. In France, the sauce usually had wine in it, and it was used to boil the fish. In Cajun Country, the sauce is as important as the fish, and it is always eaten over rice. It's easy, and the blended flavors will drive you wild!

Calories—501; Fat—11 g; Protein—37.4 g; Carbohydrates—56 g; Cholesterol—98 mg; Fiber—2.1 g; Sodium—1651 mg

99 of the 501 calories are from fat.
20% of the calories come from fat.

CHICKEN AND ANDOUILLE GUMBO

1/4 cup peanut oil
1 1/4 cups all-purpose flour
2 large onions, chopped
1 large bell pepper, seeded and chopped
2 stalks celery, finely chopped
5 cloves garlic, minced
5 whole chicken breasts, skin and bones removed
2 tsp. Cajun Spice Mix (see page 274)
6 14.5-oz. cans low sodium and fat chicken broth
2 tbsp. Worcestershire sauce

1 tsp. Tabasco® Sauce
1 tsp. onion powder
1/2 tsp. cayenne pepper
1/2 tsp. garlic powder
1 tsp. sweet basil
1/4 tsp. thyme
2 large bay leaves
1/2 lb. lean andouille sausage, sliced very thin
1 cup finely chopped green onions
1/2 cup finely chopped fresh parsley
8 cups cooked white long grain rice
Filé powder to taste

In a very heavy gumbo pot or large, heavy saucepot, heat the oil over medium heat. When it is hot, add the flour. Cook over medium-high heat, stirring constantly, until the roux (flour-and-oil mixture) turns dark brown. When the dark brown color is reached, add the onions, bell pepper, celery, and garlic. Sauté the vegetables in the roux for 6 minutes. Cut the chicken breasts in half and season with all the Cajun Spice Mix. Add the seasoned breasts, and cook in the hot roux mixture for 10 more minutes, stirring constantly. Carefully add the chicken broth (it has a tendency to steam and bubble up when added to the hot roux), Worcestershire sauce, and Tabasco® Sauce. Stir until the roux has completely dissolved into the liquid. Add the onion powder, cayenne pepper, garlic powder, basil, thyme, and bay leaves; bring the gumbo to a boil. When it begins to boil, reduce the heat to low, add the andouille sausage and let the gumbo cook at a simmer for 40 minutes. Adjust the seasonings to taste with the Cajun Spice Mix, and cook for 10 more minutes. Add the green onions and parsley and cook for 5 more minutes over low heat. Serve with plenty of filé powder over cooked white rice in individual serving bowls. Serves 10.

Lagniappe: This gumbo cooks this quickly because we are just using the chicken breast. The flavor is still good because we use the chicken broth, so don't try to substitute water, the gumbo will be too flat. The broth enhances the chicken flavor you get from the breast meat. Remember, this roux will be much drier than usual, so you must constantly stir it while you are cooking it and cooking the breast meat in the roux.

As usual, gumbo is an excellent make-ahead dish. The flavor is greatly enhanced if you make it the day before you serve it. To reheat, just place over medium-low heat and bring the gumbo to serving temperature, stirring occasionally. It is possible to just make Chicken Gumbo by leaving out the andouille sausage, which will lower the calories by about 71 and cut the fat by 6.1 grams. You lose that rich, smoky flavor that the andouille adds, but you still have a great-tasting gumbo. You can use this recipe to make Chicken and Okra Gumbo by adding 2 pounds of cut frozen okra to the gumbo when you add the chicken broth and by substituting 1/2 pound of very lean tasso for the andouille. Otherwise, cook the dish exactly as above. *Ça c'est beaucoup bon!*

Calories—503; Fat—15.2 g; Protein—35.4 g; Carbohydrates—53 g; Cholesterol—88 mg; Fiber—.7 g; Sodium—1165 mg

137 of the 503 calories are from fat.
27% of the calories come from fat.

CRAWFISH GUMBO

1/4 cup peanut oil
1 cup all-purpose flour
2 large onions, chopped
1 large bell pepper, seeded
  and chopped
2 stalks celery, finely
  chopped
4 cloves garlic, minced
1 15-oz. can stewed toma-
  toes
10 cups Seafood Stock
  (see page 57) or hot
  water
2 tbsp. Worcestershire
  sauce

2 tsp. Cajun Spice Mix (see
  page 274)
1 tsp. Tabasco® Sauce
1/2 tsp. sweet basil
3 large bay leaves
3 lb. crawfish tails
1 cup finely chopped green
  onions
1/2 cup finely chopped
  fresh parsley
7 cups cooked white long
  grain rice
Filé powder to taste

In a very heavy gumbo pot or large, heavy saucepot, heat the oil over medium heat until it is hot. Add the flour and cook over medium-high heat, stirring constantly, until the roux (flour and oil mixture) turns dark brown. When the dark brown color is reached, add the onions, bell pepper, celery, and garlic and sauté in the roux for 6 minutes. Add the stewed tomatoes and cook for 5 more minutes. Carefully add the Seafood Stock or water (it has a tendency to steam and bubble up when added to the hot roux), Worcestershire sauce, Cajun Spice Mix, and Tabasco® Sauce. Stir until the roux has completely dissolved into the liquid. Add the basil and the bay leaves, and bring the gumbo to a boil. When it begins to boil, reduce the heat to low and let the gumbo cook at a simmer for 1 hour.

Add the crawfish tails and cook for 30 more minutes over low heat. Adjust the seasonings to taste with the Cajun Spice Mix. Add the green onions and parsley, and cook for 5 more minutes over low heat. Serve with plenty of filé powder over cooked white rice in individual serving bowls. Serves 10.

Lagniappe: Yes, you can have gumbo on a low-fat diet. Notice that we are making the roux with just 1/4 cup of oil, but all the flour. Don't try to make a gumbo with browned flour alone. It is not a roux! It is just dark flour. While it will look similar, it does not have the chemical properties of a roux, so you won't have real gumbo. The dish will taste very pasty, almost like paper maché. Here we make a real roux, but we cut the oil down significantly. You will notice that the roux will be much drier than usual. That is okay, just be sure to stir constantly during the roux-making process.

Gumbo is an excellent make-ahead dish. In fact, the flavor improves if you make it the day before you serve. To reheat, just place over medium-low heat and bring the gumbo to serving temperature, stirring occasionally. You can use this same recipe to make Shrimp Gumbo by substituting 3 1/2 pounds of peeled and deveined shrimp for the crawfish. Just cook the dish exactly as above, except for the crawfish. *Bon appétit!*

Calories—415; Fat—7.6 g; Protein—31.2 g; Carbohydrates—53.5 g; Cholesterol—72 mg; Fiber—1 g; Sodium—950 mg

68 of the 415 calories are from fat.
16% of the calories come from fat.

CREAM OF CRAB SOUP

1 tbsp. unsalted butter
1 medium onion, finely
  chopped
1/4 cup finely chopped
  celery
1/4 cup finely diced red bell
  pepper
3 tbsp. all-purpose flour
1 cup low-sodium chicken
  broth
1 tsp. salt

1/2 tsp. black pepper
1/2 tsp. sweet basil
1/4 tsp. cayenne pepper
1/4 tsp. white pepper
1/4 tsp. Tabasco® Sauce
1 qt. skim milk
1/2 cup no-fat sour cream
1 lb. jumbo lump crabmeat
1/2 tsp. minced fresh
  parsley

Heat a large, heavy saucepan over medium heat until hot. Add the butter and let it melt, then add the onions, celery, and bell pepper. Sauté until the onions are clear and limp, about 5 minutes. Add the flour and cook, stirring constantly, for 4 minutes. Add the chicken broth, salt, black pepper, sweet basil, cayenne, and white pepper and blend in; the sauce will thicken quickly. Add the Tabasco® Sauce and skim milk and stir until smooth. Add the sour cream and stir until smooth. Add the crabmeat, reduce the heat to low, and let the soup simmer for 5 minutes, stirring occasionally. Add the parsley, blend it in, simmer for 2 more minutes, then serve. Serves 6.

Lagniappe: Anything made with crabmeat is good, but this soup is spectacular. This recipe takes skim milk and enriches it by adding the no-fat sour cream. No-fat sour cream is wonderful to cook with because it takes heat well. It doesn't curdle as much as regular sour cream, which means it can take higher heat without separating. You'll be surprised at just how much this soup resembles a high-fat version.

Calories—193; Fat—3.4 g; Protein—22 g; Carbohydrates—17.5 g; Cholesterol—67 mg; Fiber—.2 g; Sodium—655 mg

31 of the 193 calories are from fat.
16% of the calories come from fat.

HOMEMADE CHICKEN SOUP

2 large chicken breasts
1/2 gallon cold water
1 large onion, chopped
1 cup shredded fresh
cabbage
1 cup carrots, cut into thin
circles
1/2 cup minced celery,
minced
1/2 cup stewed tomatoes

2 cloves garlic, minced
1 tbsp. red bell pepper,
diced
1 1/2 tsp. Cajun Spice Mix
(see page 274)
1/2 tsp. Tabasco® Sauce
1/2 tsp. onion powder
1/2 tsp. sweet basil
2 tbsp. minced fresh
parsley

Cut the chicken into small bite-size pieces and place them in a stock pot. Add the remaining ingredients and bring to a boil over high heat. When the soup comes to a boil, lower the heat to a simmer and cook for 2 hours, covered. Remove from the heat, let it stand for 3 minutes, then serve. Serves 4.

Lagniappe: This is a simple, low-fat version of homemade chicken soup. It has all the goodness, minus the fat of regular chicken soup. It is easy to do; just put it into a pot and cook for 2 hours. It is a great soup. Soup is the perfect food to eat when you are trying to lose weight because it takes time to eat. It therefore tends to fill you up, not out. Serve with fat-free crackers, and you have a nice meal; or you can serve this soup as a first course with almost any dinner. Feel free to substitute your favorite vegetables or change the amount of each in the dish. You can either prepare this soup in advance and freeze or refrigerate it for later use. Just cover it tightly and either refrigerate or freeze. To reheat, just heat in a pot over low heat until the soup is hot.

Calories—188; Fat—3.9 g; Protein—28.4 g; Carbohydrates—10.3 g; Cholesterol—73 mg; Fiber—1.2 g; Sodium—336 mg

35 of the 188 calories are from fat.
19% of the calories come from fat.

NAVY BEAN SOUP

2 14.5-oz. cans beef broth
1 broth can cold water
1 cup raw macaroni
1 medium onion, finely
  chopped
1/2 cup minced red bell
  pepper
1/2 cup finely chopped
  celery
3 cloves garlic, minced

3 15-oz. cans navy beans,
  with liquid
1/4 cup minced parsley
1/2 cup finely chopped
  green onions
1/4 cup dry white wine
1/2 tsp. salt
1 tsp. sweet basil
1 tsp. Tabasco® Sauce

Heat the beef broth in a large saucepan over medium-high heat until it begins to boil. Add the water and raw macaroni, let it return to a boil, then reduce the heat to medium and cook for 5 minutes. Add the remaining ingredients and cook for 5 more minutes, stirring often. Serve hot. Serves 8.

Lagniappe: This is simple cooking and super taste made easy and low-fat. What you get is a complex carbohydrate (pasta) combined with an incomplete protein (beans) joining together to give you a complete protein that is very low in fat. It is almost just a "dump-dump" dish—a dish that you just open cans and dump them into the pot. This combination makes for good eating that is very satisfying. I do not recommend making this in advance because the noodles are best just after being cooked. When they sit for any length of time, they will absorb a lot of the liquid in the soup and swell to such a degree that they lose their appeal. Make it, serve it, and enjoy!

Calories—272; Fat—1.5 g; Protein—14.1 g; Carbohydrates—50 g; Cholesterol—.5 mg; Fiber—5.1 g; Sodium—1356 mg

14 of the 272 calories are from fat.
5% of the calories come from fat.

OYSTER AND ARTICHOKE SOUP

1 tbsp. unsalted butter
1 medium onion, finely chopped
2 stalks celery, finely chopped
3 tbsp. all-purpose flour
1 qt. skim milk
1 qt. chicken broth
1 cup no-fat sour cream
3 1/2-oz. packets Butter Buds
1 tsp. Tabasco® Sauce
1 tsp. salt
1/2 tsp. black pepper
1/2 tsp. cayenne pepper
1/2 tsp. sweet basil
1/4 tsp. thyme
2 large bay leaves
1 qt. oysters and their liquid
2 14-oz. cans artichoke hearts
1/4 cup finely minced fresh parsley

Heat the butter in a large nonstick saucepan over medium heat. When the butter has melted, sauté the onions and celery for 5 minutes, then add the flour and cook for 5 more minutes stirring constantly. Add the skim milk, chicken broth, sour cream, and Butter Buds and stir until well blended. Add the remaining ingredients, except for the parsley, and let the soup come to a low boil. Reduce to a low simmer and cook for 15 minutes. Add the parsley and cook for 3 more minutes. Serve hot. Serves 8.

Lagniappe: This is a low-fat version of a very popular Louisiana soup. Oyster soup or oyster broth is an ambrosial dish, but oysters with artichokes are divine! You can make this soup in advance and refrigerate for later use. The flavor actually improves if you make it the day before you want to serve it, and refrigerate it until you are ready to serve. The flavors blend in the cold, making a more intense dish. To serve, just heat it over low heat until it is hot enough to eat.

Calories—282; Fat—4.5 g; Protein—20.5 g; Carbohydrates—37.7 g; Cholesterol—56 mg; Fiber—1 g; Sodium—1223 mg

41 of the 282 calories are from fat.
15% of the calories come from fat.

POTAGE AUX POMME DE TERRE

4 large white potatoes,
  peeled and sliced
2/3 cup finely chopped
  celery
1 cup finely minced green
  onions
1 clove garlic, minced
2 cups low-fat chicken
  broth
1 tsp. salt

1/2 tsp. fresh ground black
  pepper
1 1/2 cups skim milk
1 1/2-oz. packet Butter
  Buds
1/4 tsp. Tabasco® Sauce
3 tbsp. no-fat sour cream
2 tbsp. finely minced fresh
  parsley

In a large saucepot over medium heat, combine the potatoes, celery, green onions, chicken broth, salt, and black pepper. Cover and cook for 15 minutes, or until the potatoes are tender. With a slotted spoon or potato masher, mash the potatoes until there are no large pieces. Add the milk, Butter Buds, and Tabasco® Sauce. Return to the heat and stir together until well blended. Add the sour cream and parsley, and blend in until the sour cream is completely dissolved. Serve hot or cold. Serves 6.

Lagniappe: This is a simple potato soup recipe. The Butter Buds and no-fat sour cream help to make this soup taste as rich as rich can be. I like it because it is made in one pot from start to finish. Potatoes are a great complex carbohydrate that go a long way toward filling you up.

You can make this soup ahead of time and refrigerate it for up to 3 days. I don't like to freeze this soup because it separates too much after it is thawed.

Calories—166; Fat—.6 g; Protein—5.6 g; Carbohydrates—38.5 g; Cholesterol—1.3 mg; Fiber—3.3 g; Sodium—777 mg

5 of the 166 calories are from fat.
3% of the calories come from fat.

RED BELL PEPPER SOUP

2 large red bell peppers,
   cut into large pieces
2 cups cold water
1 1/2 tsp. salt
1 large onion, chopped
1/2 cup chopped celery
3 14.5-oz. cans beef broth

2 cups no-fat sour cream
1/2 tsp. Tabasco® Sauce
1/2 tsp. sweet basil
1/4 tsp. oregano
1/8 tsp. thyme
1/2 tsp. fresh ground black
   pepper

Boil the bell peppers in the water with one teaspoon of the salt for 10 minutes over medium-high heat. Drain the bell peppers and remove them from the salted water. Reserve for later use. In a large sauce pot, combine the onions, celery, and beef broth; then bring to a boil over medium heat. When it begins to boil, reduce the heat to a simmer and cook for 10 minutes. Remove from the heat, let the mixture cool for a few minutes, then place in a food processor or blender. Blend at high speed until completely blended, about 2 minutes. Return to the sauce pot and add the remaining ingredients, except for the reserved bell pepper; return to medium-low heat. Cook, stirring often, until the soup is well blended and starting to bubble. Add the reserved bell pepper and let it heat through. Do not let the soup come to a boil. Serve warm or, if you like, chilled. Serves 6.

Lagniappe: This is a beautiful and unusual soup. The red pepper is so very pretty in the white broth of the soup. The taste is sweet and wonderful. You can substitute 2 large yellow bell peppers for the red to make Yellow Bell Pepper Soup. Just make as above with that one substitution.

Calories—106; Fat—.5 g; Protein—7.7 g; Carbohydrates—17.9 g; Cholesterol—.3 mg; Fiber—.6 g; Sodium—641 mg

5 of the 106 calories are from fat.
5% of the calories come from fat.

SEAFOOD GUMBO

2 tbsp. peanut oil
1/2 cup all-purpose flour
1 large onion, chopped
1 large bell pepper, seeded
and chopped
1 stalk celery, finely
chopped
2 cloves garlic, minced
1 15-oz. can stewed
tomatoes
4 cups seafood stock (see
page 57) or defatted
chicken stock
1 tbsp. Worcestershire
sauce
1 1/2 tsp. Cajun Spice Mix
(see page 274)

1/2 tsp. Tabasco® Sauce
1 large bay leaf
1 lb. okra, trimmed and
sliced (fresh or frozen)
6 large live blue crabs
1 lb. small shrimp (51-60
size), peeled and deveined
1/2 pt. shucked oysters,
with their liquid
1/2 cup chopped green
onions
1/4 cup chopped fresh
parsley
2 tsp. filé powder (or to
taste)
4 cups cooked white rice

Heat a large, heavy stockpot over medium heat. Add the peanut oil.
When the oil begins to smoke, add the flour and cook, stirring constantly, until the mixture turns dark reddish brown, 3 to 5 minutes. Reduce the heat to low; add the onions, peppers, celery, and garlic. Cook, stirring constantly, for 5 minutes. Add the tomatoes and cook, stirring, for 5 minutes more. Add the stock, Worcestershire sauce, Cajun Spice Mix, Tabasco® Sauce, and bay leaf; bring to a boil. Simmer, covered, over low heat for 15 minutes. Add the okra and simmer, covered, for 30 minutes.

Cover a cutting board with several thicknesses of newspaper. Holding a crab with a pair of tongs, rinse it under cold running water. Place the crab upside down on the paper-covered cutting board. Using a heavy cleaver or knife, cut through the middle, leaving one point on each side. Crack the claw at the second joint with the blunt side of the cleaver or knife. Rinse the crab halves under cold running water and remove the gills and viscera. Add the crabs to the gumbo and cook for 10 minutes. Add the shrimp and cook for 2 minutes. Add the oysters, oyster liquid, green onions, and parsley; simmer for 3 more minutes, or until the seafood is opaque. Remove the bay leaf and stir in the filé powder. Taste and adjust the seasonings, adding more Cajun Spice Mix if desired. Spoon rice into each soup bowl, and ladle the gumbo over the rice. Makes about 12 cups; serves 8.

Lagniappe: Gumbo is Cajun Louisiana's premier dish. We eat it as a main dish more often than not. Whenever there is a slight chill in the air, it's time for gumbo. Gumbo is truly an example of Cajun cooking's blended nature. The name is from the Congo *quingombo,* meaning okra. The dish is a remote cousin of bouillabaisse. The filé powder, which is used to thicken and to flavor, is ground sassafras leaves and the gift of the Choctaw Indians. The onion-pepper-tomato sauté is similar to a sofrito, showing a Spanish Creole influence. The style of cooking is both the braising technique of the French and the smoke pot of Haitians.

If you cannot find whole crabs, you can substitute 1 pound of lump crabmeat or 2 1/2 pounds of Alaskan king crab legs. If you use the lump crabmeat, add it to the gumbo with the oysters; if you use the crab legs, add them as you would the blue point crabs. If you like, you can prepare the dish up to the point of adding the crabs and refrigerate for up to 2 days before continuing. The dish tends to intensify and improve in taste when you do this. This is an example of saving time and actually improving the dish. Gumbo is such a tasty soup, you can't imagine just how good it is unless you have tasted it. This much lower fat version is outstanding.

Calories—378; Fat—7 g; Protein—29 g; Carbohydrates—49 g; Cholesterol—161 mg; Fiber—1.4 G ; Sodium—700 mg

62 of the 378 calories are from fat.
16% of the calories come from fat.

SHRIMP AND OKRA GUMBO

3 tbsp. peanut oil
1 cup all-purpose flour
2 large onions, chopped
1 large bell pepper, seeded
   and chopped
2 stalks celery, finely
   chopped
3 cloves garlic, minced
2 lb. chopped okra, cooked
   or frozen
1 15-oz. can stewed
   tomatoes
2 qt. hot water
2 tsp. Cajun Spice Mix (see
   page 274)

1 tsp. Tabasco® Sauce
1/2 tsp. sweet basil
3 large bay leaves
3 lb. shrimp, medium (41-
   50 size), peeled and
   deveined
1 cup finely chopped green
   onions
1/2 cup finely chopped
   fresh parsley
7 cups cooked white long
   grain rice
Filé powder to taste

In a very heavy gumbo pot or large, heavy saucepot, heat the oil over medium heat. When it is hot, add the flour. Cook over medium-high heat, stirring constantly until the roux (flour-and-oil mixture) turns dark brown. When the dark brown color is reached, add the onions, bell pepper, celery, garlic, and chopped okra; smother the vegetables in the roux until the okra loses most of it's slime, about 10 to 12 minutes. Add the stewed tomatoes and cook for 5 more minutes. Add the water carefully (it has a tendency to steam and bubble up when added to the hot roux and okra mixture), then add the Cajun Spice Mix and Tabasco® Sauce. Stir until the roux has completely dissolved into the okra mixture. Add the basil and the bay leaves, bring the gumbo to a boil over medium heat, and cook stirring constantly for 10 minutes. Add the peeled shrimp, reduce the heat to low-medium, and cook for 30 more minutes. Adjust the seasonings to taste with the Cajun Spice Mix. Add the green onions and parsley, and cook for 5 more minutes over low heat. Serve in individual bowls over cooked white rice with plenty of filé powder. Serves 8.

Lagniappe: All gumbo is named for okra because gumbo is the African name for okra. Today, all gumbos don't necessarily contain okra. It depends on the mood and taste of the cook. This is an okra gumbo to write home about!

Calories—604; Fat—9 g; Protein—45.5 g; Carbohydrates—74.9 g; Cholesterol—260 mg; Fiber—2.6 g; Sodium—1205 mg

81 of the 604 calories are from fat.
14% of the calories come from fat.

SEAFOOD STOCK

3 lb. fish heads and bones
  or uncooked shrimp or
  lobster shells
2 cups dry white wine
2 medium onions, chopped
1 bunch green onion
  bottoms only, chopped
2 stalks celery

2 medium carrots, washed
  and chopped
2 cloves garlic, crushed
4 stems fresh parsley
3 sprigs fresh thyme
2 large bay leaves
Water to cover

Rinse the fish bones and heads (or shrimp or lobster shells) under cold water. Place in a large nonreactive stockpot; combine all the vegetables and spices and add enough cold water to completely cover, about 4 quarts. Bring to a boil, then immediately reduce the heat to low. Skim off any foam, and simmer uncovered for 40 minutes, skimming occasionally. Strain the stock through a fine sieve. Remove from the heat and allow to cool. Place in the refrigerator until ready to use. Makes about 3 quarts of seafood stock.

Lagniappe: I know this sounds a bit eccentric, but it will make your seafood dishes taste heavenly. This stock can be stored in the refrigerator for up to two full days, or you can freeze it for up to six months. A great time to make this stock is any time you get fresh fish. If you go to the trouble of cleaning and filleting fish, why not get the benefits for many other dishes to come. Seafood stock is not like chicken or beef stock, it is not good to eat by itself. It is to be used only to enhance a sauce or soup.

Nutritional data cannot be determined because only trace amounts of nutrients remain after the fish, vegetables, and herbs are removed.

SHRIMP BISQUE

1 lb. large shrimp, (21-25 size) peeled and deveined
1 large onion, finely chopped
2 ribs celery, finely chopped
1 tbsp. unsalted butter
1 medium red bell pepper, finely diced
2 cloves garlic, minced
1/4 cup all-purpose flour
2 tsp. sweet paprika
2 tbsp. tomato paste
1 qt. low-sodium chicken broth
2 1/2-oz. Butter Buds
1/2 cup cream sherry
2 whole bay leaves
1/4 tsp. thyme
1/2 tsp. sweet basil
1/2 tsp. black pepper
1/4 tsp. white pepper
1/4 tsp. Tabasco® Sauce
2 tbsp. fine brandy
2/3 cup no-fat sour cream
1/4 cup finely chopped fresh parsley

Sauté the shrimp, onion, and celery in the butter over medium heat in a large saucepan for 4 minutes, then add the red bell pepper and garlic and continue to sauté for 2 more minutes. Add the flour and cook, constantly stirring, for 4 more minutes. Add the paprika and tomato paste and blend it in well. Let the sauce stay at a simmer, then add the chicken broth, Butter Buds, sherry, bay leaves, thyme, basil, fresh ground black pepper, white pepper, and Tabasco® Sauce. Cook for 1 hour at a low simmer. Add the brandy and sour cream and blend it in until smooth (use a wire whisk). Add the parsley, stir it in, and heat for 1 minute. Serve at once. Serves 4.

Lagniappe: This is uptown gourmet, but low-fat. The taste is delicate and opulent. You can make this dish in advance and refrigerate it for later use. In fact, I think the flavors actually improve and blend together better. I do not like to freeze this dish. You can keep it in the refrigerator for up to three days, but keep it very cold and tightly covered.

Calories—351; Fat—6.6 g; Protein—53.4 g; Carbohydrates—24.9 g; Cholesterol—183 mg; Fiber—.9 g; Sodium—997 mg

59 of the 351 calories are from fat.
17% of the calories come from fat.

SUMMER SQUASH SOUP

3 large yellow summer
squash, washed and stem
removed
3 large zucchini, washed
and stem removed
1 large onion
3 14.5-oz. cans chicken
broth
1/4 tsp. salt

1 1/2-oz. packet Butter
Buds
1/2 tsp. Tabasco® Sauce
1 tbsp. White Wine
Worcestershire sauce
1/2 cup chopped green
onions
1/4 cup finely minced fresh
parsley

Place the squash and onion in a large saucepan and cover with the chicken broth. Add the salt and place the pan over medium heat. Cover and let the squash simmer for 15 minutes. Remove from the heat and let the pan cool.

Place the squash and onion in a blender or food processor and blend until finely puréed. Add the remaining ingredients to the blender or processor, and blend until well mixed. Return the mixture to the saucepan and place over medium heat until the mixture comes to a low boil. Reduce the heat and simmer for 10 minutes to blend the flavors. Serve hot. Serves 4.

Lagniappe: This is a light soup that has a wonderful fresh flavor. Don't let the name *summer* in summer squash throw you. We can now get summer squash year-round. It is a less dense squash than winter squash. It loves to grow in the warm summer sun, and it grows very fast from the flower to harvest size. It is loaded with vitamin A and numerous minerals and a good supply of vitamin C as well. It is definitely good for you and is so very scrumptious too. I also like it because it is easy to prepare and to cook. No matter what time of the year you eat it, it'll have you thinking the summer sun is shining.

Calories—104; Fat—2.2 g; Protein—9.8 g; Carbohydrates—21.3 g; Cholesterol—2 mg; Fiber—2.4 g; Sodium—1523 mg

20 of the 104 calories are from fat.
19% of the calories come from fat.

TURTLE SOUP AU SHERRY

1 gallon water
1 1/2 lb. lean turtle meat
1 whole garlic, crushed but
   left unpeeled
1 large onion, cut into
   quarters
2 stalks celery, broken in
   half
1 1/2 tsp. salt
12 whole black peppercorns
3 whole bay leaves

1 tbsp. olive oil
1/4 cup all-purpose flour
1 cup chopped onions
1/2 cup chopped leeks
1 cup stewed tomatoes
1 cup cream sherry
1 cup finely chopped green
   onions
1/2 cup finely minced fresh
   parsley
4 large boiled egg whites

In a large soup or gumbo pot over medium heat, bring the water to a boil. When the water is boiling, add the turtle meat, garlic, onion, celery, salt, black pepper, and bay leaf. Bring the soup back to a boil, then reduce the heat to a rolling simmer and cook for 30 minutes. Heat a small nonstick skillet over medium-high heat until it is hot. Add the olive oil and, when it begins to smoke, add the flour. Cook, stirring constantly, until a dark brown color is reached. Add the chopped onions, leeks, and stewed tomatoes and cook, stirring constantly, until the onions are clear and limp, about 5 minutes.

Strain the soup pot so that only broth is left, reserving the turtle meat and vegetables and allowing them to cool. Return the turtle broth to the soup pot and place over medium heat. When the broth comes to a boil, add the dark brown roux mixture to the broth and blend it in well. When the turtle meat is cool, pick it from the bones, chop it up, and add it back to the broth. The soup should start to thicken somewhat. Add the cream sherry, stir it in, and cook for 5 minutes. Add the green onions and parsley, cook for 3 more minutes, then serve hot. Remove the yolk from the boiled eggs and chop the egg white into small pieces; place about 1 tablespoon of chopped egg white into each bowl of soup. Serves 8.

Lagniappe: You will be surprised just how spectacular this turtle soup is. This recipe significantly reduces the amount of fat normally found in turtle soup without significantly changing the quality or taste of the soup. Some people have trouble getting past the name, but the soup by any other name will still taste as good. When you buy turtle meat, it is frozen, so just thaw it out and put it into the seasoned water as the recipe instructs. It will be easier to take the meat from the turtle bones after it has cooked in the stock for the 30 minutes. You also remove any excess fat by boiling the meat before you put it into the soup.

Calories—181; Fat—2.3 g; Protein—20.3 g; Carbohydrates—11.9 g; Cholesterol—40 mg; Fiber—.6 g; Sodium—134 mg

21 of the 181 calories are from fat.
12% of the calories come from fat.

VEGETABLE BEEF SOUP

1 lb. very lean top round steak
Olive oil-flavored nonstick vegetable oil spray
1 large onion, chopped
1 medium bell pepper, cut into strips
1 cup celery, sliced diagonally
1 cup carrots, sliced
3 cloves garlic, crushed and minced
1 14.5-oz can stewed tomatoes
2 8-oz. cans tomato sauce
1 15-oz. can cut Italian green beans, with their liquid

1 15-oz. can red kidney beans, with their liquid
2 14.5-oz. cans beef broth
1 tsp. Cajun Spice Mix (see page 274)
1 tsp. sweet basil
1/2 tsp. rosemary
1/2 tsp. oregano
1/2 tsp. Tabasco® Sauce
1 cup diced turnips
2 cups chopped green cabbage
1/2 cup tiny elbow macaroni
1/2 cup minced fresh parsley
1/2 cup chopped green onion tops

In a large nonstick stock pot or soup pot, brown the beef over medium heat. Remove the meat and wipe the bottom of the pot with clean white paper towels to remove any fat that may be present. Lightly spray olive oil spray on the bottom of the pot, then heat the pot until it is hot. Add the onions, bell pepper, celery, carrots and garlic. Sauté the vegetables for 4 minutes, stirring often. Add the beef back into the pot, then add all the remaining ingredients up through the Tabasco® Sauce.

Let the soup come to a boil, then reduce the heat to low and let the soup simmer for 30 minutes. Add the turnips, cabbage, and macaroni and cook over low for 30 more minutes, stirring occasionally. Adjust the seasonings to your taste, then add the parsley and green onions and simmer for 5 more minutes. Serve hot. Serves 8.

Lagniappe: A pound of beef can and should go a long way when cooking lower fat dishes. Historically, meat was a seasoning, not the main course. In our country of abundance, we tend to shift that around. Of course, if we eat high meat content meals, they will be higher in fat. It doesn't take an Einstein to figure out that one way to reduce fat consumption is to reduce the amount of meat that we eat. The two biggest sources of fat in our diets are oils (fats themselves) and meats. We can lower our fat intake by restricting the amount of oil and meat we have in our diet. This vegetable beef soup is an example of doing just this. It is also great tasting and can be made in advance and refrigerated or frozen for later use. Good taste, ease of preparation, and so flexible— how can you go wrong?

Calories—261; Fat—4.6 g; Protein—28.3 g; Carbohydrates—30.3 g; Cholesterol—49 mg; Fiber—5 g; Sodium—1192 mg

41 of the 261 calories are from fat.
16% of the calories come from fat.

VEGETABLE SOUP

1 lb. very lean round steak,
cut into cubes
1 gallon water
1 12-oz. can tomato paste
2 large onions, chopped
1 large bell pepper,
chopped
2 cups coarsely chopped
celery
1 head green cabbage,
chopped
3 large tender turnips,
chopped
1 lb. fresh string beans,
ends removed, cleaned,
and snapped

1 cup fresh cut yellow corn
1 tsp. salt
1/2 tsp. Tabasco® Sauce
1/2 tsp. fresh ground black
pepper
1/2 tsp. white pepper
1 tsp. onion powder
1 tsp. dried sweet basil
3 cups carrots, chopped
1 15-oz. can great northern
white beans
1 lb. fresh new potatoes,
washed
1/2 cup non-egg macaroni,
uncooked

Add the round steak pieces into the water and simmer over low heat
for 1 hour. Add the tomato paste, onions, bell pepper, celery, cabbage, turnips, string beans, and fresh corn. Cover and simmer for 1
more hour. Add the salt, Tabasco® Sauce, black pepper, white pepper,
onion powder, and basil; cover and simmer for 30 minutes. Add the
remaining ingredients and simmer over low heat for 1 more hour. Serve
hot. Serves 8.

Lagniappe: One of the mainstays of a good low-fat diet has to be high-
volume, high-flavor food that is tasty and fills you up. Nothing fits the bill
better than soups. This vegetable soup is truly exceptional. Make it in
advance and refrigerate it or freeze it for use as you desire. I like to keep
it frozen by the bowlful. I freeze it in the zip-lock freezer bags. They hold
the soup nicely and are easy to store and easy to heat once you remove them from the freezer. Make a big pot of soup and eat some now,
but plan to freeze the rest.

*Calories—354; Fat—4.5 g; Protein—31 g; Carbohydrates—52.4 g;
Cholesterol—48 mg; Fiber—5.2 g; Sodium—412 mg*

41 of the 354 calories are from fat.
12% of the calories come from fat.

Salads and
Salad Dressings

APPLE-CARROT SALAD

**2 large red delicious apples,
cored and shredded
1 1/2 cups shredded
carrots
Juice of 1 small lemon**

**2 tbsp. sugar
1/4 tsp. Tabasco® Sauce
2/3 cup raisins
1/4 cup Miracle Whip Free
salad dressing**

In a large mixing bowl, mix together the apples, carrots and lemon juice until well blended. Add the sugar and stir until dissolved. Add the raisins, Tabasco® Sauce, and salad dressing and blend together until completely blended. Serve at once or chill. Serves 4.

Lagniappe: This is a wonderful salad. It is fast, simple, and so luscious. This is one of those recipes that is almost too easy to really believe. It keeps well in the refrigerator for up to three days. After that, you lose too much of the crispness, which takes away much of the quality. You can also add celery to this salad if you want; celery adds a nice crunch to the salad and a good, fresh, clean taste.

Calories—175; Fat—.1 g; Protein—1.3 g; Carbohydrates—41 g; Cholesterol—0 mg; Fiber—2.3 g; Sodium—117 mg

1 of the 175 calories is from fat.
Less than 1% of the calories come from fat.

CABBAGE SALAD A LA DAN JOSEPH

2 cups finely shredded
  green cabbage
2 cups finely shredded
  purple cabbage
2 large apples, grated with
  skin
1 tbsp. fresh lemon juice
2 tbsp. sugar

1 cup Mircale Whip Free
  salad dressing
2/3 cup crushed pineapple
1 tsp. Cajun Spice Mix (see
  page 274)
1 tsp. white wine
  Worcestershire sauce
1/2 tsp. Tabasco® Sauce

In a large bowl, mix together the green and purple cabbage with the apple until well blended. Sprinkle the lemon juice and sugar over the mixture and toss a bit to mix the lemon juice and dissolve the sugar. In a small mixing bowl, combine the remaining ingredients until well blended. Pour this dressing mixture over the cabbage-apple mixture, and toss until the cabbage-apple mixture is well coated. Chill in the refrigerator for at least 3 hours. Serve cold. Serves 8.

Lagniappe: This is a super make-ahead salad. Cabbage and apples are a natural mixture. This salad can be used with almost any meal; it is full of color contrasts and loaded with gusto. You can make it up to 48 hours in advance and still have it crisp and fresh.

Calories—98; Fat—.3 g; Protein—.7 g; Carbohydrates—22.9 g; Cholesterol—0 mg; Fiber—1.5 g; Sodium—333 mg

3 of the 98 calories are from fat.
3% of the calories come from fat.

CABBAGE SALAD MARKSVILLE

1 medium red cabbage head	1/2 cup chopped green onion
2 cups boiling water	1/4 cup chopped fresh parsley
1/4 cup red wine vinegar	1 tsp. Tabasco® Sauce
3 tbsp. sugar	1/2 tsp. salt
1/2 cup Miracle Whip Free salad dressing	1/2 tsp. onion powder
1 small onion, chopped	1 tbsp. fresh lemon juice
1/2 cup chopped celery	

Remove the outer leaves of the cabbage and cut the cabbage into very thin slices. Put the cabbage into a large bowl that has a cover. Pour the hot boiling water on top of the cabbage and let it stand for 5 minutes. While the cabbage is standing, put all the remaining ingredients into a food processor or a blender and chop at high speed until all the ingredients are well blended and smooth. Drain off all the water from the cabbage, then add the dressing from the food processor to the cabbage and mix together well. Cover the bowl tightly, and let it stand in the refrigerator for six hours or overnight. Serve chilled. Serves 6.

Lagniappe: This is a good substitute for coleslaw. It has a real tang, yet it has the sweetness that cabbage so dearly loves. It is easy to make and stores well in the refrigerator. It has all the makings for a super dish!

Calories—71; Fat—.1 g; Protein—1.4 g; Carbohydrates—16.4 g; Cholesterol—0 mg; Fiber—.7 g; Sodium—354 mg

1 of the 71 calories is from fat.
1% of the calories come from fat.

CAJUN SHRIMP REMOULADE

2 stalks celery, finely
minced
1 cup finely minced green
onions
3 cloves garlic, finely
minced
1 cup Miracle Whip Free
salad dressing
1/2 cup Creole mustard
2 tbsp. chili sauce
2/3 tsp. Tabasco® Sauce
1 tbsp. paprika

1/2 tsp. cayenne pepper
1/4 tsp. black pepper
1/2 tsp. salt
1 tsp. garlic powder
1 tsp. onion powder
1 tsp. sweet basil
1 tsp. Worcestershire sauce
2 lb. Spicy Boiled Shrimp,
peeled and deveined (see
page 108)
1 head finelly shredded
iceberg lettuce

Combine all the ingredients except the last two in a large mixing bowl until well mixed. Blend in the shrimp and refrigerate for at least 4 hours. Spoon over the shredded lettuce and serve chilled. Serves 6.

Lagniappe: This is an easy remoulade sauce that comes close to the real thing. Because shrimp is so low in fat, yet high in protein, this is a wonderfully healthy choice. Shrimp is always a great choice for entertaining company. You can make this sauce the day before you are going to serve and let it stand in the refrigerator with the shrimp for up to 36 hours before serving. It will actually taste better! This sauce alone also makes an excellent Remoulade Salad Dressing. You can also serve this sauce over fresh lump crabmeat to make Cajun Crabmeat Remoulade; substitute 1 pound of lump crabmeat for the two pounds of shrimp. It will still serve six because crabmeat has a tendancy to taste richer than shrimp.

Calories—323; Fat—3.2 g; Protein—33 g; Carbohydrates—16 g; Cholesterol—231 mg; Fiber —1.2 g; Sodium—865 mg

29 of the 323 calories are from fat.
9% of the calories come from fat.

CHERRY TOMATO SALAD

2 qt. cold water
1 pt. cherry tomatoes
2 qt. iced water
2 tbsp. fat-free salad
  dressing
2 tbsp. no-fat sour cream
2 tbsp. white wine vinegar
2 tbsp. fresh basil, very
  finely chopped
1 tsp. dijon mustard

1/2 tsp. salt
1/2 tsp. Tabasco® Sauce
2 tsp. sugar
1 large cucumber, thinly
  sliced
1/2 cup finely chopped
  green onions
Bed of chopped lettuce
1 tbsp. finely minced fresh
  parsley

Heat the water in a large saucepan over high heat and bring to a rolling boil. Add the tomatoes to the water and let them heat for 30 seconds. Remove them from the water with a slotted spoon, and put them into a bowl of iced water. This should make it easy to remove the peeling from the tomatoes. Using a paring knife, just remove the thin tomato skins and set the tomatoes aside for later use.

In a medium-sized mixing bowl, combine the salad dressing, sour cream, white wine vinegar, basil, mustard, salt, Tabasco® Sauce, and sugar. Whip together with a wire wisk or fork until well blended. Add the reserved tomatoes, cucumbers, and green onions to the dressing, and toss until all are coated. Serve equally on a bed of chopped lettuce, and garnish with the parsley. Serve just after mixing, or refrigerate and serve chilled. Serves 4.

Lagniappe: This is a nice alternative to a regular lettuce, cucumber, and tomato salad. By tossing with the dressing before serving, you have a greater control over the amount of dressing used—and it makes for a pretty salad. This is a beautiful salad that will nicely accompany any meal. Cherry tomatoes are a good choice for tomatoes because they actually still taste like the tomatoes of old. You can make this salad in advance and refrigerate it for up to 2 days with no loss of quality.

Calories—47; Fat—trace; Protein—2.2 g; Carbohydrates—10.1 g; Cholesterol—0 mg; Fiber—1.3 g; Sodium—415 mg

Less than 1 of the 47 calories is from fat.
2% of the calories come from fat.

CRABMEAT STUFFED TOMATOES

8 large ripe fresh tomatoes
1 recipe Creamy Crabmeat
  Spread (see page 281)

1 tsp. paprika
1 small head lettuce,
  shredded

Wash and clean the tomatoes and remove the small brown spots on each end. Cut the top third off each tomato and reserve for later use. Scoop about half of the pulp out of each of tomato. Fill each tomato with a generous amount of the crabmeat spread. Place each tomato on a bed of shredded lettuce, and garnish with the paprika. Use the leftover crabmeat spread, placing spoonfuls on the lettuce. Stick the reserved tomato top into the crabmeat spread on the lettuce. Serve chilled. Serves 8.

Lagniappe: This is a quick and easy salad that can serve as a side salad or a main course. It is exquisite and filling. The time needed to make and put both recipes together is nothing. Crabmeat is so lavish that it can't fail to please. I have also served this as a side dish on a plate with grilled fish and noodles, by cutting the tomato in half before stuffing and just stuffing half the tomato. Any way you serve it, you'll get kudos!

Calories—73; Fat—.7 g; Protein—11.5 g; Carbohydrates—5 g; Cholesterol—44 mg; Fiber—.8 g; Sodium—175 mg

6 of the 73 calories are from fat.
8% of the calories come from fat.

CRANBERRY SALAD

1 1/2 cups fresh
   cranberries, chopped
1 1/3 cups sugar
1 1/2 cups miniature
   marshmallows
1 1/3 cups crushed
   pineapple, drained of
   most liquid

1 tbsp. pecans, chopped
1 8-oz. pkg. fat-free cream
   cheese
1 cup no-fat sour cream
1/8 tsp. Tabasco® Sauce

Mix together the cranberries, 1 cup of the sugar, marshmallows, pineapple, and pecans in a medium-sized mixing bowl, and let it stand in the refrigerator for at least 24 hours. When you are ready to serve, beat the cream cheese, sour cream, Tabasco® Sauce, and the remaining sugar together until smooth, light, and fluffy. Fold the cranberries into the creamed mixture until well blended. Serve chilled. Serves 8.

Lagniappe: This salad has quite a bite to it. It is somewhat tart, but the true flavors of the cranberries come alive. It can be used as a festive holiday salad or just as an easy salad for almost any meal. I also like it as a semi-sweet snack to help kill your appetite if dinner is a few hours away. It keeps very well in the refrigerator for about 5 to 7 days. Beautiful color and great taste—what more can you ask for?

Calories—199; Fat—.5 g; Protein—4.4 g; Carbohydrates—45.1 g; Cholesterol—5 mg; Fiber—.8 g; Sodium—175 mg
5 of the 199 calories are from fat.
3% of the calories come from fat.

HOT ITALIAN CHICKEN PASTA SALAD

2 whole chicken breasts,
    skin removed
2 tsp. Italian seasoning
1 tbsp. olive oil
1/2 cup diced red bell
    pepper
1/4 cup diced bell pepper
1/2 cup finely chopped
    onion
3 tbsp. finely minced celery
2 cloves garlic, crushed and
    minced
1/4 cup dry red wine
    (Italian preferred)

1 tbsp. cornstarch
1/2 tsp. dried basil leaves
1/4 cup chopped fresh
    parsley
1 cup Italian-style stewed
    tomatoes
1/4 cup ripe olives, sliced
1 cup red kidney beans,
    drained
3 cups cooked tri-colored
    corkscrew noodles

Wash the chicken breasts in cold water and pat dry with a white paper towel. Season equally with the Italian seasoning, then pan-broil the chicken breasts for 6 minutes on each side in a nonstick skillet over medium heat. Remove from the heat, chop into bite-sized pieces, and reserve for later use.

In a large skillet over medium heat, heat the olive oil. When it is hot, add the red bell pepper, green bell pepper, onions, celery, and garlic. Sauté, stirring constantly, for 4 minutes or until the vegetables are limp and the onions clear. Mix together the dry red wine and the cornstarch until the cornstarch has dissolved. Add the basil, parsley, tomatoes, olives, and beans to the skillet and cook, stirring constantly, for 3 minutes. Add the wine-cornstarch mixture. The sauce should thicken. Quickly add the chopped chicken breasts and the noodles, then stir until the chicken and noodles are completely coated and the noodles are warm. Serve at once. Serves 6.

Lagniappe: Hot pasta is in—especially if you want low-fat dishes that are hearty and filling. The beans and the pasta (a great complex carbohydrate) combine to give you even more complete protein than you would get from just chicken alone. This dish should be eaten right after it is cooked. The noodles break down and are only really at maximum quality right after being first cooked.

Calories—192; Fat—5.4 g; Protein—24.7 g; Carbohydrates—34.8 g; Cholesterol—49 mg; Fiber—2.1 g; Sodium—318 mg

49 of the 192 calories are from fat.
26% of the calories come from fat.

GREEN ONION DRESSING

1 cup Miracle Whip Free
  salad dressing
2 tbsp. red wine vinegar
2 cups green onions,
  coarsely chopped
1/4 cup minced fresh
  parsley
1 tbsp. chopped fresh basil

1 tbsp. chopped chives
2 tbsp. fresh lemon juice
2 tbsp. sugar
1/2 tsp. Tabasco® Sauce
1/2 tsp. salt
1/2 tsp. freshly ground
  black pepper

Put all the ingredients into a blender or a food processor and blend at high speed until the dressing is smooth, about 3 minutes. Refrigerate until you are ready to use. Makes about 1 pint of dressing.

Lagniappe: This is a nice, fresh-tasting dressing that keeps well in the refrigerator and gives you a homemade taste. This dressing is not only low-fat, but also very low in calories. I recommend labeling the bottle with the date the dressing is made and the name of the dressing to ensure proper use of the dressing. I don't like to keep homemade dressings for more than ten days to two weeks. Be sure to keep the dressing refrigerated when not serving.

Per tablespoon:
Calories—15; Fat—trace; Protein—.2 g; Carbohydrates—3.4 g; Cholesterol—0 mg; Fiber—trace; Sodium—91 mg

Less than 1 of the 15 calories is from fat.
Less than 1% of the calories come from fat.

JUDE'S LOW-FAT HERBAL DRESSING

1 cup Miracle Whip Free
salad dressing
1/4 cup nonfat cottage
cheese, small curd
1/4 cup minced fresh
parsley
2 tbsp. fresh lime juice
2 tbsp. green onions,
coarsely chopped
2 tbsp. chopped fresh basil
1 tbsp. Romano cheese
1 tbsp. fresh rosemary,
leaves only

1 tbsp. fresh oregano
leaves
1 tbsp. chopped chives
1 tbsp. sugar
1 tsp. Tabasco® Sauce
1/2 tsp. salt
1 tsp. freshly ground black
pepper
1/4 tsp. white pepper
1 tsp. garlic powder
1 tsp. onion powder
1/4 tsp. ground nutmeg

Put all the ingredients into a blender or a food processor and blend at high speed until the dressing is smooth, about 3 minutes. Refrigerate until you are ready to use. Makes about 1 pint of dressing.

Lagniappe: Blender dressings are easy to make and wonderful to use. I recommend labeling the bottle with the date the dressing is made and the name of the dressing. That will ensure proper use of the dressing. I don't like to keep homemade dressings for more than ten days to two weeks. Be sure to keep the dressing refrigerated when not serving. This herb blend will really be best if the dressing is made at least 24 hours before you plan to use it, to allow the flavors to spread throughout the dressing. This dressing is not only low-fat; it is also low in calories.

Per tablespoon:
Calories—13; Fat—.1 g; Protein—.4 g; Carbohydrates—2.5 g; Cholesterol—less than 1 mg; Fiber—trace; Sodium—101 mg

1 of the 13 calories is from fat.
8% of the calories come from fat.

PINEAPPLE-LIME SALAD

1 12-oz. container Cool
Whip Light
1 3-oz. box lime jello
1 8-oz. pkg. fat-free cream
cheese

1 tsp. fresh lime juice
2 16-oz. cans pineapple
chunks, drained
1/4 cup thinly sliced celery
8 large lettuce leaves

Empty the Cool Whip into a large mixing bowl and add the lime jello and the cream cheese. Blend together well with an electric mixer, or whip it by hand until well blended. Fold in the lime juice, pineapple, and celery until well mixed. Chill the mixture for at least 4 hours, then serve on the middle of a large leaf of lettuce. Serve chilled. Serves 8.

Lagniappe: This is easy, very low-fat, and so good. I can almost eat this as a dessert instead of a salad. It will help anyone that has an overactive sweet tooth—I know it helps me. I have often found that eating a sweet salad or a sweet at the end of the meal has a tendency to leave me more satisfied. If you are trying to lose weight, it is important that you leave the dinner table full. If you are still hungry when you finish eating, you are more likely to snack on a high-fat food. You can make this salad 24 hours in advance if you like. Just keep it tightly covered in the refrigerator until you are ready to serve it. You can also feel free to change the flavor of the jello and change the fruit you use. You can make any number of excellent and tasty sweet salads without really putting yourself out.

Calories—156; Fat—.4 g; Protein—5.6 g; Carbohydrates—28.5 g; Cholesterol—5 mg; Fiber—.4 g; Sodium—204 mg

4 of the 156 calories are from fat.
3% of the calories come from fat.

POTATO SALAD

2 lb. red new potatoes
5 large eggs
1 tsp. salt
5 whole black peppercorns
Water to cover
2/3 cup finely chopped
  green onions
1/2 cup finely chopped
  celery
2/3 cup sweet pickle relish

3/4 cup Miracle Whip Free
  salad dressing
1/4 tsp. Tabasco® Sauce
2 tbsp. prepared yellow
  mustard
3 tbsp. finely diced red bell
  pepper
1/2 tsp. salt
1/2 tsp. freshly ground
  black pepper

Place the potatoes, eggs, salt and peppercorns in a large pot. Cover with cold water, then place on medium-high heat and bring to a hard boil. Reduce to a low boil and cook until the potatoes are cooked, about 12 minutes after the pot begins to boil. Check the potatoes by piercing each potato with a fork to be sure they are cooked through. If the fork goes into the center easily, then the potatoes are ready.

Drain the water from the potatoes and eggs and allow them to cool for 5 minutes. Peel the potatoes and cut them into bite-size pieces, then place them in a large bowl. Peel the eggs, remove the egg yolks, and discard the yolks. Use only the white of the egg. Chop the boiled egg whites and place them into the bowl. Add the remaining ingredients and stir together well. Serve immediately or refrigerate and serve chilled. Serves 6.

Lagniappe: Remember, you can use the white of the egg in fat-free dishes all you want. It is the yolk that has all the fat. The white of the egg is loaded with protein and gives you the feel of egg in a dish. The mustard will color the potato salad and make you think the yolk is in the dish. I personally like my potato salad made just before serving because I like it somewhat warm. If there is any left, I refrigerate to eat as leftovers. Another great way to serve this potato salad is to add two pounds of peeled and deveined spicy boiled shrimp. This makes Spicy Shrimp Potato Salad—a wonderful one-dish salad meal served on a nice bed of lettuce. This also serves 6 as a meal or 10 as a side dish.

Calories—212; Fat—.5 g; Protein—6.5 g; Carbohydrates—45 g; Cholesterol—0 mg; Fiber—1.2 g; Sodium—770 mg

4 of the 212 calories are from fat.
2% of the calories come from fat.

For the Spicy Shrimp Potato Salad—6 servings
Calories—372; Fat—3.1 g; Protein—37.2 g; Carbohydrates—46.5 g; Cholesterol—231 mg; Fiber—1.2 g; Sodium—1153 mg

28 of the 372 calories are from fat.
7% of the calories come from fat.

RED PINEAPPLE SALAD

1 8-oz. can crushed
   unsweetened pineapple
1 6-oz. box raspberry
   gelatin
1 12-oz. container Cool
   Whip Light

2 cups nonfat cottage
   cheese
1/2 tsp. vanilla extract
2 tbsp. Grand Marnier
   liqueur
1/2 head shredded lettuce

In a medium saucepan over medium heat, bring the crushed pineapple and gelatin to a boil. Let the mixture cool completely, and mix in the Cool Whip until smooth. Stir in the cottage cheese until it is completely mixed. Pour into the mold of your choice and chill for 4 to 5 hours or until firmly set. Serve chilled on a bed of lettuce. Serves 8.

Lagniappe: It is natural and informal, but it is exquisite and delectable. This dish has almost no fat so you can really enjoy yourself. It is high in protein and loaded with excellent energy sources. I like to put this into individual molds, but you can use a large pan and cut it into squares if you like. It is colorful enough for company, yet simple enough for every day.

Calories—197; Fat—6.5 g; Protein—7.5 g; Carbohydrates—28.3 g; Cholesterol—0 mg; Fiber—.4 g; Sodium—264 mg

59 of the 197 calories are from fat.
30% of the calories come from fat.

SALAD CRYSTAL

1 3 3/4-oz instant pistachio
pudding and pie mix
1 20-oz. can crushed
sweetened pineapple
1 9-oz. container Cool Whip
Light

1 1/2 cups miniature
marshmallows
1/2 cup maraschino
cherries, chopped
2 tbsp. chopped pecans

Combine the first three ingredients in a large mixing bowl, stirring until the pudding is completely dissolved. Add the marshmallows, cherries, and pecans and stir in well. Chill in the refrigerator for at least 3 hours. Spoon into pudding cups and serve chilled. Serves 8.

Lagniappe: This is a salad that is pretty, unusual, and luscious. The new Cool Whip Light is a nice, quick, and easy low-fat product when used in combination with other products that have calories but no fat. I like to serve this in a lettuce leaf or on a bed of shredded lettuce. It not only makes an exceptional salad, but it can stand in for a palatable dessert as well.

Calories—211; Fat—4.6 g; Protein—.7 g; Carbohydrates—44.6 g; Cholesterol—0 mg; Fiber—.8 g; Sodium—180 mg

41 of the 211 calories are from fat.
19% of the calories come from fat.

SWEET COLESLAW

1 cup shredded green
   cabbage
1 cup shredded purple
   cabbage
1/4 cup finely minced green
   onions
2 large red delicious apples,
   cored and shredded

Juice of 1 lemon
1 tbsp. red wine vinegar
1/2 tsp. Tabasco® Sauce
3 tbsp. light brown sugar
1/3 cup Miracle Whip Free
   salad dressing

In a large mixing bowl, combine the green cabbage, purple cabbage, green onions, apples, lemon juice, and red wine vinegar until well blended. Add the brown sugar and Tabasco® Sauce; stir in until dissolved. Add the Miracle Whip Free salad dressing and blend together until completely blended. Serve at once or chill. Serves 4.

Lagniappe: This is an awesome salad. It is so elementary and tasty. A recipe does not have to be difficult to be good; this is just such a recipe. It keeps well in the refrigerator for up to three days. After that, you sacrifice much of the crispness and quality.

Calories—155; Fat—3 g; Protein—.9 g; Carbohydrates—28 g; Cholesterol—0 mg; Fiber—1.9 g; Sodium—153 mg

3 of the 155 calories are from fat.
2% of the calories come from fat.

THREE BEAN SALAD

2 15-oz. cans dark red
  kidney beans, drained
1 15-oz. can cut green
  beans, drained
1 15-oz. can lima beans,
  drained
1 cup sugar
1/2 cup red wine vinegar
1/2 cup cider vinegar
1 small onion, chopped
1/2 small red bell pepper,
  diced
1/4 cup fresh parsley, finely
  minced
1 tbsp. extra virgin olive oil
1 tsp. salt
1 tsp. fresh ground black
  pepper
1 tsp. onion powder
1/2 tsp. sweet basil
1/2 tsp. Tabasco® Sauce

In a large mixing bowl, combine all ingredients except the lettuce leaves and stir until the sugar is mostly dissolved. Refrigerate for 8 hours, stirring the salad a few times. Serve chilled on lettuce leaves. Serves 8.

Lagniappe: This is a great way to get fiber, taste, and very little fat. I like to keep this salad in the refrigerator and use it as a snack. It is like having a sweet icebox pickle. This is also great on a buffet table and a great dish to bring to a covered dish supper. It keeps well in the refrigerator and is quick and easy to prepare. It is necessary to let the salad stand for a least 8 hours or the beans will not have enough time to absorb all the wonderful flavors.

Calories—285; Fat—2.3 g; Protein—10.8 g; Carbohydrates—58 g; Cholesterol—0 mg; Fiber—5.6 g; Sodium—1078 mg

21 of the 285 calories are from fat.
7% of the calories come from fat.

Bread and
Breakfast Foods

BARLEY BREAD

1/2 cup barley grains
2 cups self-rising flour
2 tbsp. sugar
2 tbsp. cornstarch
1 1/2-oz. packet Butter
  Buds

1/2 tsp. baking powder
1/2 tsp. salt
1 12-oz. can light beer, at
  room temperature

Preheat the oven to 350 degrees. Put the barley in a food processor or blender and blend for 1 minute. The grains should be broken. In a large mixing bowl, mix the barley and all the dry ingredients with a wire whisk or a fork until well blended, then pour in the beer and stir it into the flour mixture. Pour the batter into a 9 x 5 x 3-inch loaf pan. Set the pan in a large paper bag, and let it proof in a warm, dry place for 20 minutes. Bake at 350 degrees for 1 hour, or until the bread has a nicely browned top. Remove from the oven, allow the bread to stand for 2 minutes, then remove from the pan, slice, and serve. Serves 6.

Lagniappe: This is a whole grain bread that is quick and easy to make. Just throw away that bread machine; you don't need it. All you need is a loaf pan and a regular oven. You can find barley at most supermarkets; but if you have trouble, you will find it at a health food store. The barley will give the bread a wonderful and indescribable flavor. It is really worth trying.

Calories—258; Fat—.2 g; Protein—6.2 g; Carbohydrates—55.2 g; Cholesterol—0 mg; Fiber—1.9 g; Sodium—754 mg

2 of the 258 calories are from fat.
Less than 1% of the calories come from fat.

BLUEBERRY MUFFINS

2 large egg whites
1/2 cup skim milk
1/2 cup unsweetened
   applesauce
1 1/2 cup all-purpose flour
2/3 cup sugar

2 tsp. baking powder
1/4 tsp. baking soda
1/8 tsp. nutmeg
1/2 tsp. salt
1 cup fresh blueberries,
   washed and drained dry

Preheat the oven to 400 degrees. Beat the eggs until they begin to foam in a large glass bowl. Stir in the milk and applesauce; beat until well blended. In another mixing bowl, combine the remaining ingredients, except the blueberries. Mix the egg mixture into the flour mixture, just until it is moist. Do not over mix. Fold in the berries. Bake at 400 degrees for 20 to 25 minutes, or until a toothpick inserted into the center of the muffin comes out clean. Makes 8 muffins.

Lagniappe: This muffin mix makes a muffin that tastes every bit as good as one made with oil. Muffins are wonderful for breakfast, they make great breads at lunch or dinner, and they are great as a snack throughout the day. These nonfat muffins make a great alternative to fat-laden foods. You can make these in advance and either store them covered on the kitchen cabinet or freeze them. If you freeze them, just let them thaw at room temperature before heating them in a microwave for 20 seconds at full power if you like hot muffins. I like them both hot and at room temperature.

This is a great muffin to make when the fresh blueberries come in. This recipe can be doubled if you like. One word of warning: do not stir the muffin mixture to much. It should not be as smooth as cake batter, but rather quite stiff and unmixed in appearance.

Per muffin:
Calories—165; Fat—.4 g; Protein—3.7 g; Carbohydrates—44 g; Cholesterol—.3 mg; Fiber—.8 g; Sodium—273 mg

3.5 of the 165 calories are from fat.
2% of the calories come from fat.

CRACKED WHEAT BREAD

1/3 cup whole grain wheat
2 1/3 cups self-rising flour
1 tbsp. sugar
2 tbsp. cornstarch
1 1/2-oz. packet Butter
  Buds

1/2 tsp. baking powder
1/2 tsp. salt
1 12-oz. can light beer, at
  room temperature

Preheat the oven to 350 degrees. Place the whole grains of wheat in a food processor and chop a few times to crack the wheat grains. In a large mixing bowl, mix together all the dry ingredients with a wire whisk or a fork until well blended. Pour in the beer, and stir it into the flour mixture. Pour the batter into a 9 x 5 x 3-inch loaf pan. Set the pan in a large paper bag, and let it proof in a warm, dry place for 20 minutes. Bake at 350 degrees for 1 hour, or until the bread has a nicely browned top. Remove from the oven, allow the bread to stand for 2 minutes, then remove from the pan, slice, and serve. Serves 6.

Lagniappe: This is a wonderful full-grain bread. The whole wheat flavor is delicious as well as good for you. You can get whole wheat grains from a health food store if your supermarket doesn't have any. If you don't have a food processor, a blender will do, or you can just put the grains in a double fold of plastic wrap and roll over them with a rolling pin until the grains crack open. This is such an easy recipe, I know you will enjoy making it as much as eating it.

Calories—213; Fat—.1 g; Protein—5.3 g; Carbohydrates—44.5 g; Cholesterol—0 mg; Fiber—1.8 g; Sodium—803 mg

1 of the 213 calories is from fat.
Less than 1% of the calories come from fat.

DROP BISCUITS

2 1/2 cups no-fat biscuit
  mix
1/2 tsp. baking powder
1/2 cup skim milk

1/4 cup no-fat sour cream
1 tbsp. unsweetened
  applesauce
1/4 cup nonfat mayonnaise

In a large mixing bowl, combine the biscuit mix and baking powder and blend them together with a wire whisk or fork. Add the milk, sour cream, applesauce, and mayonnaise. Stir together with the whisk or fork until the mixture is blended; do not over stir. Drop a heaping tablespoon of the batter on a nonstick baking sheet, and bake at 400 degrees for about 18 minutes, or until the biscuits are golden brown. Serve hot. Makes about 12 biscuits.

Lagniappe: Serve with plenty of jelly, jam, or preserves. All three are fat-free, so enjoy. There is also a fat-free margarine that is not bad if you just have to have that feel and taste on your biscuits. I've learned to forego the margarine and/or butter and just load the preserves or jam on. It is really hard to taste the butter anyway with all that jelly on the biscuit. This is an example of how altering what you do just a little can have big results. I can honestly say that I enjoy these biscuits (perhaps because I really like a little biscuit with my jelly).

Per biscuit:
Calories—99; Fat—trace; Protein—1.1 g; Carbohydrates—23.2 g; Cholesterol—.2 mg; Fiber—.2 g; Sodium—220 mg
Less than 1 of the 99 calories is from fat.
Less than 1% of the calories come from fat.

EASY YEAST BREAD

2 1/3 cups self-rising flour
2 tbsp. sugar
2 tbsp. cornstarch
1 1/2-oz. packet Butter
  Buds

1 1/4-oz. packet All Natural
  Rapidrise yeast
1 1/2 cups club soda

Preheat the oven to 350 degrees. With a wire whisk or a fork, mix to-gether all the dry ingredients until well blended. Pour in the club soda and stir it into the flour mixture. Pour the batter into a 9 x 5 x 3-inch loaf pan. Set the pan in a large paper bag, and let it proof in a warm, dry place for 35 minutes. Bake at 350 degrees for 1 hour, or until the bread has a nicely browned top. Remove from the oven and allow the bread to stand for 2 minutes, then remove from the pan, slice, and serve. Serves 6.

Lagniappe: This recipe is so easy and good tasting that you'll throw away your bread machine! Why go to all the trouble and expense when you can make good fresh bread that is basically nonfat. It's easy, deli-cious, and eye-pleasing. Enjoy!

Calories—187; Fat—trace; Protein—5.2 g; Carbohydrates—41.2 g; Cholesterol—0 mg; Fiber—1.6 g; Sodium—492 mg
None of the 187 calories are from fat.

MEXICAN CORN BREAD

Nonstick vegetable oil spray
1 large onion, chopped
1 large red bell pepper,
  finely chopped
2 cloves garlic, minced
2 1/2 cups cornmeal
2 cups all-purpose flour
3 tbsp. sugar
1 tbsp. light brown sugar
2 tsp. salt
1 tbsp. baking powder
1 tsp. baking soda
1 tsp. onion powder

1 tsp. fresh ground black
  pepper
1/4 tsp. cayenne pepper
1/2 tsp. Tabasco® Sauce
3 tbsp. picante sauce
5 large egg whites, lightly
  beaten
2 cups skim milk
1/2 cup unsweetened
  applesauce
1 15-oz. cream-style corn
1 1/2-oz. packet Butter
  Buds

Preheat the oven to 400 degrees. Spray a nonstick skillet with the vegetable oil spray, and heat the skillet over medium heat. When the skillet is hot, add the onions, red bell pepper, and garlic and sauté for 4 minutes, stirring constantly. Remove from the heat and let stand for later use.

In a large mixing bowl, combine the cornmeal, flour, sugar, baking powder, soda, salt, onion powder, black pepper, and cayenne pepper. Mix together well with a wire whisk. In another mixing bowl, add the remaining ingredients and mix together well. Slowly stir the liquid mixture into the dry mixture, stirring after each addition with the whisk. Continue until all is used. Pour the mixture into a baking pan, muffin pan, or special cornbread molds. Bake at 400 degrees for about 25 minutes, or until nicely browned and you can insert a toothpick into the center and have it come out clean. Let the bread cool for 2 minutes, then serve. Serves 10.

Lagniappe: Who says you can't have cornbread on a low-fat diet? This bread is divine and full of flavor. Use this Mexican cornbread any time you would serve cornbread or bread. It is an excellent accompaniment, and it makes a nice, light supper served with plenty of nonfat butter or fat-free margarine.

Calories—309; Fat—1.1 g; Protein—9.9 g; Carbohydrates—64.4 g; Cholesterol—1 mg; Fiber—2.2 g; Sodium—965 mg

10 of the 309 calories are from fat.
3% of the calories come from fat.

OLD-FASHIONED POPOVERS

6 large egg whites
1 cup skim milk
1 tbsp. no-fat sour cream
1 cup all-purpose flour

1 tbsp. unsweetened
   applesauce
1/8 tsp. salt

Preheat the oven to 500 degrees. In a large mixing bowl, beat the egg whites until they start to foam. Add the remaining ingredients and beat at high speed until all the batter is well mixed and light. Pour into a nonstick popover pan or a nonstick deep muffin tin. Place in the preheated 500-degree oven, bake for 20 minutes, then reduce the temperature to 300 degrees and bake for 20 more minutes. Popovers should be light and fluffy. Serve warm or at room temperature. Makes 6 popovers.

Lagniappe: Popovers are a lot like eating air, but they are beautiful and complement any meal. Use these as you would a roll or bread. Never open the oven door while they are baking. It will cause them to fall, perhaps never to rise again. Be sure you have fresh eggs. The whites won't rise as much if the eggs are older. You can double this recipe by doubling everything but the eggs. Use ten egg whites with a doubled recipe. I like to store popovers in the refrigerator if any are left. You can make the batter ahead of time, and hold it in the refrigerator for up to 24 hours prior to baking. Just pour the batter right into the tins; do not beat the mixture again.

Calories—100; Fat—.2 g; Protein—7 g; Carbohydrates—21 g; Cholesterol—.7 mg; Fiber—.1 g; Sodium—85 mg
2 of the 100 calories are from fat.
2% of the calories come from fat.

ONION-HERB BREAD

2 1/3 cups self-rising flour
2 tbsp. sugar
1 tsp. dried basil
1/4 tsp. dried oregano
1/8 tsp. dried thyme
2 tbsp. cornstarch
1 1/4-oz. packet All Natural
  Rapidrise yeast

1 1/2 cups club soda
1/4 tsp. Tabasco® Sauce
2 tsp. white wine
  Worcestershire sauce
1/2 cup finely chopped
  onion
2 tbsp. finely minced fresh
  parsley

Preheat the oven to 350 degrees. In a large mixing bowl, mix together all the dry ingredients with a wire whisk or a fork until well blended. Pour in the club soda and stir it into the flour mixture. Add the Tabasco® Sauce, white wine Worcestershire sauce, onion, and fresh parsley. Blend together well. Pour the batter into a 9 x 5 x 3-inch loaf pan. Set the pan in a large paper bag and let it proof in a warm, dry place for 35 minutes. Bake at 350 degrees for 1 hour, or until the bread has a nicely browned top. Remove from the oven, allow the bread to stand for 2 minutes, then remove from the pan, slice, and serve. Serves 6.

Lagniappe: When you want a flavored bread to go with a meal, this is a wonderful choice. It is tasty, easy, and fun to make. Although it takes an hour to bake, it only takes about 2 minutes of preparation time. You can make this bread in advance and reheat it later, but it is so very good right after baking it. I always plan to have it come out of the oven just before serving.

Calories—195; Fat—trace; Protein—1.4 g; Carbohydrates—42.9 g; Cholesterol—0 mg; Fiber—1.7 g; Sodium—495 mg
Less than 1 of the 195 calories is from fat.
Less than 1% of the calories come from fat.

ORANGE-WALNUT BREAD

2 cups all-purpose flour
1 cup sugar
2 tbsp. light brown sugar
1 tsp. baking powder
1/2 tsp. baking soda
1/4 tsp. nutmeg
1/4 tsp. salt
2 tbsp. walnuts, chopped
1/3 cup unsweetened
    applesauce

1 tsp. vanilla extract
1/2 cup no-fat no-
    cholesterol egg substitute
2 tbsp. fresh orange peel
    zest
1 cup fresh orange juice
Vegetable oil and flour
    spray

Preheat the oven to 350 degrees. In a large mixing bowl, combine the first seven ingredients and mix together well with a wire whisk or a fork. Add the chopped walnuts and mix them in. In another large bowl, blend together the applesauce, egg substitute, vanilla, and orange peel zest until well blended. Add the orange juice, and blend it in well. Pour the liquid ingredients into the bowl with the dry ingredients, and mix together just until the dry ingredients are moist. Do not overmix.

Pour the mixture into two 8 x 4-inch bread pans that have been sprayed with the vegetable oil and flour spray. Bake for 50 minutes to an hour. Remove and allow the bread to stand for 10 minutes before slicing. Serve warm. Serves 8.

Lagniappe: This is a wonderful make-ahead bread. It can be made the day before you use it and refrigerated. I like to slice it, then heat it up quickly in the oven or microwave. You can also freeze this bread well. I wrap it tightly in plastic wrap, label and date it, then freeze it for later use. You can use this recipe to make Orange-Walnut Muffins by pouring the batter into muffin tins and cutting the baking time down to about 20 to 25 minutes.

Calories—223; Fat—.8 g; Protein—4.5 g; Carbohydrates—50.1 g; Cholesterol—0 mg; Fiber—.3 g; Sodium—174 mg

7 of the 223 calories are from fat.
3% of the calories come from fat.

QUICK BAKED BREAD

2 1/3 cups self-rising flour
2 tbsp. sugar
2 tbsp. cornstarch
1 1/2-oz. packet Butter Buds

1/2 tsp. baking powder
1/2 tsp. salt
1 12-oz. can light beer, at room temperature

Preheat the oven to 350 degrees. With a wire whisk or fork, mix together all the dry ingredients until well blended. Add the beer and stir it into the flour mixture. Pour the batter into a 9 x 5 x 3-inch loaf pan. Set the pan in a large paper bag, and let it proof in a warm, dry place for 20 minutes. Bake at 350 degrees for 1 hour, or until the bread has a nicely browned top. Remove from the oven, allow the bread to stand for 2 minutes, then remove from the pan, slice, and serve. Serves 6.

Lagniappe: Baking bread is truly a specialized art. Baking *this* bread is a task an idiot can accomplish. That may sound a little harsh, but it is nonetheless true. It is so easy and the product is so good that it is truly a must for those who think they can't begin to bake bread. You don't need any specialized equipment, just a bread pan, an oven, and a little light beer. The action of the beer and the yeast in the beer gives the bread a true yeast taste without all usual process of baking yeast bread. Try this bread; it is fat-free, easy, and most importantly it tastes scrumptious.

You can bake this bread in advance, wrap it, and store it like you would regular bread. It also freezes well. However, the absolute best way to serve this bread is right from the oven; it is so wonderful fresh.

Calories—200; Fat—trace; Protein—4.8 g; Carbohydrates—41.5 g; Cholesterol—0 mg; Fiber—1.6 g; Sodium—753 mg

None of the 200 calories are from fat.

QUICK CHEESE BREAD

2 1/3 cups self-rising flour
1 tbsp. sugar
2 tbsp. cornstarch
1/2 tsp. salt
1 1/2-oz. packet Butter Buds
1 1/4-oz. packet All Natural Rapidrise yeast
1 cup nonfat cottage cheese

1/2 cup nonfat parmesan cheese
2 tbsp. romano cheese
1/4 cup skim milk
1/4 tsp. Tabasco® Sauce
1 cup club soda
Vegetable oil and flour spray

Preheat the oven to 350 degrees. In a large mixing bowl, combine all the dry ingredients with a wire whisk or a fork until well blended. Add the cottage cheese, Parmesan, and Romano cheese, and blend them in. Add the milk and Tabasco® Sauce, then pour in the club soda and stir together the whole mixture. Pour the batter into a 9 x 5 x 3-inch loaf pan that you have lightly sprayed with vegetable oil and flour. Cover the loaf pan with a damp cloth, and put it in a warm, dry place to proof for about 35 minutes. Bake at 350 degrees for 1 hour, or until the bread has a nicely browned top. Remove from the oven, allow the bread to stand for 2 minutes, then remove from the pan, slice, and serve. Serves 6.

Lagniappe: The taste of this bread will stupefy you. You'll think you are eating bread that is loaded with fat grams. It seems somewhat high in calories, but when compared to other cheese breads it is not. This is a wonderful bread to serve with any spicy meal. I also like to eat this bread for supper when I want a meatless meal that is savory and filling. A nice glass of wine like a Chardonnay or a Bordeaux will have you thinking you are just a little south of heaven.

Calories—239; Fat—.9 g; Protein—11.2 g; Carbohydrates—43.7 g; Cholesterol—2 mg; Fiber—.1 g; Sodium—591 mg

8 of the 239 calories are from fat.
3% of the calories come from fat.

SWEET POTATO BREAD

3 cups all-purpose flour
1 tsp. baking soda
1/2 tsp. baking powder
1/2 tsp. salt
2 tsp. cinnamon
1 tsp. nutmeg
1/4 tsp. allspice
2 cups sugar
2 1/2 cups sweet potatoes, cooked and mashed

1 cup no-fat no-cholesterol egg substitute
1 1/4 cup sweetened applesauce
1/4 cup chopped pecans
Vegetable oil and flour spray

Preheat the oven to 350 degrees. In a large mixing bowl, combine the first eight ingredients and blend with a wire whisk or fork until well mixed. In another bowl, mix all the other ingredients, except for the pecans, until well creamed and smooth. Add the pecans to the flour mixture, then pour the liquid ingredients into the flour. Mix until the mixture is just moist, but not over mixed.

Spray two 9 1/2 x 5 1/2-inch loaf pans with the vegetable oil and flour spray, then pour the batter into the loaf pans. Bake at 350 degrees for about 45 to 50 minutes, or until done when tested with a toothpick. The pick should come out clean when inserted into the center of the bread. Remove the bread from the oven and let it set for five minutes before removing from the pan and slicing. Serve warm. Serves 8.

Lagniappe: This is a great breakfast bread or a bread you can eat as a snack in the evening. I also like it with coffee. You can use this recipe to make Sweet Potato Muffins by pouring the batter into muffin tins and baking for about 20 minutes. It should make about 16 muffins.

Calories—521; Fat—2.6 g; Protein—8.8 g; Carbohydrates—114.2 g; Cholesterol—0 mg; Fiber—1.1 g; Sodium—279 mg
23 of the 521 calories are from fat.
4% of the calories come from fat.

CREPES

3 large egg whites	**2/3 cup skim milk**
6 tbsp. all-purpose flour	**1 tbsp. brandy**
1 tbsp. sugar	**Butter-flavored nonstick**
Dash nutmeg	**vegetable oil spray**
1/8 tsp. salt	

In a medium-sized mixing bowl, lightly beat the eggs. Add the flour, sugar, nutmeg, and salt. Beat together until well blended. Add the milk and brandy, and beat until smooth.

Lightly spray a small nonstick skillet with the butter-flavored spray, then heat the skillet over medium heat until it is hot. When hot, pour 1/4 cup of batter into the skillet and tilt the skillet around until the entire bottom is covered. Return to the heat for 35 seconds, then turn the crêpe over and cook for 25 seconds on the other side. Turn the crêpe onto a plate or waxed paper. Repeat the process 3 more crêpes, then spray again and cook the remaining 4 crêpes in the same manner. This will make 8 crêpes.

Lagniappe: Crêpes can be eaten alone or with syrup for breakfast. These crêpes can also be used in other recipes (see index for recipes). Crêpes keep very well in the refrigerator for up to 4 days. Just put them on a plate and cover them with plastic wrap, or wrap them in waxed paper and put them into a zip-lock bag. You can also freeze them in a zip-lock bag. To use them later, let the crêpes thaw completely at room temperature, then separate them as needed. I find it easier to make a lot of crêpes at one time and freeze them for later use. Just double or triple the recipe, and make as many as you can. These nonfat crêpes can be used in numerous recipes and will give your dishes quite a touch of distinction.

Per crêpe:
Calories—34; Fat—.2 g; Protein—2.5 g; Carbohydrates—5.2 g;
Cholesterol—.4 mg; Fiber—0 g; Sodium—66 mg
2 of the 34 calories are from fat.
6% of the calories come from fat.

DATE-NUT MUFFINS

1 cup all-purpose flour
1/2 cup whole wheat flour
2/3 cup sugar
1 tbsp. dark brown sugar
2 tsp. baking powder
1/2 tsp. salt
1 cup chopped dates
1/4 cup pecan pieces
1/2 cup no-fat no-
  cholesterol egg substitute

1/2 cup evaporated skim
  milk
1/3 cup unsweetened
  applesauce
1 tsp. vanilla extract
Vegetable oil and flour
  spray

Preheat the oven to 425 degrees. In a large mixing bowl, combine the first six ingredients until well mixed. Stir in the dates and pecans to coat them well with the flour. In a small bowl, mix together the remaining ingredients until well blended. Add the liquid ingredients to the dry ingredients, and stir just until dry ingredients are moist; do not over mix. Pour into muffin tins that have been sprayed with vegetable oil and flour spray. Bake at 425 degrees for 15 to 20 minutes, or until golden brown and the center is cooked. Check with a toothpick, which should come out clean when inserted into the center of the muffin. Serve warm. Makes 10 muffins.

Lagniappe: This is not only a good breakfast muffin, but also a great dessert or snack food. The pecans don't hurt this recipe in the fat content because the pecans are about the only significant source of fat in the recipe. You could really add about 2 tablespoons of oil to this recipe, and the fat gram count would only go up to about 3.7 grams of fat. That would account for only 33 calories coming from fat. The calorie count would slightly rise to about 224 calories, making this version of the recipe have about 15% of its calories from fat. It gives you lots of room for play. Try it once as above, then try it with the little added oil. Decide which way you like best.

Per muffin:
Calories—200; Fat—1 g; Protein—5.2 g; Carbohydrates—42.4 g; Cholesterol—1 mg; Fiber—1.3 g; Sodium—248 mg
9 of the 200 calories are from fat.
5% of the calories come from fat.

HUEVOS RANCHEROS

4 whole white corn tortillas (no oils)
1/2 cup no-fat no-cholesterol egg substitute
1/4 cup finely minced onions
1/4 cup finely chopped bell peppers
1 tbsp. chopped fresh cilantro (or fresh parsley)
1/2 tsp. salt
1/4 tsp. Tabasco® Sauce
1/8 tsp. nutmeg
1/4 tsp. black pepper
1/4 cup diced fresh tomatoes
1/4 cup no-fat Swiss cheese
1/2 cup no-fat sour cream
Picante sauce to taste

In a nonstick skillet over medium heat, heat the corn tortillas until they are warm and somewhat pliable, about 30 seconds on each side. Set aside on a warm plate for later use. Mix together the egg substitute, onions, bell pepper, cilantro, salt, Tabasco® Sauce, nutmeg, and black pepper until well blended. Heat the nonstick skillet over medium heat, and pour the egg substitute mixture into the skillet. Cook, stirring often, for 1 minute, then add the fresh diced tomatoes and cook until the egg is firm. Add the Swiss cheese, and fold it into the hot egg mixture. Place the cooked egg mixture into the center of each tortilla and generously cover with sour cream. Fold the tortilla closed. Serve two tortillas on each plate, topped with picante sauce. Serve at once. Serves 2.

Lagniappe: This is a wonderful, completely healthy breakfast. It will fill you up and leave you thinking you have really had a delicious breakfast. Only you need to know that it was nonfat. In fact, when you make a non-fat dish, don't tell people that it is nonfat (especially when you think they won't like nonfat). Just let them enjoy! If you like, instead of the tortilla, you can just use the same recipe to make an omelet, then cover it with the no-fat sour cream and top with picante sauce. What a meal!

Calories—295; Fat—2.3 g; Protein—23.7 g; Carbohydrates—44.5 g; Cholesterol—4 mg; Fiber—2.6 g; Sodium—1224 mg
21 of the 295 calories are from fat.
7% of the calories come from fat.

NONFAT FRENCH TOAST
PAIN PERDU SANS GRAISSE

1 4-oz. container no-fat egg
   substitute
2 large egg whites
1/2 cup skim milk
1/2 cup sugar
1 tsp. vanilla extract

1/2 tsp. cinnamon
1/2 tsp. nutmeg
1/8 tsp. salt
8 slices stale bread
Butter-flavored nonstick
   vegetable oil spray

In a large mixing bowl, combine the egg substitute and egg whites and beat them together for 30 seconds; it should begin to foam. Add the milk, sugar, vanilla, cinnamon, nutmeg, and salt. Beat well with a fork or wire whisk until well blended. Place one slice of bread in the bowl at a time, and let the bread soak up some of the mixture on each side.

Very lightly spray the bottom of a nonstick skillet with the butter-flavored spray, then place the skillet over medium-low heat until the pan is hot. Add the bread and cook for about 1 minute on each side, or until the bread has browned nicely. Spray the skillet again after you have cooked 4 slices of bread. Serve warm, right from the skillet or sprinkle with additional powdered sugar or serve with syrup. Serves 4.

Lagniappe: It would be hard to give up Pain Perdu on any food schedule. I had to find a low-fat version of this premier breakfast dish. Pain perdu (lost bread) is the Louisiana version of French toast. Do not make this dish in advance; make this dish just before you are ready to serve. You can freeze pain perdu, but it is nowhere near the quality of just-made pain perdu. This is a sensational breakfast dish.

Calories—266; Fat—2.3 g; Protein—9.4 g; Carbohydrates—69.6 g; Cholesterol—.5 mg; Fiber—1.2 g; Sodium—613 mg
20 of the 266 calories are from fat.
7.5% of the calories come from fat.

NONFAT OMELET

Butter-flavored nonstick
  spray
1/4 cup chopped green
  onions
2 large mushrooms
3 large egg whites
1/8 tsp. nutmeg

1/4 tsp. Tabasco® Sauce
1/4 tsp. salt
1/4 cup skim milk
1 tsp. Molly McButter
  Natural Cheese-flavored
  Sprinkles

Lightly spray the bottom of a nonstick skillet with the butter-flavored spray. Place the skillet on medium heat and heat until the skillet is hot. Add the onions and mushrooms, sauté for 2 minutes, then slide them onto a plate. While the vegetables are sautéing, briskly beat the egg whites with a wire whisk or fork until they foam up and triple in volume. Add the nutmeg, Tabasco® Sauce, salt, and skim milk and beat again.

When the vegetables are cooked, remove them and reheat the skillet for 30 seconds, then pour the egg whites into the skillet. Heat for 1 minute then tear little openings in the center of the omelet to let the excess liquid drain onto the skillet. Add the vegetables evenly on top of the omelet. Sprinkle with the cheese-flavored sprinkles and continue to cook until the omelet is completely set. Gently loosen the sides of the omelet and fold it in half. It should float easily around in the pan. Cook for 30 more seconds, then slide it onto your serving plate. Eat at once. Serves 1.

Lagniappe: You can repeat the process for more than one omelette. This is a large, fluffy omelet. It fills the plate and looks scrumptious.

Calories—108; Fat—1.5 g; Protein—13.4 g; Carbohydrates—11.2 g; Cholesterol—31 mg; Fiber—1.0 g; Sodium—871 mg
13.5 of the 108 calories are from fat.
12.5% of the calories come from fat.

TURKEY FRITTATA

1 3 1/2-oz. turkey tenderloin piece (99% fat-free)
1/2 tsp. Cajun Spice Mix (see page 274)
1/2 cup no-fat no-cholesterol egg substitute
2 cups boiled new potatoes, thinly sliced (washed but not skinned)
1/2 cups chopped green onions

1/4 cup chopped red bell peppers
2 tbsp. skim or nonfat milk
1 tbsp. dry white wine
1/4 tsp. Tabasco® Sauce
1/2 tsp. salt
1/8 tsp. nutmeg
1/2 cup nonfat mozzarella cheese

Place the turkey tenderloin piece under plastic wrap. Using a kitchen mallet, pound the tenderloin until it has increased in size by about one-third. Cut the tenderloin into bite-sized pieces and season with the Cajun Spice Mix. Heat a heavy, nonstick skillet over medium-high heat until it is hot. Add the turkey pieces and cook, stirring often, until the turkey is cooked, about 3 to 4 minutes. Remove from the skillet and set aside. Preheat the oven to 425 degrees. Arrange the thinly sliced potato slices on the bottom of a 1 1/2-quart casserole. Sprinkle the turkey pieces evenly over the potato slices. Mix together the remaining ingredients, except for the mozzarella cheese, until well mixed; then pour the egg mixture on top of the potatoes.

Bake at 425 degrees until the egg has set and begins to brown, about 8 minutes. Sprinkle with the nonfat cheese, and bake uncovered until the cheese melts. Remove from the oven, let the dish cool for 2 minutes, then serve hot. Serves 4.

Lagniappe: What a wonderful breakfast dish. It is filling and it looks divine. Your guests will think you really went to trouble, but you'll know better. While there is a little fat in this dish from the turkey, it is negligible, and the taste is worth it.

If you want to change the taste, you can substitute chicken or even very lean chopped pork. For a completely different taste, one that could change the dish to an entree, use 1/2 pound of shrimp instead of the turkey. What a delight! It does increase the cholesterol, but there is almost no change in the fat level. The dish can be baked for 8 minutes, removed and allowed to cool, then refrigerated until you are ready to use. To serve, just add the mozzarella cheese and bake at 300 degrees for 3 minutes or until the cheese has melted. This is a great make-ahead breakfast for when you have guests.

Calories—143; Fat—.5 g; Protein—19.2 g; Carbohydrates—14.8 g; Cholesterol—11 mg; Fiber—.9 g; Sodium—594 mg

5 of the 143 calories are from fat.
3% of the calories come from fat.

Seafood

BAKED FISH

4 6-oz. fillets fish (use your favorite kind of fish)
1 tsp. Cajun Spice Mix (see page 274)
1 recipe Butter Sauce (see page 272)

1/4 cup finely minced fresh parsley
Paprika to garnish
8 large lemon wedges

Preheat the oven to 375 degrees. Season the four fish fillets equally with the Cajun Spice Mix, dip the seasoned fish into the Butter Sauce, then place the fillets in a shallow baking dish large enough to hold the four fillets. Cover the fish with the remaining sauce, sprinkle with the parsley, and dust lightly with the paprika. Bake at 375 degrees for 25 minutes, or until the fish flakes easily and is very moist. Serve each fish fillet with two wedges of lemon and generously spoon the sauce from the baking dish over the fish fillets. Serve at once. Serves 4.

Lagniappe: This is a simple and easy way to serve fish. Don't let the ease of preparation make you think that the taste is not superb; it is sumptuous! Fish is so easy to cook and so good for you. We know that just eating fish three times a week will significantly decrease our chances for heart disease and cancer. This is a case of something tasting great and being good for you as well.

Calories—210; Fat—2.3 g; Protein—35.4 g; Carbohydrates—7.3 g; Cholesterol—62 mg; Fiber—trace; Sodium—864 mg

21 of the 210 calories are from fat.
10% of calories come from fat.

BEER-BRAISED OYSTERS

Butter-flavored nonstick
  vegetable oil spray
4 cloves garlic, crushed
  then minced
1 bunch green onions,
  finely chopped
1/4 cup finely chopped
  celery
1 small red bell pepper,
  finely diced
1 12-oz. can light beer
1/2 lb. fresh mushrooms,
  sliced

1 qt. oysters, with their
  liquid
1/2 tsp. salt
1/2 tsp. cayenne pepper
1/4 tsp. Tabasco® Sauce
1 tbsp. white wine
  Worcestershire sauce
1/4 tsp. black pepper
1 tsp. sweet basil
1/4 cup finely chopped
  fresh parsley

Spray a large nonstick skillet lightly with the butter-flavored spray. Place the skillet over medium heat, and when the skillet is hot, add the garlic, green onions, celery, and red bell pepper. Sauté for 2 minutes, stirring constantly. Add the beer and mushrooms and let the mixture come to a boil. When it begins to boil, lower the temperature to a simmer and allow the mixture to braise in the beer for 5 minutes. Add the oysters and the remaining ingredients, except for the parsley, and let the oysters braise for 12 minutes, stirring often. Add the parsley, and continue to cook for 1 more minute. Serve hot with plenty of French bread. Serves 4.

Lagniappe: This is a tasty way to get real oyster flavor without much fat. I like to sop up the juice with plenty of fresh French bread, but I have also served this sauce over rice or over pasta. If you serve it with either rice or pasta, you are increasing the complex carbohydrates, which not only adds bulk, but keeps you filled and full of energy without adding fat grams. You will notice that I add the parsley after the cooking is through. I do that to keep the fresh green taste of the parsley from breaking down. If it cooks too long, you only get added color without much fresh herbal taste. You will notice that is pretty much a Cajun way of cooking with parsley. My grandmother taught me to add parsley at the end. She just said "Cher, it tastes better!" It really does!

Calories—187; Fat—5 g; Protein—13.3 g; Carbohydrates—17.4 g; Cholesterol—92 mg; Fiber—.9 g; Sodium—528 mg

45 of the 187 calories are from fat.
24% of the calories come from fat.

BOILED CRABS

3 gallons water
1 26-oz. box salt
2 heads garlic, left whole
2 whole jalapeños, crushed
30 whole black
   peppercorns
6 large onions, peeled
6 stalks celery, whole
1/4 cup Tabasco® Sauce

20 whole bay leaves
10 whole allspice
10 whole cloves
1/4 cup dried sweet basil
5 lb. whole red potatoes
7 dozen whole live crabs
12 ears frozen whole corn
   on the cob

In a large stock pot (10 to 12 gallons), bring the water and salt to a boil. Add the garlic, jalapeños, black peppercorns, onions, celery, Tabasco® Sauce, bay leaves, allspice, cloves, and sweet basil. Let the water boil for 20 minutes, then add the potatoes and let them boil for 20 minutes. Add the crabs and corn and bring the water back to boiling. Let the crabs cook for 15 minutes after the liquid begins to boil. Remove the crabs, onions, potatoes, and corn and serve at once. Serves 8.

Lagniappe: This is a very low-fat and filling dinner. You get the meat and vegetables all in one. There is no oil. You can use a seafood dipping sauce if you like, or serve the crabs with Butter Sauce (see page 272).

Calories—592; Fat—3.7 g; Protein—34.5 g; Carbohydrates—109.4 g; Cholesterol—88 mg; Fiber—6.6 g; Sodium—510 mg

33 of the 592 calories are from fat.
6% of the calories come from fat.

SPICY BOILED SHRIMP

2 gallons water
1/2 26-oz. box salt
1 head garlic, left whole
2 whole cayenne or
  jalapeño peppers,
  crushed but whole
30 whole black peppercorns
2 large onions, peeled and
  quartered
6 stalks celery, whole

2 tbsp. Tabasco® Sauce
10 whole bay leaves
10 whole allspice
10 whole cloves
1/4 cup dried sweet basil
1/2 bunch parsley, washed
6 lb. large (31-36 size)
  whole shrimp, with
  heads on

In a large stock pot (7 to 10 gallons), bring the water and salt to a boil. Add the garlic, peppers, black peppercorns, onions, celery, Tabasco® Sauce, bay leaves, allspice, cloves, sweet basil, and parsley. Let the water boil for 20 minutes, then add the shrimp and bring the water back to boiling. Let the shrimp boil for 5 minutes, then turn the heat off and let the shrimp stand in the hot water for 5 more minutes. Remove the shrimp, drain well, and serve at once; or put the shrimp on ice and chill to serve cold. Serves 8.

Lagniappe: Boiled shrimp is a wonderful low-fat dinner. If you like you can add five pounds of red potatoes and 16 ears of cleaned corn on the cob to the pot and you will have a complete meal. Just add the potatoes when you add all the other initial ingredients and let them boil for 20 minutes. Add the corn when you have 6 minutes of boiling left, and proceed as above. You'll get the meat and vegetables all in one. There is no oil, therefore you have very little fat in the dish. You can use a seafood dipping sauce if you like, or you can make a low-fat tartar sauce. You can also use this recipe to boil shrimp for use in other recipes.

Calories—362; Fat—6 g; Protein—69 g; Carbohydrates—3.6 g; Cholesterol—520 mg; Fiber—0 g; Sodium—1081 mg
54 of the 362 calories are from fat.
15% of the calories come from fat.

Note: I need to point out that the American Heart Association recommends no more than 6 ounces of a cooked lean meat or fish per day. They also recommend no more than 300 mg of cholesterol per day. This recipe exceeds both of those recommendations. To stay within these guidelines you would have to eat no more than the 6 ounces of cooked shrimp.

BROILED RED SNAPPER
AUX CHAMPIGNON

4 6-oz. fillets red snapper
1 tsp. Cajun Spice Mix (see
    page 274)
Butter-flavored nonstick
    vegetable oil spray
1 recipe Mushrooms Marie
    LeBlanc (see page 227)

1/2 cup (about 4 oz.) fresh
    lump crabmeat, frozen
    snow crab, or even the
    artificial crabmeat
1 large lemon
Paprika to garnish

Preheat the oven to broil. Season the fillets with the Cajun Spice Mix and place them in a pan for broiling. Spray lightly with the butter-flavored spray, and broil about 3 inches from the heat for 4 minutes on the skin side then turn the fish over and broil for 8 more minutes on the other side.

While the fish is cooking, make the mushroom recipe. Add the lump crabmeat to the mushroom mixture, and blend together. When the fish is cooked, remove to four warm plates. Cut the lemon in half. Squeeze one-half of the lemon for its juice, then drop a little lemon juice on top of each piece of fish. Cut the remaining half lemon into thin circles for a garnish; set aside. Spoon generous amounts of the mushroom-crab mixture on top of each fish fillet. Dust lightly with paprika and garnish with the lemon circles. Serve at once. Serves 4.

Lagniappe: This is an exquisite dish! The plate would be finished with a nice stuffed tomato and a green vegetable. Serve with a chilled Sauvignon Blanc or perhaps a Johannisberg Riesling. You will have a dinner worth raving over. This is quick and easy, so don't try to do anything in advance, except for perhaps seasoning the fish. When you season the fish and refrigerate it, the seasonings have an increased impact on the fish. Relish this dish; it is so delicate!

Calories—286; Fat—3.3 g; Protein—41 g; Carbohydrates—37 g; Cholesterol—84 mg; Fiber—7 g; Sodium—893 mg

286 of the 30 calories are from fat.
10% of calories come from fat.

BROILED RED SNAPPER
WITH SAUTEED CRABMEAT

4 6-oz. fillets red snapper
1 1/4 tsp. Cajun Spice Mix
  (see page 274)
Butter-flavored nonstick
  vegetable oil spray

1 recipe Sautéed Crabmeat
  (see page 29)
2 large lemons, cut into
  wedges

Preheat the oven to broil. Wash the fillets of red snapper with cold water and pat them dry with white paper towels. Season them equally with the Cajun Spice Mix. Place them on a nonstick baking dish, and lightly spray them with the butter-flavored nonstick vegetable oil spray. Broil about 3 inches from the heat source for 4 to 5 minutes on each side. Remove to a warm serving plate and cover with the Sautéed Crabmeat. Garnish with lemon wedges and serve at once. Serves 4.

Lagniappe: You can use any firm flesh fish for this recipe. The fillet should be about 1-inch thick. If it is thicker or thinner, you will have to adjust the cooking time either up or down. It really helps to use a nonstick baking dish because it allows you to use just one spray of butter-flavored vegetable oil spray. You will be amazed at how well the fish cooks without any oil. The fish should be plump and white when ready.

Calories—282; Fat—4.4 g; Protein—45.9 g; Carbohydrates—35.7 g; Cholesterol—350 mg; Fiber—.2 g; Sodium—708 mg

40 of the 282 calories are from fat.
14% of the calories come from fat.

CHAMPAGNE TROUT

4 6-oz. fillets freshwater
trout
1 tsp. Cajun Spice Mix (see
page 274)
1 tbsp. minced fresh basil

1 cup julienned carrots
1 cup julienned celery
2 cups champagne
1/2 tsp. Tabasco® Sauce

Preheat the oven to 450 degrees. Season the four trout fillets with the Cajun Spice Mix, and place the fish in a shallow 2-quart baking dish. Cover the fish with the minced basil, carrots, and celery. Mix together the champagne and Tabasco® Sauce and pour on top of the fish. Bake for 25 minutes at 450 degrees. Serve at once with the julienned vegetables and some of the broth from the baking dish. Serves 4.

Lagniappe: Champagne and trout—how can you go wrong? Well for that matter, champagne and just about anything will steer you in a delicious direction. This is one of those easy recipes that combines great ingredients and produces raves. The worst part of this recipe is julienning the vegetables, which may take a few extra minutes, but the finished product looks so pretty it's well worth it. Be sure to use freshwater trout and not sea trout (or saltwater trout) for this recipe. The Champagne calls for a fine and delicate meat. The wonderful thing about the widespread availability of seafood is that we have the world at our feet. Don't let the "previously frozen" label over the fish scare you. The quick freezing processes that are used today help to keep the fish very fresh, ensuring top quality.

Remember, eating seafood just a few extra days a week produces great health benefits as long as you don't load the fish down with fats. This recipe is virtually fat-free, except for the small amount of fat we get from the fish itself.

Calories—306; Fat—5.9 g; Protein—35.8 g; Carbohydrates—7.2 g; Cholesterol—96 mg; Fiber—.4 g; Sodium—278 mg

53 of the 306 calories are from fat.
17% of the calories come from fat.

CHILLED CRABMEAT CREPES
ST. MARTINVILLE

2 recipes Crêpes (see pages 96-97)
1 recipe Creamy Crabmeat Spread (see page 281)
1/4 cup no-fat sour cream

1 tsp. fresh lime juice
1/4 tsp. Tabasco® Sauce
1 tsp. paprika
Fresh parsley as a garnish

Fill each of the 16 crêpes equally with the Creamy Crabmeat Spread, until all the crabmeat is used. Roll the crêpes and place two on each plate with the seam down. Mix together the remaining ingredients in a small mixing bowl. Lightly top each crêpe with the sour cream mixture. Garnish with fresh parsley. Serve at once or you can chill until you are ready to serve. Serves 8.

Lagniappe: This is a light dish that tastes so sumptuous you will be amazed. This dish would be nice with a fresh green vegetable. Lump crabmeat may seem costly, but when you realize you can easily serve eight people with just one pound, you realize just how economical it really is. It also has a reputation for being expensive, so your guests get the idea that you really went "all out" for them.

I wouldn't tell anyone that this is a very low-fat dish unless you want to brag! Just let the dish carry itself; sit back and wait for the compliments.

Calories—106; Fat—.9 g; Protein—14.2 g; Carbohydrates—10.7 g; Cholesterol—45 mg; Fiber—.2 g; Sodium—194 mg

1.8 of the 106 calories are from fat.
1.7% of calories come from fat.

CRAB CREPES SEGURA

1/2 recipe Crab Dip
  Kimberly, without the
  crackers (see page 114)
1/3 cup dry white wine
2 recipes Crêpes (see pages
  96-97)
1/4 cup finely minced fresh
  parsley

1/4 cup finely minced green
  onions
1/2 tsp. Tabasco® Sauce
Paprika to garnish
Fresh lemon wedges to
  garnish

Preheat the oven to 350 degrees. Place about 1/2 cup of the Crab Dip Kimberly in a medium-sized saucepan. Add the dry white wine and set aside. Place about 1/4 cup of the crab dip mixture into the center of each crêpe, then roll the crêpes, placing the seams down in a nonstick baking pan. Repeat the process until all 16 crêpes are filled. Place the crêpes in the oven and bake for 15 minutes at 350 degrees.

While the crab crêpes are baking, place the saucepan with the reserved crab dip over low heat. Stir constantly until the sauce is hot. Add the fresh parsley, green onions, and Tabasco® Sauce and blend in well. When the crêpes are ready, place two crêpes on each plate and generously spoon the crab-wine sauce on top of the crêpes. Sprinkle with paprika, and garnish with lemon wedges. Serve at once. Serves 8.

Lagniappe: This is a great party dish. Serving crêpes always wows the crowd. No one has to know that it was so simple—not to mention good for you. I like to make my Crab Dip Kimberly in advance and make my Crêpes way in advance and refrigerate until I am ready to use them. There are so many wonderful ways that this crab dip can be used, I can't even think of them all. I not only like to serve these crêpes as a main dish, but I also think they are wonderful on a buffet. I keep them in a warming tray and place the warm sauce next to them. You can also make miniature crêpes and use them as finger foods for a larger party. Go ahead, come up with your own idea. If it's good, mail it to me; the next book could use it!

Calories—110; Fat—1.4 g; Protein—11.1 g; Carbohydrates—5.3 g; Cholesterol—28 mg; Fiber—.3 g; Sodium—263 mg

12 of the 110 calories are from fat.
11% of calories come from fat.

CRAB DIP KIMBERLY

1 tbsp. unsalted butter
1/2 cup finely chopped
green onions
3 tbsp. finely diced green
bell pepper
3 tbsp. finely diced red bell
pepper
3 tbsp. finely minced celery
2 cloves garlic, finely
minced
2 1/2 tbsp. all-purpose
flour
8 large mushrooms, sliced
2/3 cup evaporated skim
milk

2 tbsp. cream sherry
1 tsp. white wine
Worcestershire sauce
1/2 tsp. Tabasco® Sauce
1/2 tsp. black pepper
1/4 tsp. white pepper
1/2 tsp. salt
1 tsp. onion powder
1/2 tsp. sweet basil
1 8-oz. container fat-free
cream cheese
1 lb. lump crabmeat or
backfin lump crabmeat
Nonfat crackers or chips for
dipping

Heat a medium-sized nonstick surface skillet over medium heat until hot, then add the butter and let it melt. Add the green onions, green and red bell pepper, celery, and garlic. Sauté in the butter for 5 minutes. Add the flour and cook, stirring constantly, for 3 minutes. Add the mushrooms and blend them in for 1 minute. Remove from the heat and add the milk, wine, Worcestershire sauce, and the Tabasco® Sauce, return to the heat and cook while constantly stirring until the sauce thickens, about 1 1/2 minutes.

Season with the black pepper, white pepper, salt, onion powder, and sweet basil and blend in the seasonings well. Add the cream cheese, and stir until it has melted and blended into the sauce. Add the crabmeat and stir gently until the crabmeat is heated through, about 2 minutes. Serve hot with plenty of crackers or chips to dip. Serves 10 generously as a party dip or appetizer.

Lagniappe: If you notice in this recipe I want to cook the flour for at least 3 minutes while stirring. This is necessary to make a true roux. If we don't cook the flour in the butter for 3 minutes, it will be pasty-tasting—kind of like paper maché—so don't cut the time short on this step.

This is a good recipe to teach the various steps in cooking. It starts out as a light vegetable sauté. Then we add the flour and make a roux. Then we make a light basic white sauce. From that point we make it a "heavy" cream sauce (in this case it is a fat-free heavy cream sauce). Then we add a meat (crabmeat) and we have a sauced meat. When you get through this dish, you can see just how easy cooking can be! I also like to use this dip as a base for other dishes; it is good either way. Be ready for rave reviews with this one.

Calories—115; Fat—1.8 g; Protein—13.4 g; Carbohydrates—6.7 g; Cholesterol—43 mg; Fiber—.4 g; Sodium—306 mg

17 of the 115 calories are from fat.
15% of calories come from fat.

CRAB PENNE

1 tbsp. extra virgin olive oil
8 cloves garlic
1 tbsp. minced shallots
3 large onions, finely chopped
1 small diced red bell pepper
1 small diced green bell pepper
1/2 cup finely chopped celery
1 cup minced fresh parsley
1 cup dry white wine
2 8-oz. cans tomato sauce
2 6-oz. cans tomato paste
1 tbsp. Worcestershire sauce
2 tsp. salt
1/2 tsp. fresh ground black pepper
3/4 tsp. cayenne pepper
1/2 tsp. white pepper
1/2 tsp. Tabasco® Sauce
2 dozen crabs, cleaned and broken in half
1/2 gallon water
3 large bay leaves
1 12-oz. pkg. penne pasta

In a 4-gallon or larger pot over medium heat, heat the oil until it is hot. Add the garlic and shallots and sauté until the garlic is nicely browned, about 5 minutes. Add the onions, red and green bell peppers, and celery. Sauté for 5 minutes, then add the parsley and white wine and cook for 20 more minutes, stirring often. Add the tomato sauce and tomato paste. Cook over medium heat for about 30 more minutes, stirring often. Add the Worcestershire sauce, salt, black pepper, cayenne, white pepper, and Tabasco® Sauce, and crabs. Cover and cook for 15 minutes. Add the water and bay leaves, bring to a boil, then reduce to a simmer and cook for 15 more minutes, stirring often. Add the penne pasta and cook until the pasta is al dente. Serve hot. Serves 8.

Lagniappe: This is a one-pot dish. It makes a complete meal. Cooking the crab shells in the dish creates a wonderful stock that makes the pasta most flavorful. This is sort of like a crab boil with the rest of the meal included—all for the price of one.

Calories—308; Fat—3.4 g; Protein—19 g; Carbohydrates—48 g; Cholesterol—44 mg; Fiber—2.3 g; Sodium—856 mg

31 of the 308 calories are from fat.
10% of the calories come from fat.

CRABMEAT AU GRATIN

1 tbsp. unsalted butter
1/2 cup chopped green
  onions
2 cloves garlic, crushed and
  minced
1 lb. lump crabmeat
1 tsp. Cajun Spice Mix (see
  page 274)
1/4 cup evaporated skim
  milk

2/3 cup no-fat sour cream
1/2 cup no-fat no-
  cholesterol egg substitute
1/2 tsp. Tabasco® Sauce
2/3 cup grated no-fat
  cheddar or American
  cheese
Paprika
Lemon wedges

Preheat the oven to 350 degrees. Heat a large nonstick skillet over medium heat until hot, then add the butter. When the butter is melted, add the onions and garlic. Sauté for 2 minutes, then add the crabmeat and Cajun Spice Mix. Sauté for 5 minutes, carefully stirring to prevent breaking the crabmeat apart. In a mixing bowl, beat together the skim milk, sour cream, egg substitute, and Tabasco® Sauce until well blended. Remove the skillet from the heat, and pour the sour cream mixture into the skillet. Stir it into the crabmeat, return to low heat, and cook for 5 minutes, stirring constantly. Pour the mixture into a 2-quart casserole or individual serving dishes, and cover with the nonfat cheese. Dust lightly with the paprika and bake at 350 degrees for 20 minutes or until the cheese is melted and begins to brown. Serve hot with lemon wedges. Serves 4.

Lagniappe: This is an example of a dish that is so very close to the heavy fat recipe that it will be hard to tell the difference. Almost anything you fix with fresh crabmeat is sure to please. If you can't get fresh crabmeat, you can use frozen, but be sure to let it completely thaw in the refrigerator before you use it, and be sure to drain off any liquid that drains from the meat. I'm often asked about canned crabmeat. I don't recommend using it in an au gratin dish. You might be able to use it to flavor a dish, but I never recommend using the canned product when crabmeat is the focal point of the dish. If you can't find either fresh or frozen crabmeat, you can use the artificial crabmeat available in most seafood markets or at the seafood counter at large groceries. It is not a crab product at all, but rather flavored white fish. It is a very low-fat product and is actually lower in cholesterol than crabmeat. It does have a bit more of a tang than crabmeat and sometimes has a fishy smell, but overall it is a suitable alternative when the real thing is not obtainable.

Calories—219; Fat—4.3 g; Protein—28.4 g; Carbohydrates—12.4 g; Cholesterol—100 mg; Fiber—.2 g; Sodium—462 mg
39 of the 219 calories are from fat.
18% of calories come from fat.

CRABMEAT PICARD

2 tbsp. unsalted butter
1 large onion, finely
  chopped
1/2 cup finely chopped
  celery
1/4 cup carrots, finely
  chopped
1 medium red bell pepper,
  finely diced
1/2 tsp. sage
1/2 tsp. sweet basil
1/4 tsp. thyme
1/4 tsp. nutmeg

2 tbsp. flour
1 13-oz. can evaporated
  skim milk
1/4 cup dry vermouth
1/2 tsp. salt
1/2 tsp. Tabasco® Sauce
2 cups corn flakes, toasted
  in the oven
1 lb. lump crabmeat
1 cup fat-free cracker
  crumbs
Paprika

Preheat the oven to 375 degrees. In a large skillet over medium heat, heat the butter until it is completely melted. Add the onions, celery, carrots, and red bell pepper and sauté for 5 minutes. Add the sage, basil, thyme, and nutmeg and mix until well blended. Add the flour and cook for 4 minutes, stirring constantly until blended. Add the skim milk, vermouth, salt, and Tabasco® Sauce; stir until well blended. Mix together the toasted corn flakes and crabmeat, then stir it into the sauce mixture. Fold together until well blended. Pour into six individual baking dishes or casserole dishes. Sprinkle the cracker crumbs on top of the casseroles, and dust them lightly with the paprika. Bake at 375 degrees for 20 minutes, or until golden brown. Serve hot. Serves 6.

Lagniappe: This is a quick and easy casserole dish that enhances the singular flavor of crabmeat. I like to use this as an entree with a large glass of very cold white zinfandel, a green vegetable, and a wilted green salad with a light vinaigrette. I also like plenty of hot fresh nonfat bread. What a delightful dinner! You can make this recipe in advance, tightly cover it, and refrigerate or freeze it. To reheat, just thaw in the refrigerator and bake at 300 degrees for about 12 to 15 minutes, or until the dish is hot enough to serve.

Calories—282; Fat—5.1 g; Protein—21.2 g; Carbohydrates—35.6 g; Cholesterol—72 mg; Fiber—.6 g; Sodium—458 mg

46 of the 282 calories are from fat.
16% of the calories come from fat.

CRAWFISH CASSEROLE ETIENNE

Butter-flavored nonstick
  vegetable oil spray
1 medium onion, finely
  chopped
1 cup finely chopped celery
1/2 cup finely diced bell
  pepper
3 cloves garlic, crushed and
  minced
1/4 cup dry white wine
1 lb. crawfish, peeled and
  deveined
1 can low-fat cream of
  mushroom soup

1 cup water
1/2 cup diced pimentos
1/2 cup finely chopped
  green onions
1/4 cup finely chopped
  fresh parsley
2 cups cooked long grain
  white rice
1 tsp. Cajun Spice Mix (see
  page 274)
1/2 tsp. Tabasco® Sauce
1 tbsp. Worcestershire
  sauce
1/2 cup fresh bread crumbs

Preheat the oven to 350 degrees. Lightly spray a large, heavy nonstick skillet with the butter-flavored vegetable oil spray, then place on medium heat. When the skillet is hot, add the onion, celery, bell pepper, and garlic. Sauté for 3 minutes, then add the wine and bring to a boil. Reduce to a simmer and cook for 3 more minutes. Add the crawfish, simmer for 4 minutes, then add the remaining ingredients, except for the bread crumbs. Stir in well and cook for 5 minutes. Pour into a 2-quart casserole dish, and cover with the bread crumbs. Lightly spray once with the butter-flavored nonstick vegetable oil spray, and bake at 350 degrees for 30 minutes. Serve right from the oven. Serves 4.

Lagniappe: This is not only a low-fat dish; it is also a quick and easy recipe. Crawfish is an excellent food value. One pound of crawfish easily feeds four people. You buy the meat by the pound—already peeled and deveined. It is pure meat. It is very low in fat (only about 4.8 grams of fat per pound) and reasonable in cholesterol. Crawfish meat is tender and sweet and very delicate. You can make this dish up to the baking point and refrigerate it for up to 2 days until you are ready to serve. If you want to hold it longer than that, completely bake it, then wrap the casserole dish tightly with plastic wrap, label it (so you'll know just what it is), date it, then freeze for later use. I also like to serve this in individual au gratin or casserole dishes. This is a super recipe to make in double or triple batches. Put the extra into individual freezer-to-oven dishes, tightly wrap, label, and date, then freeze. You'll have a great Cajun TV dinner. To use the frozen dinners, just thaw in the refrigerator and bake at 300 degrees for 12 to 15 minutes, or until the dish is hot enough to serve.

Calories—379; Fat—3.6 g; Protein—28.4 g; Carbohydrates—55.4 g; Cholesterol—65 mg; Fiber—1.2 g; Sodium—1226 mg

32 of the 379 calories are from fat.
8% of the calories come from fat.

CRAWFISH ETOUFFEE

2 tbsp. unsalted butter
1 large white onion, finely chopped
1/2 cup finely chopped celery
1 medium bell pepper, finely diced
2 cloves garlic, crushed and minced
3 tbsp. all-purpose flour
1 lb. fresh crawfish tails, peeled and deveined
1 tsp. salt
1/2 tsp. cayenne pepper

1/2 tsp. Tabasco® Sauce
1/4 tsp. fresh ground black pepper
1 tsp. onion powder
1/2 tsp. sweet basil
1/2 tsp. sweet paprika
1 1/2 cups water or seafood stock
1 bunch green onions, finely chopped
1/4 cup finely minced fresh parsley
5 cups cooked white long grain rice

Heat a large nonstick skillet over medium heat until it is hot, then add the butter. When the butter has melted, add the onion, celery, bell pepper, and garlic. Sauté for 4 minutes, stirring constantly. Add the flour and cook it for 4 minutes, stirring constantly. This will make a light roux which will enhance the flavor of the étouffée and thicken the gravy. Add the crawfish tails and all the spices. Cook, stirring often, for 3 minutes, then slowly add the water. The sauce should thicken nicely and take on a beautiful orange color. Reduce the heat to low and cook for 10 minutes, stirring occasionally. Add the green onions and parsley, blend it in, and cook, stirring often, for 2 more minutes. Serve hot over cooked white rice. Serves 6.

Lagniappe: Yes, you can have an étouffée that is much lower in fat than the regular étouffée. You will be pleasantly surprised with the taste, even though the dish is low in fat. Part of the problem in cutting fat from recipes is that it can cut taste. Fat helps to carry taste and have it float over your taste buds. We counteract that lack of fat by using other flavors to enhance the food, like spices and seasonings. Give it a try, I think you will be impressed. This recipe is a good example of how a few changes in your cooking methods can produce excellent food at significantly improved health benefits.

Calories—332; Fat—5.3 g; Protein—19 g; Carbohydrates—51 g; Cholesterol—51 mg; Fiber—.7 g; Sodium—1018 mg

48 of the 332 calories are from fat.
14% of the calories come from fat.

CRAWFISH MATERNE

1 lb. crawfish tails, peeled and deveined
1 10 3/4-oz. can cream of mushroom soup
1 10 3/4-oz. can cream of chicken soup
1/2 cup finely chopped onion
1/2 cup finely diced red bell pepper
1/4 cup finely chopped celery
1/2 cup finely chopped green onions
1 tsp. Cajun Spice Mix (see page 274)
1/2 tsp. Tabasco® Sauce
1 cup dry white wine
1 cup raw long grain white rice

Preheat the oven to 350 degrees. Stir together all the ingredients until well mixed. Pour into a 2-quart covered casserole, and bake for 30 minutes. Remove the cover and stir well, then cover and bake for 30 more minutes, or until the rice is cooked. Serve hot. Serves 6.

Lagniappe: This is simple, easy, and no-fuss. The taste is superb. You can make this in advance and refrigerate it for later use, or you can freeze it. To reheat, just cover and bake at 300 degrees until the dish is hot. This type of dish is great when you have to throw something together because you are short on time. Don't let the ease fool you; it tastes great.

Calories—231; Fat—4 g; Protein—17 g; Carbohydrates—24.3 g; Cholesterol—48 mg; Fiber—.3 g; Sodium—863 mg

35 of the 231 calories are from fat.
15% of calories come from fat.

LOBSTER THERMIDOR

2 2-lb. live lobsters
Water to cover
1 tbsp. salt
4 whole bay leaves
20 whole black
   peppercorns
1 tbsp. unsalted butter
1 tbsp. finely chopped
   shallots
2 1/2 tbsp. flour
2/3 cup evaporated skim
   milk

1 cup no-fat sour cream
1 tsp. hot dry mustard
1/4 tsp. Tabasco® Sauce
1 1/2-oz. packet Butter
   Buds
1/4 tsp. salt
1/4 tsp. cayenne pepper
6 large mushrooms, sliced
2 tbsp. minced fresh
   parsley
1/2 cups nonfat parmesan
   cheese

Preheat the oven to 350 degrees. In a large pan, cover the lobsters with water. Add the salt, bay leaves, and peppercorns. Place on high heat and bring to a boil. Boil the lobsters for 5 minutes. Remove the lobsters from the water and let them cool. Remove the meat from the shells, chop it into large bite-sized pieces, then set it aside for later use.

Make a sauce by melting the butter in a medium nonstick skillet over medium heat. When the butter is melted, add the shallots and sauté the shallots for 3 minutes. Add the flour and stir constantly over the medium heat for 3 more minutes. Mix together the skim milk, sour cream, mustard, and Tabasco® Sauce until blended, then slowly pour it into the flour-butter mixture. Blend together well, and let the mixture reach the boiling point, stirring constantly. Add the Butter Buds, salt, cayenne, and mushrooms; mix in well. Add the lobster meat and parsley, then stir it in and cook for 1 minute. Spoon the lobster and sauce into 4 individual baking dishes, sprinkle equally with the nonfat parmesan, and bake at 350 degrees for 20 minutes. Serve at once. Serves 4.

Lagniappe: This dish can be made in advance up to the baking point and refrigerated or frozen for later use. Just thaw it in the refrigerator and follow the baking directions above. As an alternate way of serving, you can cut the lobster in half lengthwise after it has cooked and clean the meat out of the shell. Stuff the shell with the Thermidor sauce and bake for the same amount of time as above. It makes a beautiful presentation and you can just throw the "dish" away when you are finished eating!

Calories—398; Fat—5.7 g; Protein—31.8 g; Carbohydrates—28 g; Cholesterol—53 mg; Fiber—.5 g; Sodium—1319 mg

1 of the 398 calories is from fat.
13% of the calories come from fat.

LUMP CRABMEAT MARIE LOUISE

Butter-flavored nonstick
  vegetable oil spray
2/3 cup diced red bell
  pepper
1/2 cup finely chopped
  white onions
1/2 cup chopped celery
2 cloves garlic, crushed and
  minced
3 tbsp. all-purpose flour
8 large fresh mushrooms,
  sliced
1 cup low-fat and low
  sodium chicken broth
2/3 cup cream sherry
1 5-oz. can light evaporated
  skim milk
1/4 tsp. Tabasco® Sauce

1 tbsp. white wine
  Worcestershire sauce
8 oz. fat-free cream cheese
1 tsp. Cajun Spice Mix (see
  page 274)
1 lb. lump crabmeat
2 1/2-oz. packets Butter
  Buds
1/2 cup chopped green
  onions
1/4 tsp. minced fresh
  parsley
2 tbsp. fresh lemon juice
2 cups cooked non-egg
  fettuccine noodles
2 cups cooked non-egg
  spinach fettuccine
  noodles

Spray a large nonstick skillet for about 5 seconds (twice as much as usual) with the butter-flavored nonstick vegetable oil spray, then place the skillet over medium heat. Add the red bell pepper, white onions, celery, and garlic. Sauté, stirring constantly, for 4 minutes. Add the flour, and blend it in well. Cook the flour, stirring constantly for 4 minutes, then add the mushrooms and mix them in well. Pour in the chicken broth and cream sherry, and stir until the sauce begins to thicken. Add the evaporated skim milk, Tabasco® Sauce, and Worcestershire sauce and stir in until the liquid is incorporated into the sauce. Add the cream cheese, and stir until it is completely melted through the dish. Season the crab with the Cajun Spice Mix, and add the seasoned lump crabmeat. Fold the crab in carefully, trying not to break the large lumps of crabmeat. Cook over medium heat for about 2 minutes, stirring occasionally. Add the Butter Buds, green onions, and the fresh parsley; blend in well. Finally, add the lemon juice and stir until the sauce begins to bubble. Reduce the heat, and simmer for 1 minute, stirring constantly. Serve hot over a mixture of cooked plain and spinach fettuccine noodles. Serves 6.

Lagniappe: Ah, crabmeat! *Ça c'est beaucoup bon!* It is so very good! This is a luxurious and luscious dish that will please even someone who scoffs at the idea of eating healthy food. It is low-fat, but it looks and tastes like the real thing. Food needs to taste good for you to keep coming back for more; but great food needs to look exquisite as well. You get both with this dish. I like to mix the two noodles after they are cooked to be sure that I have enough and equal amounts of each. It is sometimes difficult to judge just how much cooked noodles you will get from dried noodles, so I like to measure the finished product.

Calories—478; Fat—2.8 g; Protein—31.4 g; Carbohydrates—73.4 g; Cholesterol—66 mg; Fiber—1.7 g; Sodium—787 mg

25 of the 478 calories are from fat.
5% of the calories come from fat.

LUMP CRABMEAT SAUTE

Butter-flavored nonstick
  vegetable oil spray
2 tbsp. finely minced
  shallots
3 cloves garlic, crushed and
  finely minced
2 tbsp. finely minced celery
1/4 cup diced red bell
  pepper
2 tbsp. all-purpose flour
8 large mushrooms, sliced
1 cup dry white wine

1 lb. lump crabmeat
1/4 tsp. black pepper
1/4 tsp. red pepper
1/4 tsp. white pepper
1/2 tsp. salt
1/4 tsp. Tabasco® Sauce
1 1/2-oz. packet Butter
  Buds
1 tsp. sweet basil
1/4 cup finely minced fresh
  parsley

Lightly spray a good nonstick skillet with the butter-flavored vegetable oil spray, then place the skillet over medium heat. When the pot is hot, add the shallots, garlic, celery, and red bell pepper; sauté, stirring constantly, for 5 minutes. Add the flour and cook for 3 minutes, stirring constantly, then add the mushrooms and white wine. Allow the sauce to thicken, then let it simmer for 2 minutes. Add the remaining ingredients, and stir together carefully. Serve at once. Serves 6.

Lagniappe: This is wonderful by itself or in combination with other recipes. You can use this crabmeat recipe to top just about any meat, from chicken or veal to a variety of seafoods. It is simple to fix—in fact, it is almost too simple. The results are anything but simple. It is low-fat, but it is outstanding. This is the recipe to use when making Veal LeBlanc. Blending crabmeat with almost anything is good. If you decide to just eat the Sautéed Crabmeat by itself and not as part of another entree, I like to serve it over cooked noodles. The crabmeat is rich in taste, but relatively low in fats. Don't freeze this dish because the crabmeat falls apart when you defrost it. Prepare this dish when fresh crabmeat is easy to get and the price is reasonable.

Calories—133; Fat—1.2 g; Protein—21.1 g; Carbohydrates—9.6 g; Cholesterol—59 mg; Fiber—.6 g; Sodium—365 mg

11 of the 133 calories are from fat.
8% of the calories come from fat.

MUSSELS WITH TOMATO SAUCE

Olive oil-flavored vegetable oil spray
1 bunch green onions, finely chopped
1/2 cup diced yellow bell pepper
1/4 cup diced celery
2 cloves garlic, minced
1 14.5-oz. can nonfat stewed tomatoes
1 4-oz. can nonfat tomato sauce
1 tsp. dried sweet basil
1/2 tsp. dried thyme
1/2 tsp. rosemary
1/2 tsp. onion powder
1/2 tsp. garlic powder
1/2 tsp. Tabasco® Sauce
1/2 tsp. medium or mild paprika
1 tsp. Cajun Spice Mix (see page 274)
2 tsp. Worcestershire sauce
1 1/2 cups dry white wine
1/2 tsp. salt
3 whole bay leaves
36 fresh mussels in their shells, scrubbed and debearded
1/2 cup chopped fresh parsley
6 cups cooked spaghetti
Lemon wedges as needed

Spray the olive oil spray on the bottom of a large skillet. Heat the skillet over medium-high heat until it is hot, then add the onions, bell peppers, celery, and garlic and sauté for 4 minutes, stirring constantly. Add the stewed tomatoes, tomato sauce, basil, thyme, rosemary, onion powder, garlic powder, Tabasco® Sauce, and paprika. Cook for 3 more minutes, then add the Cajun Spice Mix and Worcestershire sauce; blend in well. Reduce the heat to a low simmer and cook uncovered for 30 minutes; stirring constantly. The sauce should begin to thicken nicely.

While the tomatoes are cooking, put the wine, salt, and bay leaves in a large pot and bring the mixture to a boil. Add the mussels and cook for 2 minutes, or until all the shells open. Transfer the mussels to the tomato sauce liquid, add the fresh parsley, and cook for 2 more minutes. Place the cooked spaghetti on a large platter, arrange the mussels on the noodles, then spoon the sauce evenly over the entire platter. Serve at once, garnished with the fresh wedges of lemon. Serves 6.

Lagniappe: To a Louisiana boy, a mussel looked strange the first time I saw one. It looked like an oyster with an attitude! The taste was scrumptious. You know the Cajun philosophy of choosing food: "If it moves, breathes, or can be chewed with minimal effort, cook it and eat it!" Remember, it was a Cajun who looked at a crayfish (pronounced *crawfish* in Louisiana no matter how it's spelled) and said, *"Mais, cher dat looks like an étouffée to me!"* To the untrained eye, it just looked like a mudbug! In the hands of a Cajun cook, it became a delicacy. I guess I am trying to say, "Mais, cher dat mussel looks enuf good to eat, yea."

Calories—343; Fat—3.7 g; Protein—19.6 g; Carbohydrates—49 g; Cholesterol—24 mg; Fiber—1.7 g; Sodium—940 mg

33 of the 343 calories are from fat.
10% of the calories come from fat.

OVEN-FRIED CATFISH FILLETS

4 6-oz. catfish fillets
1/2 cup yellow cornmeal
1/2 cup bread crumbs
1 tbsp. all-purpose flour
1 1/2 tsp. Cajun Spice Mix
  (see page 274)
1/2 tsp. sweet basil

1/2 cup evaporated skim
  milk
1 egg white, slightly beaten
1 tsp. Tabasco® Sauce
Butter-flavored nonstick
  vegetable oil spray

Preheat the oven to 450 degrees. Wash the catfish fillets well with cold water and dry with white paper towels. Combine the cornmeal, bread crumbs, flour, Cajun Spice Mix, and sweet basil until well blended. Mix together the skim milk, egg white, and Tabasco® Sauce until well blended. Dip the fish in the milk-egg mixture until well covered, then coat with the cornmeal-bread crumb mixture, pressing the fish into the crumbs ensure that they stick. Spray a baking dish with the butter-flavored spray and place the fish on the pan. Lightly spray the top of the fish with the butter-flavored spray. Bake at 450 degrees for 13 to 15 minutes or until the fish flakes when touched with a knife. Serve hot, right from the oven. Serves 4.

Lagniappe: This is not fried fish at all, but it is about as close as you can get without the fat. The flavor of the fish comes through, and the catfish is such a sweet and mild fish that the taste is delightful. Don't make this in advance because it will start to get soggy when it sits for a while. I batter it up and place it on the baking dish in advance, but I bake it just before dinner.

Catfish is such a good cost value as well as a good source of low-fat protein. Cooking time and preparation time are negligible. Try this recipe when you get the craving for fried fish. This recipe works well with other fish as well. You might have to slightly adjust the cooking time for a firmer fleshed fish, but other than that, the recipe will work fine.

Calories—388; Fat—8 g; Protein—41.9 g; Carbohydrates—32.6 g; Cholesterol—101 mg; Fiber—.9 g; Sodium—952 mg

72 of the 388 calories are from fat.
19% of calories come from fat.

OYSTER STEW

1 qt. skim milk
1 cup no-fat sour cream
2 1/2-oz. packets Butter
  Buds
1/4 tsp. Tabasco® Sauce
1/4 cup Sauterne wine

2 cups oysters, with their
  liquid
1/4 cup minced fresh
  parsley
1 tbsp. minced fresh chives

Place all the ingredients into a large saucepan over medium heat and let the stew come to a boil. Reduce the heat to low and simmer for 5 minutes. Serve at once. Serves 4.

Lagniappe: The taste of oysters, cream, and butter comes through in this recipe. Everything but the fat is for real. Don't let the simplicity of the dish throw you, it is spectacular. The flavors really blend in this soup to create a heavenly dish. You can make it in advance if you need to, but I find that it is best just after cooking the first time. You can also freeze the dish without much loss of taste. However, I really recommend making it when you want it and just refrigerating or freezing leftovers. The flavor peaks the first time around, and you still have a wonderful leftover for later.

Calories—245; Fat—2.5 g; Protein—.3 g; Carbohydrates—30.8 g; Cholesterol—50 mg; Fiber—trace; Sodium—647 mg

23 of the 245 calories are from fat.
9% of calories come from fat.

OYSTERS DANIEL

1 qt. oysters, with their
liquid
1/2 cup dry vermouth
1/2 cup chicken broth
1 tbsp. extra virgin olive oil
4 cloves garlic, crushed and
minced
2 tbsp. shallots, finely
chopped
1/4 cup all-purpose flour
1 cup finely chopped green
onions

1/2 cup minced fresh
parsley
2 tbsp. white wine
Worcestershire sauce
1/4 tsp. Tabasco® Sauce
1/2 tsp. salt
1/2 tsp. fresh ground black
pepper
1/2 tsp. onion powder
4 cups cooked spaghetti

In a medium-sized saucepan over medium heat, combine the oysters with their liquid, the vermouth, and chicken broth. Heat just until the liquid begins to boil, stirring gently. Cook until the oysters become puffy and white and begin to curl. Remove the oysters from the liquid, and reserve both the oysters and the liquid for later use.

In another medium-sized nonstick saucepan over medium heat, heat the olive oil, then add the garlic and shallots. Sauté for 3 minutes, then add the flour and cook, stirring constantly for 4 minutes. Slowly add the oyster liquid-wine mixture into the flour mixture. The sauce should begin to thicken nicely. Add the green onions, parsley, Worcestershire sauce, Tabasco® Sauce, salt, black pepper, and onion powder; mix in well. Cook, stirring constantly, for 10 minutes over low-medium heat. Add the cooked oysters to the liquid and heat for 2 minutes. Place 1 cup of cooked spaghetti on each of four plates. Spoon the oyster sauce over the cooked spaghetti and serve at once. Serves 4.

Lagniappe: This is a marvelous alternative to spaghetti sauce and an unrivaled way to serve oysters. This sauce will have you licking the plate! Oysters do well when their liquid is the base for the sauce in which they are served. Oyster liquid is, for the most part, a seafood stock that is made by the oyster itself. It is hard to duplicate without using the oyster liquid.

I remember the first time I ate oysters; I was about eight years old. They looked so terrible to a kid, but the taste—especially a cooked oyster—was singular and delectable. I've been hooked ever since. I'm still trying to get my seventeen-year-old to try her first oyster! She just can't seem to get past the initial presentation. Oh well, I might have missed on her, but my four-year-old will be eating oysters before she is six!

Calories—395; Fat—8.5 g; Protein—19.7 g; Carbohydrates—65.3 g; Cholesterol—92 mg; Fiber—1.3 g; Sodium—646 mg

77 of the 395 calories are from fat.
19% of the calories come from fat.

OYSTERS PARLANGE

Butter-flavored nonstick vegetable oil spray
2 qt. oysters, drained on white paper towels
1 cup finely chopped green onions
1/2 cup minced fresh parsley
3 cloves garlic, finely minced
1 1/2 tsp. Cajun Spice Mix (see page 274)
1/2 tsp. Tabasco® Sauce
2 tbsp. white wine Worcestershire sauce
2 tbsp. fresh lemon juice
2 1/2-oz. packets Butter Buds
2 cups no-fat cracker crumbs
1 cup no-fat sour cream
1/4 cup cream sherry
1 tsp. paprika

Preheat the oven to 375 degrees. Lightly spray a shallow 2-quart casserole with the butter-flavored vegetable oil spray. Spread about 1 quart of the oysters evenly on the bottom of the casserole. Spread about half of each of the following: green onions, parsley, garlic, Cajun Spice Mix, Tabasco® Sauce, Worcestershire sauce, and lemon juice. Open one of the packets of Butter Buds and sprinkle it evenly on top of the oysters and seasonings. Cover with one cup of the cracker crumbs, spreading them evenly. Repeat the process beginning with the second quart of oysters. Spread the seasonings, then the Butter Buds and crackers. Mix together the sour cream and the sherry, then pour the mixture on top of the cracker-covered oysters. Sprinkle the paprika on top of the casserole, place in the 375-degree oven, and bake for 30 minutes. Serves 8.

Lagniappe: This is an oyster lover's delight. It is full of oyster goodness and can serve as a wonderful main course. I also like to put it in individual casseroles. It makes the seasoning process a little more difficult (it is hard to split the seasonings up into eight equal parts), but it does make serving much easier and ensures that each serving has an equal amount of the wonderful cream sauce that is created from baking the oysters and the sour cream. The flavor is heavenly.

Calories—199; Fat—4.3 g; Protein—15.6 g; Carbohydrates—32.9 g; Cholesterol—92 mg; Fiber—.3 g; Sodium—677 mg

39 of the 199 calories are from fat.
20% of calories come from fat.

RED SNAPPER LANNETTE

Olive oil-flavored vegetable
  oil spray
1 medium green bell
  pepper, cut into strips
1 medium red bell pepper,
  cut into strips
1 cup thinly chopped leeks
1/4 cup chopped celery
2 cloves garlic, minced
1 26 1/2-oz. can no-fat
  spaghetti sauce
2/3 tsp. Tabasco® Sauce
1 tsp. dry sweet basil

1/2 tsp. fennel seeds
1/2 tsp. dried oregano
2 cups zucchini, thinly
  sliced
3 8-oz. fillets red snapper,
  cut into bite-sized pieces
4 cups cooked tricolored
  noodles (rotini or rotelle)
1/2 cup nonfat parmesan
  cheese
1/2 cup fresh Italian
  parsley, finely chopped

Spray a large nonstick saucepan with the olive oil-flavored vegetable oil spray, then place the pan over medium-high heat and heat until hot. Add the green and red bell peppers, leeks, celery, and garlic. Sauté for 4 minutes, stirring often. Add the spaghetti sauce, Tabasco® Sauce, basil, fennel, and oregano and blend together well. Simmer for 10 minutes, then add the zucchini and red snapper. Simmer over low heat for 10 more minutes, stirring a few times. Add the remaining ingredients and cook, covered for 3 more minutes. Serve at once. Serves 6.

Lagniappe: This is a remarkable, flavorful, and elementary dish. The ease should not fool you, it is a luscious dish that will please even the hard-to-please. Feel free to substitute the fish of your choice for the snapper. Any fish will do.

Because this is a one-pot meal, you just serve it with a salad and bread and your meal is prepared. Scrumptious!

Calories—314; Fat—2.4 g; Protein—32 g; Carbohydrates—43 g; Cholesterol—42 mg; Fiber—7.9 g; Sodium—560 mg

22 of the 314 calories are from fat.
7% of calories come from fat.

SCALLOPS ANGELA

1 lb. bay scallops
1/4 cup finely chopped
   green onions
2 cloves garlic, minced
1 1/2 tsp. Cajun Spice Mix
   (see page 274)
2 tbsp. Butter Buds

1 tbsp. Worcestershire
   sauce
2 tbsp. fresh lime juice
2 tbsp. dry white wine
1/2 tsp. Tabasco® Sauce
1/2 tsp. freshly ground
   black pepper

Preheat the the broiler. In a 2-quart shallow casserole, mix together all the ingredients. Broil about 3 inches from the heat until the scallops are nicely browned. Serve at once with hot French bread. Serves 4.

Lagniappe: It's quick; it's easy. It tastes so good. It is hard to believe that it is low-fat and so good. This dish does not need to be made in advance, but you can mix it all together and place it in the casserole in the refrigerator up to 15 hours prior to cooking. That means all you have to do is preheat the oven to broil.

Calories—127; Fat—.9 g; Protein—19.5 g; Carbohydrates—7.5 g; Cholesterol—38 mg; Fiber—.1 g; Sodium—691 mg

8 of the 127 calories are from fat.
6% of calories come from fat.

SCALLOPS GRAND ISLE

1 tbsp. extra virgin olive oil
5 cloves garlic, crushed and
  finely minced
1/4 cup finely minced
  parsley
1/2 tsp. cayenne pepper
1/4 tsp. fresh ground black
  pepper

1 tsp. fresh oregano (or 1/3
  tsp. dried)
1 lb. fresh sea scallops
1/3 cup dry sherry
1 tbsp. fresh lemon juice
3 cups cooked non-egg
  fettuccine noodles

Heat a large nonstick skillet over medium-high heat until it is hot. Add the olive oil, and let it begin to smoke, then add the garlic, parsley, cayenne, black pepper, and oregano. Sauté for 2 minutes, stirring often. Add the sea scallops and sauté on both sides until they are plump, lightly browned, and juicy, about 5 minutes. Deglaze the pan with the sherry and lemon juice, then add the noodles to the skillet and toss until they are coated with the juices and warmed. Serve at once. Serves 4.

Lagniappe: You can serve this as an appetizer without the noodles if you like. The noodles add a nice complex carbohydrate and lower the percentage of fat in each serving by adding low-fat bulk. While the dish has the same fat gram content, it is a smaller portion of the overall caloric content of the dish when we add low-fat bulk to the meal. This helps to fill you up without filling you out!

Calories—470; Fat—5.7 g; Protein—30.2 g; Carbohydrates—71.3 g; Cholesterol—38 mg; Fiber—1 g; Sodium—193 mg

51 of the 470 calories are from fat.
11% of the calories come from fat.

SCALLOPS RICHARD

Olive oil-flavored nonstick
   vegetable oil spray
1 lb. fresh sea scallops
1 tsp. Cajun Spice Mix (see
   page 274)
1 tbsp. peanut oil
1 cup carrots, thinly sliced
   diagonally
2 cloves garlic, minced
1 cup fresh snow peas and
   pods, cleaned and ends
   snapped
8 large mushrooms, sliced

1 cup green onions, cut
   diagonally
1 1/2 tbsp. fresh grated
   ginger
1 cup chicken broth
1 tbsp. soy sauce
1/2 tsp. Tabasco® Sauce
1 1/2 tbsp. cornstarch
2 tbsp. minced fresh
   parsley
4 cups cooked white long
   grain rice
Lemon wedges as garnish

Spray a large nonstick skillet with a quick spray of the nonstick olive oil-flavored vegetable oil spray; place the skillet on medium-high heat. Season the scallops with the Cajun Spice Mix. When the skillet is hot, sear both sides of the scallops until nicely browned. Remove the scallops to a warm platter for later use. Add the peanut oil and, when it is hot, add the carrots and sauté for 1 minute. Add the garlic and snow peas and sauté for 30 seconds. Add the mushrooms and sauté for 1 minute. Add the green onions and ginger and sauté, stirring constantly, for 30 more seconds. Mix together the broth, soy sauce, Tabasco® Sauce, and cornstarch until well mixed, then pour into the skillet. Add the scallops back to the pan and stir in well. The sauce should begin to thicken. Add the parsley, heat for 1 minute, then serve over cooked white rice. Serve hot, garnished with lemon wedges. Serves 4.

Lagniappe: Seafood is easy to cook and helps make you look like quite a professional. Just the light spray of oil is enough to make the scallops come out perfect. The searing of the meat leaves the scallops plump and juicy. Seafood cooks quickly, so you get great taste in a short period of time. You can make Shrimp Richard by substituting 1 1/3 pounds of large (21-25 size) peeled and deveined shrimp for the scallops and proceeding with the rest of the recipe as above. You can substitute just about any seafood to make the dish you like best. Enjoy!

Calories—438; Fat—5.3 g; Protein—31 g; Carbohydrates—68 g; Cholesterol—38 mg; Fiber—2.7 g; Sodium—1524 mg

47 of the 438 calories are from fat.
11% of calories come from fat.

SEA SCALLOPS MICHAEL

Butter-flavored nonstick vegetable oil spray
1/4 cup seasoned bread crumbs
1 1/3 lb. fresh sea scallops, washed and cleaned
1/4 cup minced fresh parsley

1/2 recipe Crab Dip Kimberly, without the crackers (see page 114)
Paprika to taste
Lemon wedges as garnish

Preheat the oven to 425 degrees. Lightly spray the bottom and sides of 8 individual ramekins with the butter-flavored vegetable oil spray. Spread the bread crumbs evenly over the bottom of each ramekin. Add the equal amounts of scallops to each ramekin, then sprinkle the fresh parsley over the scallops. Spoon generous amounts of the Crab Dip Kimberly on top of the scallops, filling the cups to about 1/4-inch from the top. Dust the top of each ramekin with the paprika and bake for 15 to 20 minutes at 425 degrees, or until the sauce is bubbling and lightly browned. Serve hot as an appetizer, and garnish with lemon wedges. Serves 8.

Lagniappe: Scallops are so easy to cook, and this recipe gives you the richness of a sauce that will bring raves to your dinner. Bringing crabmeat and scallops together is a marriage that heaven will long bless. No one will ever guess that this is a low-fat item. Sometimes that's really what low-fat cooking is all about. Making a few little changes can have little impact on the taste of the dish, but great impact on your health and well being. Try eating this dish and thinking that you are deprived! You'll surprise and please yourself.

Calories—158; Fat—1.9 g; Protein—21.9 g; Carbohydrates—10 g; Cholesterol—77 mg; Fiber—.3 g; Sodium—440 mg

17 of the 158 calories are from fat.
11% of calories come from fat.

SHRIMP AND EGGPLANT MARIE LOUISIE

1 recipe Eggplant Thomas (see page 222)
1 1/2 lb. shrimp, peeled and deveined

1 tsp. Cajun Spice Mix (see page 274)

In a large nonstick skillet, combine the Eggplant Thomas, shrimp, and Cajun Spice Mix. Cook over medium heat until the shrimp are cooked, about 20 minutes, stirring often. Use either as a side dish or as a main course. Serve at once. Serves 6.

Lagniappe: I first made this dish because I was doing a Louisiana Seafood Class for Elderhostel at McNeese State University. I needed to make recipes that included Louisiana seafood. I also wanted to make a dish that could serve as a side course or as a vegetable with seafood. I chose this recipe because my eggplant dishes always went over well with previous Elderhostel groups. What began as a nice idea turned into a luscious recipe. Sometimes recipes are created for reasons just like this one. I think this turned out choice.

This recipe can be made in advance and either frozen or refrigerated for later use. Just reheat on low until the dish is warm, then serve. Another serving suggestion would be to serve it in scooped out eggplant shells. If you want to do this, just fill the eggplant shells with the Eggplant Thomas, lightly sprinkle the top with bread crumbs, and bake for about 20 minutes at 400 degrees. It makes an exquisite main dish, and the presentation is dazzling.

Calories—226; Fat—2.7 g; Protein—24.8 g; Carbohydrates—11.1 g; Cholesterol—173 mg; Fiber—1.6 g; Sodium—746 mg

24 of the 226 calories are from fat.
11% of calories come from fat.

SHRIMP AMANDA

1 1/3 lb. shrimp, peeled
and deveined
1 10 3/4-oz. can cream of
mushroom soup
1 10 3/4-oz. can cream of
onion soup
1/2 cup finely chopped
onion
1/2 cup finely diced bell
pepper
1/4 cup finely chopped
celery
2 cloves garlic, crushed and
minced

1/2 cup finely chopped
green onions
1/4 cup minced fresh
parsley
1 tsp. Cajun Spice Mix (see
page 274)
1/2 tsp. Tabasco® Sauce
1 cup cream sherry
3/4 cup raw long grain
white rice
1/4 cup raw brown rice

Preheat the oven to 350 degrees. Mix together all the ingredients until well blended. Pour into a 2-quart covered casserole, and bake for 30 minutes. Remove the cover and stir well, then cover the casserole and bake for 30 more minutes, or until the rice is cooked. Serve hot. Serves 6.

Lagniappe: This is uncomplicated, informal, and no-fuss. The taste is splendid. You can make this in advance and refrigerate it for later use, or you can freeze it. To reheat, just cover and bake at 300 degrees until the dish is hot. This is an "I'm short of time and in a big hurry to fix dinner" dish. Don't let the simplicity fool you, it's filled with gusto.

Calories—305; Fat—8.9 g; Protein—22.9 g; Carbohydrates—31 g; Cholesterol—57 mg; Fiber—.9 g; Sodium—830 mg

81 of the 305 calories are from fat.
26% of the calories come from fat.

SHRIMP BATON ROUGE

3 cups chicken broth
3/4 cup dry white wine
1 14 3/4-oz. can stewed
  tomatoes
1 cup chopped onions
1 cup chopped celery
1/2 cup chopped red bell
  pepper
2 cloves garlic, minced
1/2 tsp. Tabasco® Sauce
1/2 tsp. Cajun Spice Mix
  (see page 274)
1 tsp. sweet basil
1/2 tsp. dried oregano
  leaves
1/4 tsp. ground saffron

1 lb. shrimp (31-36 size),
  peeled and deveined
1 cup cooked chicken
  breast, cut into bite-sized
  pieces
1 14-oz. can artichoke
  hearts, drained and
  quartered
1 1/2 cup frozen sweet
  peas, thawed
1 1/3 cup cooked long-
  grain white rice
1/2 cup chopped fresh
  parsley
1/2 cup green onions,
  chopped

In a large saucepan over medium heat, combine the first 12 ingredients and simmer for 20 minutes. Add the remaining ingredients, except for the parsley and green onions. Lower the temperature to low, then cover and cook for 12 more minutes, stirring often. Add the parsley and green onions, stir them in, and cook for 1 more minute. Serve at once. Serves 6.

Lagniappe: This is a quick and easy jambalaya. You can make it with other meats; substitute pork tenderloin or a nice, low-fat smoked turkey sausage for the chicken. You can use other seafood in the place of shrimp as well. Lump crabmeat or sea scallops work well and have roughly similar amounts of fat grams. Use the dry wine you plan to serve with dinner, and it will blend perfectly with the dish. Serve with plenty of fresh French bread and a nice green salad with nonfat salad dressing.

Calories—175; Fat—1.6 g; Protein—20 g; Carbohydrates—21.6 g; Cholesterol—100 mg; Fiber—1.3 g; Sodium—691 mg

14 of the 175 calories are from fat.
8% of calories come from fat.

SHRIMP DEBORAH PATRICIA

Butter-flavored nonstick
  vegetable oil spray
1 tsp. Cajun Spice Mix (see
  page 274)
1/4 tsp. salt
1 1/3 lb. shrimp, peeled
  and deveined (31-36 size)
2/3 cup diced red bell
  pepper
1/2 cup chopped green
  onion bottoms
1/2 cup chopped celery
2 cloves garlic, crushed and
  minced
2 tbsp. all-purpose flour
8 large fresh mushrooms,
  sliced
1 cup low-fat and low
  sodium chicken broth

2/3 cup dry chardonnay
1 5-oz. can light evaporated
  skim milk
1/4 tsp. Tabasco® Sauce
1 tbsp. white wine
  Worcestershire sauce
4 oz. fat-free cream cheese
1 1/2-oz. packet Butter
  Buds
1/2 cup chopped green
  onion tops
1/4 tsp. fresh parsley,
  minced
2 tbsp. fresh lemon juice
4 cup cooked fettuccine
  noodles

Spray a large nonstick skillet for about 5 seconds (twice as much as usual) with the butter-flavored nonstick vegetable oil spray, then place the skillet over medium heat. Season the shrimp with the Cajun Spice Mix and salt until well coated. When the skillet is just to the smoking point, add the seasoned shrimp and sauté the shrimp over medium heat until they are mostly cooked and begin to brown, about 4 minutes. Add the red bell pepper, green onion bottoms, celery, and garlic. Continue to sauté, stirring constantly, for 3 more minutes. Add the flour and blend it in well. Cook the flour for 3 minutes, stirring constantly, then add the mushrooms and mix them in well. Pour in the chicken broth and chardonnay, and stir until the sauce begins to thicken somewhat.

Add the evaporated skimmed milk, Tabasco® Sauce, and Worcestershire sauce, and stir in until the liquid is incorporated into the sauce. Add the cream cheese and stir it in until it is completely melted through the dish. Add the Butter Buds, green onion tops, and the fresh parsley; blend in well. Finally, add the lemon juice and stir until the sauce begins to boil. Reduce the heat and simmer for 2 minutes, stirring constantly . Serve hot over cooked fettuccine noodles. Serves 6.

Lagniappe: This is a recipe that came to life very much like the recipes of old. My wife, Deborah Patricia, wanted a rich-tasting sauce to use with some fresh shrimp left over from one of my demonstrations. She loves shrimp, but with all the fat-free and low-fat eating we've been doing, she said she really wanted something that looked and tasted like it was loaded with calories and fat. When Debbie gets that craved look in her eyes, I know she really means business. What to do? No problem, I just looked in the refrigerator to see what we had. I wanted to build the rich-looking wine sauce around the shrimp and the beautiful red bell peppers I had. The rest was easy. I just created a sauce that had the consistency of a heavy cream sauce. This dish refrigerates well for a few days; simply reheat it on top of the stove in a skillet or in a covered dish in the microwave. The cream cheese helps to make the dish have the consistency of a heavy sauce. I think you will be more than pleased with this sauce; it is stupendous.

Calories—486; Fat—3.6 g; Protein—38 g; Carbohydrates—70.6 g; Cholesterol—162 mg; Fiber—1.7 g; Sodium—874 mg
32 of the 486 calories are from fat.
7% of the calories come from fat.

SHRIMP GROSS TETE

Butter-flavored nonstick
  vegetable oil spray
1 small onion, finely
  chopped
1/4 cup finely chopped
  celery
8 large mushrooms, finely
  chopped
1/4 cup finely diced red bell
  pepper
1 tbsp. unsalted butter

2 lb. shrimp, peeled and
  deveined
4 large fresh tomatoes,
  peeled and diced
2 cups no-fat sour cream
2 tbsp. all-purpose flour
2 tsp. Cajun Spice Mix (see
  page 274)
1/4 cup brandy
Paprika to garnish

Preheat the oven to 375 degrees. Spray a large skillet lightly with the nonstick vegetable oil spray and place it over medium heat. Sauté the onion, celery, mushrooms, and red bell pepper for 5 minutes, stirring constantly. Add the butter to the skillet and, when it has melted, add the shrimp and sauté for 3 more minutes. Add the tomatoes, reduce the heat to low-medium, and simmer for 12 minutes, stirring occasionally. Mix together the sour cream, flour, and Cajun Spice Mix until well blended, then fold into the shrimp mixture until smooth. Add the brandy and stir until it is incorporated into the sauce. Pour the mixture into 8 individual au gratin or casserole dishes. Sprinkle the top lightly with paprika, and bake for 30 minutes at 375 degrees. Serve hot. Serves 8.

Lagniappe: This is a simple, but delightful sauce. It is the kind of sauce you will want to sop up with plenty of hot, fat-free bread. You can make the dish in advance up to the baking point, then refrigerate for later use. When you take a cold dish from the refrigerator, you might have to add about 5 to 10 extra minutes to the cooking time. Never take food out of the refrigerator and let it stand until it gets to room temperature. That is a neither healthy nor safe habit, as it promotes harmful bacteria growth. Keep cold foods cold and hot foods hot.

Calories—243; Fat—3.9 g; Protein—28.4 g; Carbohydrates—17.1 g; Cholesterol—178 mg; Fiber—.9 g; Sodium—447 mg

35 of the 243 calories are from fat.
14% of calories come from fat.

SHRIMP JAMBALAYA

Butter-flavored vegetable oil
  spray
1 tbsp. peanut oil
1 large onion, chopped
1 large bell pepper,
  chopped
1 small red bell pepper,
  chopped
1 cup chopped celery
4 cloves garlic, minced
1/2 cup finely minced
  carrots
1 1/3 lb. shrimp, peeled
  and deveined
1/4 lb. lean (98% fat-free)
  ham
2 15-oz. cans stewed
  tomatoes

1/4 cup tomato paste
1/4 cup lemon juice
1/2 cup dry white wine
2 whole bay leaves
1 tsp. sweet basil
1/4 tsp. thyme
1 tsp. salt
1 tsp. cayenne pepper
1/4 tsp. fresh ground black
  pepper
5 cups cooked long grain
  white rice
1/2 cup finely chopped
  green onions
1/4 cup finely minced fresh
  parsley

Spray a large nonstick saucepan with the vegetable oil spray, then place the pan over medium-high heat. When it is hot, add the peanut oil and the onion, bell peppers (green and red), celery, garlic, and carrots. Sauté for 5 minutes, then add the shrimp and ham. Cook, stirring constantly, for 5 minutes. Add the stewed tomatoes, tomato paste, lemon juice, wine, bay leaves, basil, and thyme; then reduce the heat to medium-low and simmer for 15 minutes. Add the salt, cayenne, and black pepper and blend in well. Add the rice, green onions, and parsley and blend in well. Cook over low heat, stirring often, for 5 minutes. Adjust seasonings to taste; serve hot. Serves 6 as a main dish.

Lagniappe: Jambalaya is an all-time Louisiana favorite. It is most often filled with the favorite foods of the bayou. Jambalaya was originally created to clean out the ice box. It contained whatever was left over. It got its name from the French word for ham—*jambon.* Therefore, jambalaya usually had ham in it. Today, it is not a leftover by any means; it is the main course and filled with anything that catches your fancy. The term also means a mix of food or a mix of events or happenings. Use this one as-is, or change the ingredients to suit your fancy.

Calories—417; Fat—5.5 g; Protein—29.7 g; Carbohydrates—58.7 g; Cholesterol—162 mg; Fiber—1.6 g; Sodium—1640 mg

50 of the 417 calories are from fat.
12% of calories come from fat.

SHRIMP LAFAYETTE

Olive oil-flavored nonstick vegetable oil spray
1 medium onion, chopped
1/2 cup diced bell peppers
1/4 cup finely chopped celery
2 cloves garlic, finely minced
1/2 cup dry white wine
2 cups French bread, torn into small pieces
2 cups water
1 lb. shrimp, peeled and deveined

1 1/4 tsp. Cajun Spice Mix (see page 274)
1/2 cup nonfat egg substitute
1/4 tsp. Tabasco® Sauce
1 cup finely chopped green onions
1/4 cup finely minced fresh parsely
1/2 cup fat-free crackers, crushed into crumbs
Butter-flavored nonstick vegetable oil spray

Preheat the oven to 375 degrees. Spray a large nonstick skillet with the olive oil-flavored nonstick vegegetable oil spray and place the skillet over medium-high heat. Add the onions, bell pepper, celery, and garlic. Sauté for about 3 minutes, then add the wine and let it come to a boil. Simmer the vegetables in the liquid for 3 more minutes. Place the French bread into a large bowl, and add the water on top of the bread. Let the bread soak for a few minutes. Chop the shrimp and season them with the Cajun Spice Mix. Add the shrimp to the skillet and cook them, stirring often, for 5 minutes. Squeeze the water out of the soaked French bread and add it to the skillet with the shrimp. Cook for 5 more minutes, then remove from the heat. Add the egg substitute, Tabasco® Sauce, green onions, and parsley; mix it in well. Pour the mixture into a 2-quart casserole and sprinkle with the nonfat crackers. Lightly spray with the butter-flavored nonstick vegetable oil spray. Bake at 375 degrees for 20 minutes, or until the crackers are a golden brown. Serve hot as either a side dish or as the main meal. Serves 6.

Lagniappe: This is a great shrimp dish that will liven up almost any meal.

Calories—185; Fat—1.5 g; Protein—8 g; Carbohydrates—37.6 g; Cholesterol—88 mg; Fiber—.3 g; Sodium—585 mg

14 of the 185 calories are from fat.
7% of calories come from fat.

SHRIMP STEW

2 tbsp. corn oil
5 tbsp. all-purpose flour
1 large onion, chopped
1/2 cup chopped bell pepper
1/4 cup finely chopped celery
3 cloves garlic, minced
3 lb. shrimp (31-36 size), peeled and deveined
1 tsp. salt

1/2 tsp. cayenne pepper
1/2 tsp. white pepper
1/4 tsp. black pepper
1 cup water
1/2 tsp. Tabasco® Sauce
1/2 cup chopped green onions
1/4 cup minced fresh parsley
6 cups cooked white long grain rice

In a large iron pot over medium heat, heat the oil until it is hot. Add the flour and make a golden brown roux by stirring the flour constantly until the flour is a dark golden brown. Do not let the flour burn. When it reaches a deep golden brown color, add the onion, bell pepper, and celery. Cook for 5 minutes, stirring constantly, then add the garlic, shrimp, salt, cayenne, white pepper, and black pepper. Cook, stirring, for 3 minutes. Add the water, reduce the heat to low, cover, and cook for 30 minutes, stirring occasionally. Add the green onions and parsley, cook uncovered for 2 more minutes, then serve over 1 cup of cooked white rice per serving. Serve hot. Serves 6.

Lagniappe: We don't have to give up our roux based stews and gravies to cook and eat low-fat dishes, but we do have to alter the way we make the roux. A roux is, by definition, flour cooked in oil at least until the pastiness is no longer present, which takes at least 1 1/2 to 2 minutes of cooking. You can not make a roux by just browning flour in the oven. It will give you some of the taste of the toasted flour, but you get the paper maché aftertaste of flour and water. A roux is not chemically a flour; it is a new substance that has some of the properties of flour and some of the properties of oil. I'm not saying that you can't thicken, color, or get the appearance of a roux, but I am telling you it will be very pasty-tasting and not nearly as good as a roux or, as in this recipe, a light roux recipe. You will be pleasantly surprised with the quality of this dish, even compared to a high-fat version.

Calories—397; Fat—7.2 g; Protein—38.6 g; Carbohydrates—43.2 g; Cholesterol—260 mg; Fiber—.7 g; Sodium—1011 mg
65 of the 397 calories are from fat.
16% of the calories come from fat.

STUFFED BAKED RAINBOW TROUT

4 whole rainbow trout (about 10-oz. each), cleaned and heads removed

2 tsp. Cajun Spice Mix (see page 274)

1 recipe Mushroom Stuffing (see index for recipes)

Olive oil-flavored nonstick spray

Lemon wedges, to garnish

Preheat the oven to 425 degrees. Season the trout evenly, inside and out, with the Cajun Spice Mix. Stuff each of the trout with one-fourth of the Mushroom Stuffing. Lightly spray the bottom of a baking dish with the olive oil-flavored spray, then place each trout in the baking dish. Lightly spray the top of each fish, then place in a 425-degree oven and bake for 22 to 25 minutes, or until the fish flakes when pierced with a knife or fork. Serve at once with lemon wedges. Serves 4.

Lagniappe: Fish is so good for you and so easy to fix. Research tells us that replacing other foods at least three times per week with seafood fixed in a low-fat way will have a positive impact on the health of our hearts and help prevent certain cancers. That may be one reason to eat seafood, but the taste of a good fish is all the reason I need. For too long, we have overlooked a tremendous food value. Try the ease and taste of cooking with fish. This is a stuffed trout, but you can just bake it plain if you like. The cooking time will cut back by about 3 to 5 minutes. I like to use the stuffing because it makes the dish look so large, and it loads the dish with complex carbohydrates. That means this dish is good for you as well as being delicious!

Calories—342; Fat—8.1 g; Protein—98.3 g; Carbohydrates—15.2 g; Cholesterol—98.3 mg; Fiber—1.6 g; Sodium—927 mg
73 of the 342 calories are from fat.
21% of calories come from fat.

TROUT MEUNIERE

4 6-oz. fillets freshwater
   trout
1 1/4 tsp. Cajun Spice Mix
   (see page 274)
1/2 cup flour
1 tbsp. unsalted butter
2 tbsp. lemon juice
2 tbsp. white wine
   Worcestershire sauce

1/4 cup chicken broth or
   stock
1 1/2-oz. Butter Buds
1/4 tsp. Tabasco® Sauce
1/4 cup finely minced fresh
   parsley

Wash the trout fillets in cold water, then dry them with clean white paper towels and season them equally with the Cajun Spice Mix. Dredge the seasoned fillets in the flour, and shake off any excess flour. Heat a large nonstick skillet over medium heat until it is hot, then add the butter. When the butter has melted, cook the fish fillets for 3 minutes on each side, shaking the pan often. Remove the fish to warm serving plates, and keep them warm until you are ready to sauce the fish.

Add all the remaining ingredients to the skillet, and heat over medium heat until the sauce begins to bubble. Reduce the heat and let it simmer for 3 minutes. Pour an equal amount of sauce on top of each fish fillet, and serve hot. Serves 4.

Lagniappe: This recipe alters the original recipe in two main fat-heavy areas. First, the four fillets are pan-fried in only 1 tablespoon of butter instead of deep-frying the fish, which is ten times the fat content. Second, the sauce is made from the Butter Buds, which gives you the taste of real butter without the negatives. You will be pleased with just how super this dish tastes. I think the sweet taste of the trout comes through in a way that will gratify and inspire you.

Because this recipe calls for freshwater trout, like rainbow trout, you may need to use two smaller fillets per serving. The reason we must use a freshwater trout is they are lower in both fat and sodium. This recipe is basically just the fish, so there are not enough other ingredients to help lower the overall fat intake from the dish. Therefore, we must use a trout that has the lowest possible fat gram count.

Calories—304; Fat—9 g; Protein—37.3 g; Carbohydrates—21 g; Cholesterol—104 mg; Fiber—.1 g; Sodium—583 mg

81 of the 304 calories are from fat.
27% of the calories come from fat.

TROUT ROSE

1 tbsp. extra virgin olive oil
3 cloves garlic, crushed and finely minced
1 tbsp. shallots, finely minced
1 tbsp. celery, finely minced
6 large mushrooms, finely chopped
1 1/2 cups bread crumbs made from French bread
1/2 cup dry white wine
1/2 tsp. Tabasco® Sauce

3 tbsp. nonfat parmesan cheese
1 tbsp. romano cheese
1/4 cup fresh parsley
1/2 tsp. sweet basil
1/4 tsp. dried thyme
4 6-oz. trout fillets
1 tsp. Cajun Spice Mix (see page 274)
Butter-flavored nonstick vegetable oil spray
Paprika

Preheat the oven to broil. Heat a medium nonstick skillet over medium heat until it is hot, then add the olive oil. When the oil begins to smoke, add the garlic, shallots, and celery and sauté for 4 minutes. Add the mushrooms and sauté for 4 more minutes, stirring constantly. Add the bread crumbs and continue to cook for 2 more minutes, stirring constantly. Add the wine and Tabasco® Sauce, and cook the mixture for 3 minutes. Add the cheeses, parsley, basil, and thyme and mix in well.

Season each trout fillet with the Cajun Spice Mix. Spread one side of each fillet with the bread mixture, then roll the fish up like a jelly roll. Secure the fish with toothpicks. Lightly spray a broiling pan with the vegetable oil spray and place each rolled-up fillet in the dish. Spray the top and sides of each fillet lightly with the butter-flavored spray and dust lightly with the paprika. Broil the fish about 5 inches from the heat source for 15 minutes, turning the fish a few times to ensure even cooking. Carefully remove the toothpicks and serve hot. Serves 4.

Lagniappe: Divine, divine, divine is all I can say about this dish. The stuffing is outstanding, and the fish just blends with and into the stuffing. This is company cooking at its best! A nice pasta dish, a green vegetable, and fresh hot rolls and you have a delightful meal. You can make the stuffing and roll the fish in advance, and refrigerate until you are ready to serve. Just remove from the refrigerator, broil, and serve. You can also freeze the fish after you have stuffed them. I like to tightly wrap them with plastic wrap, then place each wrapped and rolled fillet into zip-lock freezer bags and freeze for later use. Just let them thaw in the refrigerator and proceed as above when they are completely thawed. I generally make a double batch of this dish; I eat half that day and freeze the other half for later use. When you are in a rolling mood, it's easier to roll a little extra all on one day.

Calories—351; Fat—11.2 g; Protein—39.8 g; Carbohydrates— 20.7 g; Cholesterol—96 mg; Fiber—1.1 g; Sodium—458 mg
101 of the 351 calories are from fat.
29% of the calories come from fat.

ZESTY TUNA

2 cups purple cabbage,
  finely chopped
2 medium carrots, finely
  chopped
3 stalks celery, finely
  chopped
10 medium radishes, finely
  chopped
1 cup golden raisins
1/4 cup green onions, finely
  chopped
2 6.5-oz. cans tuna packed
  in spring water

3/4 cup Miracle Whip Free
  salad dressing
1/4 cup no-fat sour cream
1/4 tsp. Tabasco® Sauce
1/2 tsp. salt
1/2 tsp. cayenne pepper
1/2 tsp. onion powder
1 tbsp. fresh lemon juice
1 head lettuce, shredded
3 medium ripe red
  tomatoes, cut into wedges
Lemon wedges to garnish

In a large mixing bowl, combine all but the last three ingredients
and mix together until well blended. Allow the salad to sit in the refrigerator for 1 hour to let the seasonings blend. Serve on a bed of shredded lettuce, and garnish with the tomato and lemon wedges. Serve cold.
Serves 8.

Lagniappe: A tuna salad that is loaded with fresh vegetables is a nice alternative to a tuna sandwich. It raises the bulk, flavor, and vitamins. You
can make in advance and refrigerate it for up to 3 days. I like to keep
it in the refrigerator as a quick and handy appetite killer. It is also good
on a slice of bread or with fat-free crackers.

*Calories—185; Fat—.6 g; Protein—16.4 g; Carbohydrates—28.5 g;
Cholesterol—17 mg; Fiber—2 g; Sodium—521 mg*

5 of the 185 calories are from fat.
3% of calories come from fat.

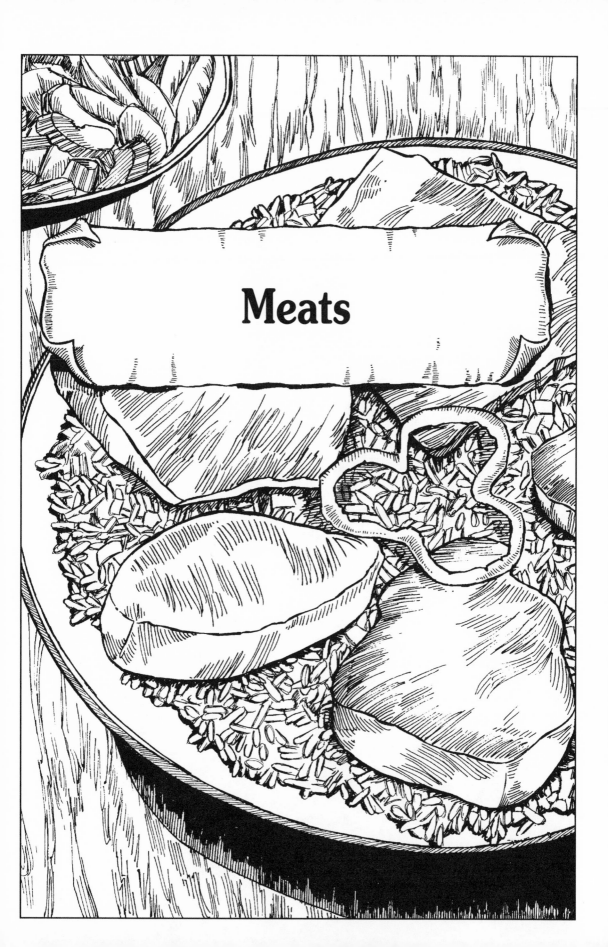

Meats

BEEF STROGANOFF DEBORAH

1/2 lb. lean beef top round
  steak
1 tsp. Cajun Spice Mix (see
  page 274)
Butter-flavored nonstick
  vegetable oil spray
1 large onion, finely
  chopped
1/2 lb. fresh mushrooms,
  sliced
2 cloves garlic, minced
2 tbsp. red bell pepper,
  diced

3 tbsp. all-purpose flour
1 14 3/4-oz. can beef broth
1/2 cup dry red wine
1/4 cup low-fat catsup
1/2 tsp. Tabasco® Sauce
1 tbsp. Worcestershire
  sauce
1 1/4 cup no-fat sour
  cream
4 cups cooked non-egg
  noodles

Cut off any pieces of fat that might remain on the meat. Place the meat between two pieces of plastic wrap and pound it until the meat increases in size by about one-third. Season the meat equally with the Cajun Spice Mix, then cut it across the grain into thin strips about 2 inches long. Lightly spray a large nonstick covered skillet with the butter-flavored spray. Place the skillet on medium-high heat, and heat until the pan is hot. Add the onions, mushrooms, garlic, and red pepper. Sauté for 3 minutes, stirring constantly. Remove the vegetables from the skillet to a plate for later use.

Spray the skillet lightly again with the butter-flavored spray and return to the heat. When hot, add the seasoned meat and cook for 5 minutes, stirring constantly. Add the flour and cook for 3 minutes more, stirring constantly. Add the cooked vegetables and blend together well. Add the broth, wine, catsup, Tabasco® Sauce, and Worcestershire sauce; mix in well. Stir to make sure all the pan drippings are dissolved into the sauce. Cover the skillet and lower the heat to simmer. Cover and cook for 25 minutes, stirring a few times. Raise the heat to medium and bring the mixture to a boil, stirring constantly. Stir in the sour cream, and reduce the heat to low. Cook uncovered for 3 minutes, stirring. Serve hot over cooked noodles. Serves 4.

Lagniappe: Stroganoff has always been one of my favorite dishes. If Debbie asks me what I want her to fix, I usually ask for stroganoff. She makes a wonderful stroganoff. This is a low-fat version of her wonderful recipe. I like this over mashed potatoes as well as noodles (see the index for a great mashed potatoes recipe). I also like to fix a baked potato, cut it open, mash it a bit, and fill it with this wonderful stroganoff. However you serve it, it is great.

Calories—443; Fat—6 g; Protein—36.5 g; Carbohydrates—72 g; Cholesterol—49 mg; Fiber—1.5 g; Sodium—1005 mg

54 of the 443 calories are from fat.
12% of the calories come from fat.

CAJUN PEPPER STEAK

1 lb. top round steak
1 tsp. Cajun Spice Mix (see page 274)
Butter-flavored nonstick vegetable oil spray
3 cloves garlic, minced
2 tbsp. minced celery
1 large onion, cut into thin strips
1 14 3/4-oz. can beef broth
2 tbsp. soy sauce
1 tbsp. Worcestershire sauce
1/2 tsp. Tabasco® Sauce

2 1/2 tbsp. cornstarch
2/3 cup dry red wine
1 large green bell pepper, cut into strips
1 large red bell pepper, cut into strips
1 8-oz. can stewed tomatoes
1 tbsp. minced fresh parsley
6 cups cooked long grain white rice or white and brown rice mixed

Cut any excess fat from the steak, then cut the meat into strips about 2 1/2 inches long and 1/2 inch wide. Season well with the Cajun Spice Mix. Spray a large covered skillet lightly with the vegetable oil spray, then heat the skillet over medium-high heat. When it is hot, add the meat and cook, stirring often, until it is well browned, about 3 minutes. Add the onions, garlic, and celery, stir together, and cook for 2 more minutes. Add the broth, soy sauce, Worcestershire sauce, and Tabasco® Sauce. Reduce the heat to low, cover, and simmer for 20 minutes, stirring a few times.

Mix together the cornstarch and wine until well blended; set aside. Add the green peppers, red peppers, and stewed tomatoes and cook, uncovered for 5 minutes. Raise the temperature to medium, and let the mixture begin to bubble. Add the cornstarch-wine mixture and blend it in well. The dish will thicken and slowly come to a boil. Add the parsley, let it boil for 1 minute, then serve over the cooked rice. Serves 6.

Lagniappe: This is similar to regular pepper steak, but it's cooked by a Cajun and it uses the seasonings and spices that Cajuns like. I've cut the amount of beef down to a little less than 3 ounces per person. This dish is best right from the skillet. I usually refrigerate the leftovers, if there are any. Do not freeze this dish; a cornstarch mixture tends to break apart in the freezer and with all these vegetables, you lose much of the crispness. I like to mix brown and white rice together when I serve pepper steak. I mix about 1/4 cup of brown rice to 3/4 cup of white rice. It gives you the taste and texture of white rice with the bran of the brown rice.

Calories—427; Fat—5.8 g; Protein—30 g; Carbohydrates—58.6 g; Cholesterol—65 mg; Fiber—1.1 g; Sodium—1522 mg

52 of the 427 calories are from fat.
12% of the calories come from fat.

GROUND ROUND STROGANOFF

1 lb. lean ground round
1 1/3 tsp. Cajun Spice Mix
(see page 274)
Butter-flavored nonstick
vegetable oil spray
2 medium onions, finely
chopped
3 cloves garlic, crushed and
minced
1 small red bell pepper,
diced
8 large fresh mushrooms,
sliced

1/4 cup celery, finely sliced
1/4 cup all-purpose flour
2 14 3/4-oz. cans beef
broth
1 cup dry red wine or
Merlot
1/2 cup low-fat catsup
1/2 tsp. Tabasco® Sauce
2 tbsp. Worcestershire
sauce
2 cups no-fat sour cream
8 cups cooked non-egg
noodles

Season the meat with the Cajun Spice Mix. Lightly spray a large non-stick covered skillet with the butter-flavored spray. Place the skillet on medium-high heat until the pan is hot, then add the onions, garlic, red bell pepper, and celery. Sauté for 3 minutes, stirring constantly. Add the seasoned meat and continue to cook over medium heat until the meat is browned. Add the mushrooms and cook for 1 more minute. Add the flour and cook for 3 minutes more, stirring constantly. Add the broth, wine, catsup, Tabasco® Sauce, and Worcestershire sauce; mix in well. Stir to make sure all the pan drippings are dissolved into the sauce. Cover the skillet and lower the heat to simmer. Cover and cook for 25 minutes, stirring a few times. Raise the heat to medium, and bring the mixture to a boil, stirring constantly. Add the sour cream, stir in, and reduce the heat to low. Cook uncovered for 3 minutes, stirring. Serve hot over cooked noodles. Serves 8.

Lagniappe: Stroganoff has always been one of my favorite dishes. This no-fuss version is a take-off on Debbie's Stroganoff but made with ground round instead of round steak or tenderloin. I like this over mashed potatoes as well as noodles (see the index for a great mashed potatoes recipe). I also like to bake a potato, then cut it open, mash it a bit, and fill it with stroganoff.

Calories—445; Fat—6 g; Protein—36.6 g; Carbohydrates—72 g; Cholesterol—51 mg; Fiber—1.6 g; Sodium—995 mg
54 of the 445 calories are from fat.
12% of the calories come from fat.

HAM STEAK AGNES

1/2 cup dark brown sugar
1/4 cup light brown sugar
6 tbsp. water
4 tbsp. cider vinegar
2 tbsp. prepared mustard
1/2 tsp. salt

1/2 tsp. Tabasco® Sauce
1/2 tsp. ground ginger
2 8-oz. low-fat ham steaks
(1 gram fat per ounce
ham)

Preheat the oven to 350 degrees. In a small mixing bowl, combine the sugars, water, cider vinegar, prepared mustard, salt, Tabasco® Sauce, and ground ginger until well mixed. Spread the mixture on top of each ham steak in a nonstick baking dish. Place in the oven and bake at 350 degrees until the sauce begins to bubble and the ham is cooked, about 10 total minutes. Serve hot. Serves 4.

Lagniappe: Serve this ham steak in any meal that you would serve ordinary ham. You can make this dish ahead of time and refrigerate or freeze it. Just thaw it in the refrigerator and, when it is completely thawed, reheat it in the oven.

There are all kinds of wonderful new products out there, like very low-fat ham and low-fat turkey chili. All in all, this type of eating is healthy and, most importantly, tasty. Be sure to read the labels. Don't be misled by the percentages on the front of the package. It's important to know what you are looking at. The label will tell you the amount of fat grams. For this recipe, look for 1 gram in the fat section of the label. What you do is multiply that 1 by 9 calories per fat gram, which equals 9 calories from the fat. Next, you are to look at he label to give you the amount of calories. Let's say there were 100 calories in the ham. Now you divide the number of calories from fat by the total calories, or 9/100 (9 divided by 100) which is equal to 9 percent fat. The ham gets 9 percent of its calories from fat. Remember that we want to stay below 30 percent fat in all the items that we eat. The best way to succeed in keeping your diet below 30 percent fat is to keep all the food you eat at or below 30 percent fat.

Calories—294; Fat—4.2 g; Protein—20 g; Carbohydrates—43.9 g; Cholesterol—66 mg; Fiber—0 g; Sodium—1740 mg

38 of the 294 calories are from fat.
13% of the calories come from fat.

HOT TAMALE PIE

BATTER:

1 cup yellow cornmeal
1 tbsp. all-purpose flour
2 cups water
1 tbsp. Worcestershire
  sauce
1 tsp. chili powder

1/2 tsp. Tabasco® Sauce
1/2 tsp. salt
1/4 tsp. cumin powder
1 1/2-oz. packet Butter
  Buds

FILLING:

1 lb. lean ground round
1 large onion, chopped
1 large bell pepper,
  chopped
1/2 cup chopped celery
3 cloves garlic, crushed and
  minced
2 14.5-oz. cans stewed
  tomatoes
1 15-oz. can cream-style
  white corn
3 tbsp. chili powder

2 tsp. cumin powder
1/2 tsp. crushed red pepper
1/2 tsp. fresh ground black
  pepper
1/4 tsp. white pepper
1/4 tsp. Tabasco® Sauce
1 tsp. salt
1 tbsp. sugar
1 cup minced green onions
1/4 cup minced fresh
  cilantro

TOPPING:

1 cup no-fat grated sharp
  cheddar-flavored cheese
1/4 cup nonfat mozzarella
  cheese
1/4 cup fat-free cracker
  crumbs

1 tsp. paprika
1/4 cup finely minced fresh
  cilantro

To make the batter, combine all the batter ingredients in a medium saucepan and place over medium heat. Cook on medium, stirring constantly, until the mixture has thickened nicely. Pour half of the batter into a 12 x 9-inch shallow baking dish, then set aside the baking dish and the remaining batter for later use.

Preheat the oven to 350 degrees. Heat a large nonstick skillet over medium heat until it is hot, then add the lean ground round and cook the meat, stirring until it is brown. Add the onions, bell pepper, celery, and garlic and sauté for 5 minutes, or until the vegetables are quite limp. Add the stewed tomatoes and cook, stirring often, for 5 more minutes. Add the corn, chili powder, cumin, red pepper, black pepper, white pepper, Tabasco® Sauce, salt, and sugar. Cook over medium heat for 4 minutes, stirring constantly, then add the green onions and cilantro and cook for 1 more minute. Spoon this filling over the batter in the center of the baking dish. Mix together all the topping ingredients, then put about 1/3 of this mixture on top of the filling. Spoon the remaining batter from the saucepan on top of the filling and topping. Cover the dish with the remaining 2/3 topping mixture, then bake at 350 degrees for 1 hour, or until well set. Allow the pie to cool for 5 minutes before serving. Serve hot. Serves 6.

Lagniappe: Don't let the long list of ingredients scare you. It is simple and very hearty. If you have ever made hot tamales, you will appreciate just how easy this recipe is. You can make this dish completely in advance and refrigerate or freeze it for later use. To serve, just thaw in the refrigerator, then bake at 350 until it is hot, about 12 to 15 minutes.

I hope you notice that I always tell you to thaw in the refrigerator. This is not just a preference of mine. We should never thaw frozen foods on the counter because it is not safe and promotes the growth of harmful bacteria. We should always keep cold foods cold and hot foods hot. If you get into a bind because you forgot to take the food out of the freezer to thaw, it is best to use the microwave and set it for defrost. It will produce enough energy to thaw the food properly without allowing the food to stand unrefrigerated for too long.

Calories—446; Fat—6.2 g; Protein—40.8 g; Carbohydrates—60.2 g; Cholesterol—70 mg; Fiber—3.2 g; Sodium—1881 mg

56 of the 446 calories are from fat.
13% of the calories come from fat.

LASAGNA

1 16-oz. box lasagna
  noodles
2 26.5-oz. cans spaghetti
  sauce
1/2 lb. very lean ground
  round
2 cups nonfat cottage
  cheese
1 10-oz. pkg. frozen
  spinach, defrosted but
  not cooked (do not
  drain)
1 8-oz. pkg. fat-free cream
  cheese

1/2 cup nonfat parmesan
  cheese
1 tsp. Cajun Spice Mix (see
  page 274)
Salt (optional)
1 tsp. garlic powder
2 tsp. onion powder
1 tsp. Italian seasoning
1/2 tsp. sweet basil
1 cup Burgundy wine or
  Chianti
2/3 cup water
1 1/2 cups nonfat
  mozzarella cheese

Select a deep covered baking dish that is about as long as the lasagna noodles. Arrange the noodles in the pan to determine how many you need to get three layers of noodles. You may have to break a few noodles to fit them in the pan. I like to crisscross the noodles, but it isn't absolutely necessary. Pour about 1 cup of sauce on the bottom of the pan, then place a layer of uncooked lasagna noodles over the sauce in the bottom of the pan. Add about 1 more cup of sauce on top of the noodles. Separate the meat into two equal parts, then spread one-half of the meat on top of the noodles. Place 1/2 of the cottage cheese by teaspoonful around the pan, followed by 1/2 of the spinach, 1/2 of the cream cheese, and 1/2 of the parmesan cheese. Season with 1/2 of the spices. Cover with about 1 cup of sauce. Add another layer as above, cover with 1 cup of sauce. Add another layer of uncooked lasagna noodles. Pour the wine and water over all the dish. Top with the remaining sauce and season with the remaining spices. Sprinkle with the nonfat mozzarella cheese. Cover and bake at 350 for 1 hour. Remove the cover and bake at 375 for 6 more minutes. Remove from the oven, let the lasagna stand and cool for 5 minutes, then serve. Serves 8.

Lagniappe: This is a marvelous dish that is easy to make, especially since you use uncooked noodles and raw meat. It's more like a Cajun lasagna than an Italian lasagna, but I like it this way; hopefully, you will too. I really like to make this dish the day before I want to eat it. I refrigerate it overnight, and it seems to pick up flavors and blend flavors together in the refrigerator. It also cuts more easily after it has been reheated. This is another example of using meat as a flavoring rather than the main ingredient. The half pound of ground round that is used is more than adequate to flavor the dish.

Calories—478; Fat—3.1 g; Protein—41.8 g; Carbohydrates—67.3 g; Cholesterol—33 mg; Fiber—4.8 g; Sodium—1358 mg

28 of the 478 calories are from fat.
6% of the calories come from fat.

PORK ROSALIE

1 1/3 lb. pork tenderloin, trimmed of visible fat
1 tsp. Cajun Spice Mix (see page 274)
1 medium onion, chopped
1 medium red bell pepper, cut into strips
1/3 cup finely chopped celery
3 cloves garlic, crushed and minced
1 cup Marsala wine
1 10 3/4-oz. can low-sodium cream of mushroom soup
1 10 3/4-oz. can low-sodium cream of onion soup

1/4 cup chicken broth
6 large fresh mushrooms, sliced
1/2 cup finely chopped green onions
1/4 cup minced fresh parsley
1/2 tsp. Tabasco® Sauce
2 tbsp. white wine Worcestershire sauce
1 cup raw long grain white rice
2 tbsp. wild rice

Preheat the oven to 350 degrees. Cut the pork into bite-sized pieces. Season the pork with the Cajun Spice Mix. Heat a large nonstick skillet over medium heat. When it is hot, add the seasoned pork. Shake the pan to see that all sides of the pork pieces are browned. Add the onions, bell pepper, celery, and garlic. Cook over medium heat for 3 minutes, stirring often and shaking the pan; then add the wine. Let the wine come to a boil, then reduce the heat to a simmer. Add all the remaining ingredients into the skillet, stirring until well mixed. Cook over low heat for 5 minutes, then pour into a 2-quart covered casserole and bake for 30 minutes. Remove the cover and stir well, then cover the casserole and bake for 30 more minutes, or until the rice is cooked. Serve hot. Serves 6.

Lagniappe: This is so good, yet so simple. It is the kind of recipe you keep secret, not because you are stingy, but because it is too easy. Let them think you killed yourself in the kitchen. You can make this dish ahead of time and refrigerate or freeze it. The only negative is the one-hour cooking time, but you aren't standing over it or having to watch it. Sometimes we need recipes that are unconstrained, and this one fits the bill.

Calories—361; Fat—9.7 g; Protein—31.9 g; Carbohydrates—31.7 g; Cholesterol—84 mg; Fiber—1.3 g; Sodium—985 mg

87 of the 361 calories are from fat.
24% of the calories come from fat.

RABBIT ETOUFFEE

2 2 to 2 1/2-lb. rabbits
2 tbsp. Cajun Spice Mix
   (see page 274)
3 tbsp. peanut oil
2 oz. andouille sausage,
   thinly sliced
2 tbsp. all-purpose flour
2 large onions, chopped
2 large red or green bell
   peppers, diced
1 stalk celery, chopped
3 cloves garlic, minced

2 cups defatted or low-fat
   chicken stock or broth
1 1/2 tbsp. Worcestershire
   sauce
1 tbsp. tomato paste
1 tsp. Tabasco® Sauce
1 bunch green onions,
   trimmed and chopped
2 tbsp. fresh parsley,
   chopped
4 cups cooked long-grain
   white rice

Cut each rabbit into eight pieces and season with the Cajun Spice Mix. Heat a large, heavy covered pot over medium-high heat until it is hot, then add 1 tablespoon of peanut oil, heating it until it begins to smoke. Add half of the rabbit pieces and cook until they are browned, 3 to 5 minutes per side. Transfer the meat to a plate and set aside. Add another tablespoon of peanut oil to the pan, and brown the remaining rabbit in the same manner. Set it aside when cooked. Add the andouille to the pan and cook, stirring, until it is lightly browned, 2 to 3 minutes. Remove from the pan and drain the sausage on white paper towels.

Add the remaining peanut oil and the flour to the pan and cook, stirring constantly, until the flour is a golden brown, 2 to 3 minutes. Add the onions, bell peppers, celery, and garlic; stir and cook for 5 minutes. Stir in the chicken stock, Worcestershire sauce, tomato paste, and Tabasco® Sauce; bring to a boil, stirring. Add the browned rabbit and andouille to the pan. Cover and simmer over low heat for 1 hour, stirring occasionally, until the rabbit is tender. Skim the fat from the surface, then stir in the green onions and parsley. Serve hot over cooked white rice. Serves 8.

Lagniappe: This étouffée can be prepared in advance, covered, and stored in the refrigerator for up to 2 days or in the freezer for up to 3 months. I have two favorite ways to prepare rabbit. My grandfather Theriot taught me how to cook rabbit atop chicken wire set in the ground at an angle. The meat was always tender, smokey, and moist. From my grandmother Borel, I learned the secret of Rabbit Etouffée. In the old days, this dish would have been dripping in lard; but today we use much less oil and our peanut oil is much lower in saturated fats.

This is a one-dish meal; I mean the vegetables, sauce, and meat are all cooked in the same pot. If you look at French cooking, you will find the French saucing their meats. The reason our culture has so many one-dish meals is our environment didn't permit the handling of so many dishes, so we just made them all together in one pot. Etouffée is served over one of Cajun Louisiana's staples: rice. *Etouffée* means "choked" or "smothered." Because we are cooking and not committing a crime, we will use the latter definition. *Ça c'est beaucoup bon!*

Calories—325; Fat—9 g; Protein—23 g; Carbohydrates—37 g; Cholesterol—55 mg; Fiber—.8 g; Sodium—686 mg
80 of the 325 calories are from fat.
25% of the calories come from fat.

RUM CHOPS

4 3-oz. boneless pork loin
chops, fat removed
1/2 cup fresh orange juice
1/4 cup dark rum
2 tbsp. fresh lime juice
3 tbsp. dark brown sugar
3 cloves garlic, crushed and
finely minced
1/2 tsp. salt
1/2 tsp. Tabasco® Sauce
1/2 tsp. fresh ground black
pepper
1/2 tsp. ground ginger
1/2 tsp. ground cloves

1/4 tsp. ground allspice
1 large onion, coarsly
chopped
1 large bell pepper, cut into
strips
1 large red bell pepper, cut
into strips
1 cup low-fat and low-
sodium chicken broth
1 tbsp. cornstarch
1/4 cup cold water
4 cups cooked long grain
white rice

Combine the chops with the orange juice, rum, lime juice, sugar, garlic, salt, Tabasco® Sauce, black pepper, ground ginger, ground cloves,
and ground allspice. Place in a tight container and marinate in the refrigerator for 3 hours (or overnight if you have the time). Remove the
chops from the marinade and reserve the marinade.

Heat a large nonstick skillet over medium-high heat until it is hot.
When hot, place each of the chops in the pan and cook for 3 minutes
on each side. Pour the reserved marinade into the skillet, bring it to a
boil, then add the onion, green pepper, and red bell pepper. Use the
chicken broth liquid to braise the vegetables and meat by reducing the
dish to a low simmer and cooking for 15 minutes. Mix together the
cornstarch and cold water until the cornstarch is completely dissolved in
the water, then add it to the hot skillet. Raise the temperature to medium, and let the sauce thicken. Once the sauce has thickened nicely,
place a cup of cooked rice and one chop on each of four plates. Cover
the rice and chops with the sauce and serve at once. Serves 4.

Lagniappe: This recipe utilizes some of the spices that make food come to life. My grandmother always used to say, "Cher, make them think they don't know what you done put in this dish!" In other words, a lot of hints of flavor come together to create an enchanting dish. Good cooking and good eating is as much about variety as it is about taste. Don't make this dish in advance. It needs to be eaten just after it is cooked.

Calories—467; Fat—5 g; Protein—29.5 g; Carbohydrates—73.5 g; Cholesterol—67 mg; Fiber—1.2 g; Sodium—1366 mg

45 of the 467 calories are from fat.
10% of the calories come from fat.

SIMPLY STROGANOFF

1 lb. lean ground round
1 tsp. Cajun Spice Mix (see page 274)
1 small white onion, thinly sliced
1/2 large red bell pepper, diced
1/4 cup celery, finely chopped
3 cloves garlic, minced
8 large fresh mushrooms, sliced

2 tbsp. Worcestershire sauce
1/2 tsp. Tabasco® Sauce
1 10 3/4-oz. can cream of mushroom soup
1 cup beef broth
1/3 cup catsup
1 cup no-fat sour cream
5 cups cooked non-egg noodles
2 tbsp. fresh parsley, finely chopped

Add the ground round to a large saucepan over medium heat. Season the meat with the Cajun Spice Mix, and stir until the meat begins to brown, about 4 minutes. Add the onions, bell pepper, celery, and garlic and continue to cook for 5 minutes. Add the fresh mushrooms, Worcestershire sauce, Tabasco® Sauce, cream of mushroom soup, beef broth, and catsup; heat just until the mixture begins to bubble. Reduce the heat to low and cook at a simmer for 5 minutes. Add the sour cream and blend it in. Cook over low heat for 2 to 3 more minutes, then serve over the cooked noodles. Garnish with fresh parsley. Serves 6.

Lagniappe: This is a quick and simple stroganoff. I couldn't decide which one of my stroganoff recipes to leave out. They are all so similar, yet so very different. It's like they are cousins; all in the same family, but each with their own personality and taste. Because I couldn't decide, even after kitchen testing all three recipes four times, I decided to leave them all in. If you decide which one you like best, drop me a line. I would like to hear your opinion.

The can of soup helps to make this somewhat of a short-cut recipe. I honestly hope you enjoy all three recipes. This recipe can be made in advance and refrigerated, but do not freeze it. It really is so easy to put together that you don't need to go to the trouble of planning and freezing for later use; just make it when you feel like eating stroganoff.

Calories—602; Fat—9.7 g; Protein—44 g; Carbohydrates—88 g; Cholesterol—69 mg; Fiber—5.1 g; Sodium—828 mg

87 of the 602 calories are from fat.
14% of the calories come from fat.

SPAGHETTI IN A RUSH

1 lb. lean ground round
1 tsp. Cajun Spice Mix (see page 274)
1 medium white onion, finely chopped
1 large red bell pepper, finely diced
1/4 cup finely chopped celery
4 cloves garlic, finely minced
8 large fresh mushrooms, sliced
2 tbsp. Worcestershire sauce
1/2 tsp. Tabasco® Sauce

2 15-oz. cans tomato sauce
1/2 cup beef broth
2 tbsp. tomato paste
1/2 cup catsup
1 tsp. dried sweet basil
1 tsp. onion powder
1/2 tsp. dried oregano
1/2 tsp. dried rosemary
1/2 tsp. garlic powder
1/4 tsp. thyme
1/2 cup nonfat grated parmesan cheese
5 cups cooked spaghetti
2 tbsp. finely minced fresh parsley

Place the ground round in a large saucepan over medium heat. Season the meat with the Cajun Spice Mix and stir until the meat begins to brown, about 4 minutes. Add the onions, bell pepper, celery, and garlic and continue to cook for 5 minutes. Add the fresh mushrooms, Worcestershire sauce, Tabasco® Sauce, tomato sauce, beef broth, tomato paste, and catsup; heat just until the mixture begins to bubble. Reduce the heat to low, cook at a simmer for 5 minutes, then add the basil, onion powder, oregano, rosemary, garlic powder, and thyme and blend it in. Simmer over low for 10 minutes. Add the parmesan cheese, simmer for 3 more minutes, then serve over cooked spaghetti. Garnish with fresh parsley. Serves 6.

Lagniappe: This is Cajun Italian cooking. I have found that spaghetti is a wonderful complex carbohydrate that goes a long way toward filling you up and staying with you for a long time, and it is low in fat. The lean ground round keeps this recipe low in fat. I like to grind my own ground round if I have time, or I like to choose a round steak and ask the butcher to trim all the obvious fat from it and grind it for me. Most meat counters will do that, so don't feel bad about asking. Remember, you are the customer and you are always right!

Calories—391; Fat—6 g; Protein—39 g; Carbohydrates—50.4 g; Cholesterol—7 mg; Fiber—2.4 g; Sodium—765 mg

54 of the 185 calories are from fat.
14% of the calories come from fat.

STUFFED RED BELL PEPPERS

6 large red bell peppers
1 lb. lean ground round
1 tsp. Cajun Spice Mix (see page 274)
1 medium white onion, finely chopped
1 large green bell pepper, finely diced
1/4 cup finely chopped celery
3 cloves garlic, finely minced
2 tbsp. Worcestershire sauce
1/2 tsp. Tabasco® Sauce

1 cup stewed tomatoes
1/4 cup beef broth
1/2 tsp. dried sweet basil
1/4 tsp. dried rubbed sage
1/2 cup finely chopped green onions
1/4 cup finely minced fresh parsley
1/2 tsp. onion powder
2 cups cooked long grain white rice
2 tbsp. Italian seasoned bread crumbs
1/2 cup grated no-fat Swiss cheese

Cut the tops off the red bell peppers and remove the seeds. Place the peppers in boiling water for about 5 minutes, then remove them and drain well. Set aside for later use.

Place the ground round in a large saucepan over medium heat. Season the meat with the Cajun Spice Mix, and stir until the meat begins to brown, about 4 minutes. Add the onions, bell pepper, celery, and garlic and continue to cook for 5 minutes. Add the Worcestershire sauce, Tabasco® Sauce, stewed tomatoes, beef broth, basil, and sage; heat just until the mixture comes to a boil. Preheat the oven to 375 degrees. Reduce the heat to low and cook at a simmer for 5 minutes. Add the green onions, parsley, and onion powder, cook for 2 minutes, then add the rice. Fill the drained red bell peppers with this rice and meat mixture, sprinkle with the bread crumbs, and place in a shallow baking dish. Bake covered at 375 degrees for 25 minutes, then sprinkle with the cheese and bake for 5 more minutes, uncovered. Serves 6.

Lagniappe: Red bell peppers are appealing, vivid, and so sweet to the taste that I love to use them. Red bell peppers are true bell peppers without the chlorophyll that the green peppers have. They have a considerable amount of extra sugar so they add a much sweeter taste and a beautiful color to this recipe. They act as the serving plate as well. Stuffed peppers can be used as either the main entree or as a side dish. No matter how you decide to use them, they are sure to please. I like to make a big batch when I decide to stuff peppers. I then serve a few and freeze the rest for later use. Before freezing them, I separate them into batches of 2 or 4, cover them tightly with plastic wrap, and label and date them (to ensure use in a timely manner).

Calories—315; Fat—5.3 g; Protein—34.3 g; Carbohydrates—34.6 g; Cholesterol—68 mg; Fiber—2.3 g; Sodium—923 mg

48 of the 315 calories are from fat.
15% of the calories come from fat.

TENDERLOIN OF PORK DAN JOSEPH

1 1/2 lb. pork tenderloin
1 1/2 tsp. Cajun Spice Mix
   (see page 274)
2 tbsp. all-purpose flour
Butter-flavored nonstick
   vegetable oil spray
1/4 cup unsweetened
   applesauce
1 tbsp. Butter Buds

4 large Granny Smith
   apples, peeled, cored,
   and sliced
1 1/2 cups beef broth or
   beef stock
1/4 cup Madeira wine
2 tsp. fresh lemon juice
1/4 tsp. Tabasco® Sauce

Remove any excess fat that may remain on the pork tenderloin, then cut the loin into 6 equal steaks, about 4 ounces each. Season steaks equally with the Cajun Spice Mix, then dredge the tenderloin steaks in the flour. Spray a large nonstick skillet that has a lid with the butter-flavored vegetable oil spray and place it over medium heat. When the skillet is hot, brown the pork on each side until nicely browned, about 3 minutes per side. Mix together the applesauce and Butter Buds and pour it into the skillet. Stir the applesauce around. Cover the pork with the apple slices. Mix together the broth, wine, lemon juice, and Tabasco® Sauce and pour on top of the apples and pork. Cover the pan, turn the heat to low, and simmer for 50 minutes, stirring occasionally. Serve hot. Serves 6.

Lagniappe: This is a matchless dish. It is both the main course meat and a side dish all in one. I serve this with a nice green salad and a potato. It makes a complete, well-balanced, and luscious meal. The tartness and sweetness of the apples really merges well with the pork. The technique is nothing more than a braise. The results will dazzle you.

You can make this dish completely in advance and refrigerate it for up to 3 days. I do not recommend freezing this recipe. This is a great example of how sweet and tangy work well with pork. Enjoy!

Calories—200; Fat—6.1 g; Protein—31.6 g; Carbohydrates—16 g; Cholesterol—90 mg; Fiber—2 g; Sodium—581 mg
55 of the 200 calories are from fat.
27.5% of the calories come from fat.

TENDERLOIN OF PORK MERLOT

Olive oil-flavored nonstick vegetable oil spray
1 lb. pork tenderloin, cut into thin sliced steaks
1 tsp. Cajun Spice Mix (see page 274)
2 small onions, skin removed and cut into quarters
1 clove garlic, crushed and minced
1 cup carrots, julienned
1/2 lb. fresh mushrooms, cut in half

1/2 cup beef broth
1/4 tsp. Tabasco® Sauce
1 cup Merlot wine
1 tbsp. Dijon mustard
1/4 cup minced green onion tops
1/2 cup finely minced fresh parsley
1 tbsp. cornstarch
2 tbsp. cold water
4 cups cooked long grain white rice or 4 cups mashed potatoes

Heat a nonstick skillet over medium heat until it is hot, then spray it lightly with the olive oil-flavored vegetable oil spray. Season the pork tenderloin steaks equally with the Cajun Spice Mix. Brown the pork in the skillet until nicely browned on both sides. Remove the pork to a warm plate for later use.

Add the onions, garlic, carrots, and fresh mushrooms to the skillet, and sauté for 5 minutes, stirring often. Return the pork tenderloin steaks to the pan and add the broth, Tabasco® Sauce, and wine. Bring the dish to a boil, then add the mustard and mix it in well. Reduce the heat to simmer, cover the dish, and cook over low heat for 10 minutes, shaking the skillet a few times. Add the green onions and parsley and cook for 1 minute.

Mix together the cornstarch and water until the cornstarch is dissolved, then add it to the skillet. Stir the cornstarch into the skillet, raise the temperature to medium, and stir until the sauce thickens. Place one cup of cooked rice on each plate with an equal amount of pork, then spoon the sauce and vegetables on top of the rice and tenderloins. Serve at once. Serves 4.

Lagniappe: Pork tenderloins are so easy to use and cook. If there is any excess fat on the loin, just cut it off. Remember any fat you take off in the preparation stage is fat that won't be in the finished product. Pork cooks quickly, it is light, and it tastes so good. I don't like to make this dish in advance, and it does not freeze well. It is easy enough to make just before serving. You can do all your cutting and chopping in advance if you like, which will speed the cooking time along.

You can use this recipe with chicken breast to make Breast of Chicken Merlot. It is similar, but using the chicken will change the overall effect. I use one-half breast of chicken per serving. You will have to cook the chicken breast for about 4 minutes on each side, instead of just browning as you do with the pork. Other than that, the recipe is the same.

Calories—509; Fat—6.6 g; Protein—37.8 g; Carbohydrates—64.5 g; Cholesterol—90 mg; Fiber—1.3 g; Sodium—183 mg
59 of the 509 calories are from fat.
12% of the calories come from fat.

TURNIP JAMBALAYA

1 1/2 lb. fresh young
    turnips
Water to cover
2 tsp. salt
3/4 lb. ground round
1 large onion, finely
    chopped
1 small bell pepper, finely
    chopped
3 cloves garlic, finely
    minced
1/2 cup celery, finely
    minced
1 1/2 tsp. Cajun Spice Mix
    (see page 274)

1 tsp. onion powder
1 cup dry red wine or
    Merlot
1 1/4 cups beef broth or
    stock
1/2 tsp. Tabasco® Sauce
1 tbsp. Worcestershire
    sauce
3 cups cooked white long
    grain rice
1/2 cup finely chopped
    green onions
1/4 cup fresh parsley, finely
    minced

Clean and wash the turnips well. Cut off the tops and the root bottoms. Place in a large saucepan and cover with water. Add the 2 teaspoons of salt and bring to a boil over high heat. Boil the turnips until they are tender, about 25 minutes, depending on the size. When a fork is easily inserted all the way through the centers of the turnips, they are done. Remove from the heat and drain. Allow the turnips to cool.

In a large nonstick skillet, sauté the ground round until it is completely browned. Remove the meat from the pan and place on a stack of about 10 white paper towels. Pat until the meat is dry and the fat is removed. Clean the skillet with paper towels and return the fat-extracted meat to the skillet. Add the onions, bell pepper, garlic, and celery; sauté for 2 minutes. There should be no oil left; you will be basically wilting the vegetables and further browning the meat. Season with the Cajun Spice Mix and the onion powder. Add the red wine and braise the meat and vegetables for 4 minutes. Add the beef broth, Tabasco® Sauce, and Worcestershire sauce, stir in well, then cover.

Finely chop the cooled turnips, then add them to the meat skillet, cover, and braise over low heat for 15 minutes. Add the rice, green onions, and parsley and mix together well. Serve hot. Serves 8.

Lagniappe: This is a great jambalaya, dressing, or stuffing. I like to eat it plain as a main dish. I find that corn complements this jambalaya well. I enjoy it with fresh, hot French bread, a glass of Merlot, a side of cream-style corn, and a little extra Tabasco® Sauce to just add that last finishing touch. I also like to use this recipe to stuff a chicken or a wild duck. Just use the Turnip Jambalaya as you would any other stuffing, and truss the bird. Bake as you would with any stuffing.

Calories—225; Fat—3.9 g; Protein—17.2 g; Carbohydrates—31.2 g; Cholesterol—37 mg; Fiber—.8 g; Sodium—722 mg

35 of the 225 calories are from fat.
16% of the calories come from fat.

VEAL AMANDA

4 3-oz. veal scallopini
1 tsp. Cajun Spice Mix (see
    page 274)
2 tsp. all-purpose flour
Butter-flavored nonstick
    spray
1 medium onion, chopped
2 cloves garlic, minced
1 tbsp. finely minced celery

6 large mushrooms, sliced
1/4 cup beef broth
1 26.5-oz. can nonfat
    spaghetti sauce
1/2 tsp. Tabasco® Sauce
1 cup no-fat sour cream
6 cups cooked spaghetti
1 tbsp. finely minced fresh
    parsley

Place the scallopini between two pieces of plastic wrap and pound it with a kitchen mallet until it increases in size by about one-third. Mix together the Cajun Spice Mix and the flour until well blended, then cover the scallopini. Spray the bottom of a large nonstick skillet with the butter-flavored spray. Heat the skillet over medium heat until hot, and cook the veal for 2 minutes on each side. Remove to a warm plate for later use. Lightly spray the skillet again, then add the onions, garlic, celery, and mushrooms. Sauté the vegetables for 3 minutes, then add the beef broth and cook for 3 more minutes, taking care to dissolve the pan drippings into the liquid (deglazing the skillet). Add the spaghetti sauce and Tabasco® Sauce; simmer over low heat for 10 minutes, stirring often. Add the sour cream and blend in well. Return the veal to the skillet, and let them heat until the sauce begins to lightly bubble. Add the parsley and stir it through. Place 1 1/2 cups of cooked spaghetti and one scallopini on each plate. Generously cover with the sauce. Serve hot. Serves 4.

Lagniappe: This is an alternative to high-fat ground beef. Veal is tender, cooks fast, and adds a touch of distinction. When you pound the veal, it becomes quite large. The three ounces of veal look like a much bigger piece of meat after being pounded. The sour cream makes this a mellow spaghetti sauce, and the color is beautiful. You can make the sauce in advance and refrigerate it for later use. Just store it tightly covered in the refrigerator for up to 4 days. When you are ready to serve, just cook the veal as directed and simmer the sauce. When the veal is cooked, add it to the sauce and continue as above. This recipe is as swift as it is savory! *Bon appétit!*

Calories—525; Fat—10 g; Protein—40 g; Carbohydrates—75 g; Cholesterol—60 mg; Fiber—1.5 g; Sodium—470 mg

90 of the 525 calories are from fat.
17% of the calories come from fat.

VEAL GERARD

1 tbsp. peanut oil
1 lb. veal round, cut into
   thin strips
1 1/2 tsp. Cajun Spice Mix
   (see page 274)
1 cup carrots, cut
   diagonally
1/4 cup celery, cut
   diagonally
1 medium onion, cut
   into strips
1 small red bell pepper, cut
   into strips
1 small green bell pepper,
   cut into strips
3 cloves garlic, minced

1 15.5-oz. can nonfat pinto
   beans, drained
1 14.5-oz. can beef broth
2 tbsp. cornstarch
1/2 tsp. onion powder
1/2 tsp. garlic powder
1/2 tsp. Tabasco® Sauce
1 tbsp. Worcestershire
   sauce
1 tsp. soy sauce
1 tsp. salt
1/2 tsp. sweet basil
1/2 cup Burgundy wine
4 cups cooked white long
   grain rice

In a wok or large skillet, heat the peanut oil until it is hot. Cut the veal into thin strips, about 1/4 inch thick and 1 1/2 inches long, then season the veal well with the Cajun Spice Mix. Add the seasoned veal pieces to the skillet, and sauté until they are nicely browned, about 3 minutes. Add the carrots, celery, and onions and sauté for 2 minutes. Add the red and green bell peppers and garlic; sauté for 2 more minutes. Add the drained beans and sauté for 1 minute.

Combine the cornstarch with about 1/2 cup of the beef broth and stir until it is dissolved. Add the remaining broth to the skillet and season with the onion powder, garlic powder, Tabasco® Sauce, Worcestershire sauce, soy sauce, salt, and sweet basil; blend in well. Add the 1/2 cup of wine and blend in well. The sauce should thicken nicely. Adjust the seasonings to taste. Serve at once over cooked white rice. Serve hot. Serves 6.

Lagniappe: This dish uses veal, which is somewhat high in fat, as meat should really be used, as a seasoning. One pound of veal now serves six people. Be sure to trim off any visible fat before you cook the veal. Every piece of fat cut off will mean less in the dish, and ultimately less on you. The beans are added to the recipe to boost the per serving protein count because they combine with the rice to form a complete protein.

Calories—461; Fat—10.5 g; Protein—29.2 g; Carbohydrates—54.4 g; Cholesterol—67 mg; Fiber—2.8 g; Sodium—1724 mg

95 of the 461 calories are from fat.
21% of the calories come from fat.

VEAL LEBLANC

1 recipe Veal Panné (see
pages 177-78)
1 recipe Lump Crabmeat
Sauté (see pages 125-26)

2 large fresh lemons, cut
into 6 wedges each

Cook the Veal Panné according to directions and place, loosely covered with aluminum foil in a 180-degree oven until you are ready to serve. Prepare the Lump Crabmeat Sauté according to recipe. Place each slice of the veal on a warm serve plate, and put a heaping serving of the Lump Crabmeat Sauté in the center of the veal. Garnish with fresh lemons. Serves 6.

Lagniappe: I think this is an example of a dish that appears to be quite gourmet. I think this is almost so easy that anyone who knows their way around the kitchen can be successful with this recipe. Be sure to sprinkle a couple squeezes of fresh lemon on the dish; lemon and this dish really go well together. This is also the dish for a nice dry white wine. Enjoy!

Calories—484; Fat—7.2 g; Protein—59.3 g; Carbohydrates—36 g; Cholesterol—160 mg; Fiber—.8 g; Sodium—807 mg

65 of the 484 calories are from fat.
13% of the calories come from fat.

VEAL LEMOINE

1 tbsp. unsalted butter
2 lb. veal top round, cut
into bite-sized cubes
4 medium onions, sliced
1 large red bell pepper,
diced
1/2 cup celery, finely
chopped
1 clove garlic, minced
1 cup beef broth or stock

1 tsp. nutmeg, grated
1 tsp. mace, grated
1 tsp. Cajun Spice Mix (see
page 274)
1/2 tsp. Tabasco® Sauce
1 1/2 cups no-fat sour
cream
4 cups cooked non-egg
noodles

Heat a large nonstick skillet over medium heat until hot, then add the butter. When the butter is melted, brown the veal. Add the onions, red bell pepper, celery, and garlic. Cook slowly until the vegetables are lightly browned, about 5 minutes, stirring constantly. Add all ingredients except the sour cream and noodles. Simmer over low heat until tender, about 20 minutes. Add the sour cream, and simmer for 15 to 20 minutes. Serve over 1/2 cup of cooked noodles. Serve at once. Serves 8.

Lagniappe: Veal is really company food. It is often passed over because of its delicate white color and lack of familiarity. Veal is a young meat, and it is very tender. Because it has not had time to load itself down with fat (except for fat from dairy products), it is, for the most part, not as fattening as beef. It can be a good food choice. The secret, when it comes to meat, is moderation. Flavor the dish with meat, but don't always try to dominate the recipe.

This dish is best when eaten right after it is prepared. However, you can refrigerate the dish for later use, if any is left. I don't recommend freezing this dish at all.

Calories—533; Fat—14.3 g; Protein—42.4 g; Carbohydrates—55.4 g; Cholesterol—84 mg; Fiber—1.1 g; Sodium—313 mg

129 of the 533 calories are from fat.
24% of the calories come from fat.

VEAL PANNE
(Pan-Fried Veal)

6 4-oz. slices veal top
  round steak
1 cup all-purpose flour
2 tsp. Cajun Spice Mix (see
  page 274)
1/2 cup egg substitute
1 1/2-oz. packet Butter
  Buds
1/4 cup evaporated skim
  milk

1 tsp. Tabasco® Sauce
1 tbsp. white wine
  Worcestershire sauce
2 cups fat-free cracker
  crumbs
butter-flavored nonstick
  vegetable oil spray

Cover each slice of veal round with plastic wrap, then pound the veal with a kitchen mallet until it is very thin, doubling the size of the original slice. Mix together the flour and 1 teaspoon of Cajun Spice Mix until well blended. Dredge the veal well in the flour and shake off any excess flour.

In a medium-size mixing bowl, mix together the egg substitute, Butter Buds, skim milk, Tabasco® Sauce, and Worcestershire sauce until blended. Dip each slice of veal in the seasoned egg substitute, then roll it in the cracker crumbs. Spray a large nonstick skillet with the butter-flavored vegetable oil spray, then heat the skillet over medium heat until hot. Sauté the breaded veal in the skillet until the veal is cooked and begins to brown, about 2 to 3 minutes on each side. Serve at once. Serves 6.

Lagniappe: The secret to this dish is a good nonstick skillet. If you have a cheap one, your veal will stick and come apart. If you have a good one the veal won't stick at all, and you will be able to turn the veal over intact with all the breading still stuck to the meat. Veal Panné is great by itself or wonderful covered with any number of sauces for a truly exquisite dining experience.

Unfortunately this dish must be eaten right after it is cooked. It does not hold long, nor does it refrigerate or freeze well. To speed things up a bit though, you can pound, flour, and bread the veal with the cracker crumbs and be all ready to sauté the meat when your guests arrive. It is also possible to hold the veal in a 180-degree oven for up to 30 minutes without much loss in texture, quality, or appearance. You will have a lot of the flour mixture and cracker mixture left after breading the veal. The excess is not counted in the nutritional analysis for the recipe because it is not eaten.

Calories—517; Fat—8.9 g; Protein—57 g; Carbohydrates—36.8 g; Cholesterol—151 mg; Fiber—.2 g; Sodium—662 mg
80 of the 517 calories are from fat.
15% of the calories come from fat.

Poultry

BREAST OF CHICKEN CHRISTINE

Olive oil-flavored nonstick
   vegetable oil spray
1 tsp. Cajun Spice Mix (see
   page 274)
1/4 tsp. salt
2 large chicken breasts, cut
   into bite-sized pieces
1/2 cup red bell pepper, cut
   into thin strips
1/2 cup green bell pepper,
   cut into thin strips
2 tbsp. minced shallots
1/2 cup chopped celery
1/2 cup julienned carrots
3 cloves garlic, crushed and
   minced
3 tbsp. all-purpose flour
8 large fresh mushrooms,
   sliced

1 1/3 cups low-fat and low-
   sodium chicken broth
1 cup dry Chardonnay
1 5-oz. can light evaporated
   skim milk
1/2 tsp. Tabasco® Sauce
2 tbsp. white wine
   Worcestershire sauce
8 oz. fat-free cream cheese
1 1/2-oz. packet Butter
   Buds
1/2 cup chopped green
   onions
1/2 tsp. minced fresh
   parsley
1/2 tsp. sweet paprika
4 cups cooked fettuccine
   noodles

Spray a large nonstick skillet for about 5 seconds (twice as much as usual) with the olive oil-flavored nonstick vegetable oil spray, then place the skillet over medium heat. Season the chicken with the Cajun Spice Mix and salt until well mixed. When the skillet is just to the smoking point, add the seasoned chicken pieces and sauté them over medium heat until they are mostly cooked and begin to brown, about 5 minutes. Add the bell peppers, shallots, celery, carrots, and garlic and continue to sauté, stirring constantly, for 3 more minutes. Add the flour and blend it in well. Cook the flour for 3 minutes, stirring constantly, then add the mushrooms and mix them in well.

Pour in the chicken broth and Chardonnay and stir until the sauce begins to thicken somewhat. Add the evaporated skimmed milk, Tabasco® Sauce, and Worcestershire sauce, then stir until the liquid is incorporated into the sauce. Add the cream cheese and stir until it is completely melted through the dish. Add the Butter Buds, green onions, and fresh parsley and blend in well. Finally, add the paprika and stir until the sauce begins to boil. Reduce the heat and simmer for 2 minutes, stirring constantly. Serve hot over cooked fettuccine noodles. Serves 6.

Lagniappe: This is a quick and easy recipe that is rich looking and has the feel of a heavy cream or cheese sauce. When we taste food, we taste it first with our eyes. Next, we taste with our sense of smell or our nose. Third, we taste the texture and feel of food; then we taste with our tongue. We also taste food with our memory. That is to say we remember how something tasted when we ate it at some time in the past. This recipe captures all our senses and makes a dish that looks great, smells great, has the feel of a real heavy sauce, and tastes so rich and tasty that it brings back to our mind all the rich sauces we might have eaten in the past. I noticed when I tested this recipe that I got full quickly. It has such the look of a fat-heavy sauce that the thought of eating it filled me up! I'm very serious about this; we need to use all of our senses to help us get the full benefit of the food we eat. You can't beat this dish for entertaining, and it is a treat for daily family eating.

Calories—496; Fat—4.1 g; Protein—35.7 g; Carbohydrates—71.8 g; Cholesterol—73 mg; Fiber—1.8 g; Sodium—802 mg

37 of the 185 calories are from fat.
7% of the calories come from fat.

BREAST OF CHICKEN GRAND ISLE

2 recipes Pan-Seared
  Chicken Breast (see page
  203)
1 recipe Crab Dip Kimberly,
  without the crackers (see
  page 114)
1/2 cup cream sherry
1/4 cup skim milk

1/2 tsp. Tabasco® Sauce
1/4 cup minced fresh
  parsley
4 cups non-egg noodles,
  cooked al dente
1 tbsp. finely minced fresh
  basil

Preheat the oven to 190 degrees. Place the cooked chicken breasts on a warm plate, cover it loosely with foil, and place it in the slow oven. Let it stand until you are ready to serve it.

Divide the Crab Dip Kimberly into two equal parts. Keep half over very low heat and stir often. Place the other half of the crab dip in a medium saucepan and add the sherry, milk, Tabasco® Sauce, and parsley. Heat the saucepan over medium heat until the contents become well blended and smooth. The cooked noodles should be warm. Toss them with the fresh basil, then pour the crab dip from the saucepan over the noodles as the sauce begins to bubble. Stir until the noodles are well coated. Place a half chicken breast and equal parts of the crab sauced noodles on each of four warm plates. Spoon generous amounts of extra crab dip on top of each chicken breast and on top of the noodles. Serve at once. Serves 4.

Lagniappe: This is just a combination of two other recipes. Crab and chicken go together very well. You can reduce caloric content, if you like, by chopping the chicken into bite-sized pieces and tossing all the crab dip with the noodles. It will then serve eight people, which will cut the calories and all other nutritional information in half. The percentage of fat in the recipe will still remain twelve of the total calories. Don't refrigerate after mixing the dip with the noodles. If you want to make this dish in advance, keep the dip separate until you are ready to serve, then toss with warm noodles. Be sure to avoid egg noodles; they will have much more fat than noodles without egg. This dish is easy enough for daily fare, but it can be fancy enough for the finest company.

Calories—644; Fat—8.5 g; Protein—66.5 g; Carbohydrates—55.5 g; Cholesterol—181 mg; Fiber—1.7 g; Sodium—1229 mg

77 of the 644 calories are from fat.
12% of the calories come from fat.

BREAST OF CHICKEN MARIE LOUISE

4 tbsp. honey
3 tbsp. dark brown sugar
2 tbsp. red wine vinegar
2 tsp. Worcestershire sauce
2 tsp. finely minced shallots

1/4 tsp. Tabasco® Sauce
1 tbsp. brown prepared
mustard
2 large chicken breasts,
skinned and cut in half

Preheat the oven to 400 degrees. Combine all the ingredients, except the chicken breasts, and mix until well blended. Place the chicken in a nonstick baking pan, and coat the breasts with all the sauce. Bake for 15 minutes, basting about 3 times. Reduce the heat to 350 degrees, and bake for 20 more minutes, basting occasionally through the baking. Remove from the oven and serve at once with plenty of the basting sauce. Serves 4.

Lagniappe: This sweet and sour mixture brings the chicken to life and adds a nice zing! For a savory meal, serve with a nice pasta dish, or with a potato or rice and a green vegetable. Although this recipe will work with a whole chicken or with other parts of the chicken equally well, the fat content will be notably increased. Current thinking on the chicken breast skin allows it to be removed after the meat is completely cooked when you are grilling, baking, or broiling chicken. Just be sure that you remember to do it! If you leave the skin on when you are baking, the meat has less tendency to dry out, and studies show that there is no more fat in the meat than there is in meat cooked with the skin removed.

Calories—251; Fat—3.2 g; Protein—27 g; Carbohydrates—28.6 g; Cholesterol—73 mg; Fiber—0 g; Sodium—106 mg

29 of the 251 calories are from fat.
12% of the calories come from fat.

CHICKEN BREASTS
A LA MARIE LEBLANC

2 large chicken breasts, skin and bones removed
1 tsp. Cajun Spice Mix (see page 274)

1 recipe Mushrooms Marie LeBlanc (see page 227)
2 tbsp. fresh parsley, minced

Preheat the oven to broil. Cut each breast into two halves. Wash the chicken breasts with cold water, then pat dry with a plain white paper towel. Season equally with the Cajun Spice Mix. Place in a pan for broiling, and broil the breasts about 3 inches from the heat for 4 minutes on the first side, then turn it over and broil on the second side for 4 more minutes. Turn it back over and cook for 2 more minutes. Remove from the oven, place on a plate, and cover with the Mushrooms Marie LeBlanc. Sprinkle the top with the minced parsley. Serves 4.

Lagniappe: This is elegant, simple, and so tasty. You'll have a beautiful entree that is low in fat and tastes great. I would serve this with a nice green vegetable and a glass of dry white wine (like a Chardonnay or a Bourdeaux Blanc). I would use the same wine in the recipe when making the Mushrooms Marie LeBlanc. This would help to marry the dish to the wine, making it a perfect blend. You would not want to make this dish in advance, it is so quick and easy, you can make it and serve it at once. Chicken that comes right from the broiler will taste superior to that which has been cooked earlier and reheated. Enjoy!

Calories—168; Fat—3.4 g; Protein—28.5 g; Carbohydrates—4.5 g; Cholesterol—18 mg; Fiber—.7 g; Sodium—402 mg

30 of the 168 calories are from fat.
18% of the calories come from fat.

CHICKEN CATHERINE

4 4-oz. chicken breast
    halves, boned but not
    skinned
Butter-flavored nonstick
    vegetable oil spray
2 tbsp. Creole mustard
2 tbsp. brown sugar
2 tbsp. honey
1 tbsp. White wine
    Worcestershire sauce
1/2 tsp. Tabasco® Sauce
3 cloves garlic, minced
1 tsp. minced shallots
3 tbsp. minced fresh
    parsley

Place the chicken in an 11 x 7 x 2-inch dish lightly coated with the vegetable oil spray. Mix together all the remaining ingredients, except for the parsley, then brush the basting mixture over chicken. Cover with a lid or aluminum foil, and bake at 375 degrees for 15 to 20 minutes or until the chicken is puffy and white. Remove the skin, baste again with the sauce, and sprinkle with the parsley. Uncover the chicken and broil 4 inches from the heat for 1 to 2 minutes or until golden. Take the chicken out of the oven and brush once more with the basting sauce. Serve at once. Serves 4.

Lagniappe: This is a fundamental dish that is filled with zest. The sugary taste of the honey and brown sugar and the acidity of the mustard set up a polarity in your mouth that makes your taste buds tingle. Chicken breast is a versatile food that can be cooked in so many ways. The basting sauce turns the chicken golden brown and fills it with a savory flavor. Serve it with a potato salad, a steamed fresh green vegetable, and hot French bread. It is splendid.

Calories—264; Fat—4.5 g; Protein—9.3 g; Carbohydrates—17.5 g; Cholesterol—97 mg; Fiber—trace; Sodium—159 mg

41 of the 264 calories are from fat.
16% of the calories come from fat.

CHICKEN CREOLE

Butter-flavored nonstick
vegetable oil spray
2 large chicken breasts, cut
in half
1 1/2 tsp. Cajun Spice Mix
(see page 274)
1 large onion, chopped
1 large bell pepper,
chopped
1/2 cup finely chopped
celery
1/2 cup finely chopped
carrots
2 cloves garlic, minced
2 15-oz cans stewed
tomatoes

8 large mushrooms, sliced
2 tbsp. Worcestershire
sauce
1/2 tsp. Tabasco® Sauce
3 tbsp. cornstarch
1/2 cup Marsala wine (or
dry white wine)
1 cup low-fat chicken broth
2/3 cup finely minced green
onions
1/2 cup finely minced fresh
parsley
4 cups hot cooked long
grain rice

Spray a large nonstick pan with a short spray of butter-flavored vegetable oil spray, then place over medium-high heat. Season the chick-
en breasts with the Cajun Spice Mix, then brown the chicken nicely on
both sides, about 3 minutes per side. Remove the chicken to a plate,
then spray the pan once more with vegetable oil spray. Add the onion,
bell pepper, celery, carrots, and garlic; sauté over medium heat for 4
minutes, stirring constantly. Add the tomatoes and mushrooms, and
cook for 5 minutes, stirring often.

Cut the chicken into bite-sized pieces, then add the chicken pieces,
Worcestershire sauce, and Tabasco® Sauce to the pan, cover, and simmer for 5 minutes. Raise the heat to high and bring the mixture to a
hard boil. Mix together the cornstarch, wine, and broth until the cornstarch is completely dissolved, then add it to the boiling chicken mixture.
Stir in well, and the mixture will thicken. Reduce the heat to low and
add the green onions and parsley. Cook for 1 minute, then serve hot
over rice. Serves 4.

Lagniappe: Creole is a favored Cajun dish. We eat chicken Creole, shrimp Creole, pork Creole, and you-name-it Creole. This Creole is a low-fat rendition that has all the marvelous flavor and goodness of regular Creole without the fat. You can make this in advance and refrigerate or freeze it for later use. When you go to reheat it, thaw in the refrigerator and heat over low until thoroughly warmed, then serve. The name Creole comes from the type of tomatoes that were used, Creole tomatoes, and not from the Creole people. This is a wonderful tomato dish that will be most engaging for any occasion.

Calories—426; Fat—5.7 g; Protein -42 g; Carbohydrates—86.4 g; Cholesterol—74 mg; Fiber—3.6 g; Sodium—1991 mg

51 of the 426 calories are from fat.
12% of the calories come from fat.

CHICKEN DUPUIS

4 12-oz. chicken breasts, bones and skin removed
2 tsp. Cajun Spice Mix (see page 274)
2 tbsp. all-purpose flour
Butter-flavored nonstick vegetable oil spray
1 10 3/4-oz. can cream of celery soup
1 cup low-fat chicken broth
1 1/2 cups no-fat sour cream
2/3 cup Madeira wine
1/2 tsp. Tabasco® Sauce
8 large fresh mushrooms, sliced
1 1/2 cups raw long grain rice
1/2 cup minced green onions
2 tbsp. minced fresh parsley

Separate the breasts into two halves each. Mix together the Cajun Spice Mix and the flour until well blended. Equally coat each breast half with the flour-spice mix. Lightly spray a large nonstick skillet with the vegetable oil spray, then place it over medium heat until it is hot.

Add the chicken and brown nicely on each side. Mix together the remaining ingredients in a large sauce pot, then cook over medium heat for 4 minutes. Pour this soup-rice mixture into the bottom of a 3-quart shallow covered casserole. Place the chicken on top of the rice mixture and cover. Bake at 375 degrees for 1 1/2 hours. Remove from the oven, allow the dish to stand for 5 minutes, then serve hot. Serves 8.

Lagniappe: You'll find that this is an easy, yet wonderful dish. You can either bake it completely in advance or just put it together and bake just before serving, which is my preference. The ease of the dish is one of its main appeals.

Calories—218; Fat—4.5 g; Protein—32 g; Carbohydrates—15 g; Cholesterol—76 mg; Fiber—.5 g; Sodium—578 mg

40 of the 218 calories are from fat.
18% of the calories come from fat.

CHICKEN ETOUFFEE

3 large chicken breasts (or
   2 1/4 lb.)
2 tbsp. Cajun Spice Mix
   (see page 274)
3 tbsp. peanut oil
3 tbsp. all-purpose flour
2 large onions, chopped
1 large green bell pepper,
   diced
1 large red bell pepper,
   diced
1 stalk celery, chopped
3 cloves garlic, minced

2 cups chicken stock or
   defatted or low-fat broth
1 1/2 tbsp. Worcestershire
   sauce
2 tbsp. tomato paste
1 tsp. Tabasco® Sauce
1 bunch green onions,
   trimmed and chopped
1/4 cup fresh parsley,
   chopped
4 cups cooked long-grain
   white rice

Cut each chicken breast into strips, then season with the Cajun Spice Mix. Heat a large, heavy covered pot over medium-high heat until it is hot, then add 1 tablespoon of peanut oil, heating it until it begins to smoke. Add half of the chicken strips, and cook until they are browned, 2 to 3 minutes per side. Transfer the meat to a plate, and set aside. Add the other tablespoon of peanut oil to the pan and brown the remaining chicken breast strips in the same manner. Set it aside when cooked.

Add the remaining peanut oil to the pan with the flour, and cook, stirring constantly until the flour is a golden brown, 3 to 5 minutes. Add the onions, bell peppers, celery, and garlic; stirring for 5 minutes. Stir in the chicken stock, Worcestershire sauce, tomato paste, and Tabasco® Sauce; bring to a boil, stirring constantly. Add the browned chicken to the pan. Cover and simmer over low heat for 30 minutes, stirring occasionally, until the chicken is tender. Skim any fat from the surface, then stir in the green onions and parsley. Serve hot over cooked white rice. Serves 8.

Lagniappe: This étouffée can be prepared ahead of time and stored, covered in the refrigerator for up to 3 days or in the freezer for up to 3 months. This is a one-dish meal; the vegetables, sauce, and meat are all cooked in the same pot. Etouffée is served over one of Cajun Louisiana's staples—rice.

This recipe cooks so quickly because chicken breasts cook quickly. You can make this with other pieces of chicken, but remember the fat content goes up dramatically when you move from the white breast meat to the dark meat of the chicken.

Calories—284; Fat—4 g; Protein—19 g; Carbohydrates—37 g; Cholesterol—73 mg; Fiber—.8 g; Sodium—697 mg

36 of the 284 calories are from fat.
13% of the calories come from fat.

CHICKEN ETOUFFEE NICHOLAS

Butter-flavored vegetable oil
  spray
1 large onion, chopped
1 large red bell pepper,
  chopped
2/3 cup chopped celery
3 cloves garlic, crushed and
  minced
2 tbsp. all-purpose flour
2 whole chicken breasts,
  cut in half
1 1/4 tsp. Cajun Spice Mix
  (see page 274)

1 cup dry red wine
1 14.5-oz. can chicken
  broth
1 tbsp. Worcestershire
  sauce
1/4 tsp. Tabasco® Sauce
1/2 cup chopped green
  onions
1/4 cup minced fresh
  parsley, minced
4 cups cooked white long
  grain rice

Heat a large nonstick saucepan over high heat until it is hot, then spray it lightly with the butter-flavored vegetable oil spray. When the oil is hot, add the onion, bell pepper, celery, and garlic and cook over high heat for 4 minutes, stirring constantly. Add the flour and cook, stirring constantly, for 2 minutes. Season the chicken breasts with the Cajun Spice Mix and add them to the skillet with the vegetables and flour. Cook them, stirring constantly, for 2 more minutes, trying to turn the breasts over so both sides will be seared and begin to turn white. Add the wine, broth, Worcestershire sauce, and Tabasco® Sauce; stir until the liquid begins to thicken. Reduce the heat to low and let the pot simmer. Cover and cook for 30 minutes, stirring a few times during the cooking process. Add the green onions and fresh parsley, and simmer uncovered for 5 more minutes. Serve hot over cooked white rice. Serves 4.

Lagniappe: This is a version of chicken étouffée that I named after my grandfather. He instilled in me my love of chicken. He raised them and started me raising them. I have to admit that getting a Cajun to give up heavy sauces and gravies seems to be impossible. However, I started experimenting with dishes like this étouffée, and I discovered that I would not have to give up anything but the fat. The taste of this dish is outstanding; you won't walk away thinking that you have had to give up anything. You can make this dish in advance and refrigerate or freeze it.

To serve, just thaw in the refrigerator and return to a saucepan over low and heat until the dish is piping hot. Serve as above. I like to serve this dish with plenty of French bread or homemade low-fat bread.

Etouffée means "smothered" or "choked." Because we are cooking rather than commiting a crime, this is smothered chicken, or perhaps you might call it chicken stew. No matter what you call it, it is out of this world.

Calories—252; Fat—4.4 g; Protein—30.4 g; Carbohydrates—14.3 g; Cholesterol—99 mg; Fiber—.9 g; Sodium—693 mg

40 of the 252 calories are from fat.
16% of the calories come from fat.

CHICKEN JOSEPH BETH

Butter-flavored nonstick vegetable oil spray
2 cups cooked chicken breast, cut into bite-sized pieces
1/2 tsp. crushed red pepper flakes
1/4 tsp. cayenne pepper
1/4 tsp. fresh ground black pepper
1 large onion, coarsely chopped
1 medium bell pepper, coarsely chopped

6 large mushrooms, sliced
2 tbsp. low-sodium soy sauce
3/4 cup pineapple juice
2 tbsp. Worcestershire sauce
1/4 tsp. Tabasco® Sauce
1/2 cup cream sherry
1 1/2 tsp. cornstarch
4 cups cooked white long grain rice
2 tbsp. minced fresh parsley

Use the nonstick vegetable oil spray to lightly coat a large, heavy nonstick skillet, then place the skillet over medium-high heat. Add the chicken, crushed red pepper, cayenne, and black pepper. Sauté for 1 minute, then add the onions, bell pepper, and mushrooms and sauté for 1 more minute. Add the soy sauce, pineapple juice, Worcestershire sauce, and Tabasco® Sauce. Cook, stirring constantly, for 2 minutes.

Combine the sherry and the cornstarch and stir until completely blended. Add the sherry mixture into the skillet. Cook, stirring constantly, until the sauce thickens. Serve hot over one cup of cooked white rice, and garnish with the parsley. Serves 4.

Lagniappe: This recipe was accidently created at Joseph Beth Bookstore in Lexington, Kentucky, in April of 1992. I was there to do a cooking demonstration, and the produce was accidentally left off the shopping list. What do you do when something like this happens? You make the best of it. The results were outstanding. I liked the finished product, and the crowd was more than pleased. Sometimes accidents make good dishes!

This recipe has to be made just before you are ready to eat it. Total cooking time is only about 10 minutes. You can use cooked turkey cut into bite-sized pieces in the place of chicken to make Turkey Joseph Beth. Either way, it is an uncomplicated and delectable dish.

Calories—442; Fat—3 g; Protein—25.9 g; Carbohydrates—69 g; Cholesterol—55 mg; Fiber—.8 g; Sodium—1415 mg

27 of the 442 calories are from fat.
6% of the calories come from fat.

CHICKEN JULIE

2 large chicken breasts, cut
  into bite-sized pieces
1 tsp. Cajun Spice Mix (see
  page 274)
1 medium onion, finely
  chopped
1/2 medium bell pepper,
  chopped
1/4 cup finely chopped
  celery
2 cloves garlic, crushed and
  minced
1 cup Madeira wine
1 10 3/4-oz. can cream of
  chicken soup

1 10 3/4-oz. can cream of
  celery soup
1/2 cup chicken broth
4 large fresh mushrooms,
  sliced
1/2 cup green onions, finely
  chopped
1/4 cup fresh parsley,
  minced
1/2 tsp. Tabasco® Sauce
1 tbsp. white wine
  Worcestershire sauce
1 cup raw long grain white
  rice
1 tbsp. wild rice

Preheat the oven to 350 degrees. Season the chicken with the Cajun Spice Mix. Heat a large nonstick skillet over medium heat. When it is hot, add the seasoned chicken. Shake the pan to be sure that all sides of the chicken are browned. Add the onions, bell pepper, celery, and garlic, then cook over medium heat for 3 minutes, stirring often. Add the Madeira wine and let the wine come to a boil, then reduce the heat to low.

Add all the remaining ingredients to the skillet, and stir until well mixed. Cook over low heat for 3 minutes, then pour into a 2-quart covered casserole and bake for 30 minutes. Remove the cover and stir well, then cover and bake for 30 more minutes, or until the rice is cooked. Serve hot. Serves 6.

Lagniappe: This is quick. This is easy. This is the kind of dish you make and don't give out the recipe. Let them think you slaved in the kitchen. Come out covered with stains and pat water on your face to make it look like you were really sweating; do it up well. You can make ahead and refrigerate or freeze. The only negative is the one-hour cooking time, but you aren't standing over it working yourself to death. Sometimes we need recipes that are effortless. This is one of them!

Calories—349; Fat—8.7 g; Protein—22 g; Carbohydrates—33.4 g; Cholesterol—59 mg; Fiber—.9 g; Sodium—1261 mg

78 of the 349 calories are from fat.
22% of the calories come from fat.

CHICKEN LIVERS AUX CHAMPIGNONS

1 lb. chicken livers, trimmed of any excess fat
1 tsp. Cajun Spice Mix (see page 274)
1/4 cup all-purpose flour
Butter-flavored vegetable oil spray
1 lb. fresh mushrooms, sliced
1 cup finely chopped green onions
1/2 cup port wine

1/2 cup evaporated skim milk
1/2 cup low-fat chicken broth
1/2 tsp. Tabasco® Sauce
1 tbsp. Worcestershire sauce
1/4 cup minced fresh parsley
1 1/2 cups no-fat sour cream
6 cups non-egg noodles

Season the chicken livers with the Cajun Spice Mix, then dredge the livers in the flour until they are well coated. Spray a large, nonstick skillet with the vegetable oil spray, then place the skillet over medium-high heat. Gently sauté the livers in the skillet until they are browned on both sides. Remove the livers from the pan, and place them in a warm plate for later use. Spray the skillet one more time, and sauté the mushrooms and green onions for 3 minutes, stirring constantly.

Deglaze the skillet with the port wine until the drippings from the bottom of the pan are dissolved, then add the evaporated milk and chicken broth; stir until well blended. Add the Tabasco® Sauce, Worcestershire sauce, and parsley; blend in well. Return the livers to the skillet and stir them in well. Lower the heat to a simmer, and cook for 12 minutes. Add the sour cream, blend in well, and simmer for 3 minutes. Serve hot with plenty of gravy and mushrooms over noodles. Serves 6.

Lagniappe: Don't miss out on chicken livers just because you are watching fat. While the liver is very high in cholesterol, it is relatively low in fat. This is a wonderfully tasty dish that lifts the liver to the sumptuous level. It is a great choice for the individual who loves the taste of chicken liver. The sauce is absolutely divine. You won't believe you are eating a low-fat dish!

Calories—426; Fat—2 g; Protein—31.4 g; Carbohydrates -114.7 g; Cholesterol—481 mg; Fiber—1.3 g; Sodium—350 mg

18 of the 426 calories are from fat.
4% of the calories come from fat.

Note: This recipe exceeds the American Heart Association guidelines for cholesterol (no more than 300 mg per day). The AHA does note that liver is rich in iron and vitamins and a small serving (no more than 3 ounces—which this recipe does meet) is okay about once a month. To meet the AHA guidelines don't serve this dish or any other organ-meat dish more than once a month.

CHICKEN LIVERS MADEIRA

1 lb. chicken livers, trimmed of any excess fat
1 tsp. Cajun Spice Mix (see page 274)
1/4 cup all-purpose flour
Butter-flavored vegetable oil spray
1 medium onion, sliced
3 cloves garlic, minced

6 medium apples, cored and thinly sliced with peels
1 cup Madeira wine
3 tbsp. light brown sugar
1/2 tsp. Tabasco® Sauce
1 tbsp. Worcestershire sauce
4 cups cooked long grain white rice

Season the chicken livers with the Cajun Spice Mix, then dredge the livers in the flour until they are well coated. Spray a large, nonstick skillet with the vegetable oil spray, then place the skillet over medium-high heat. Gently sauté the livers in the skillet until they are browned on both sides. Remove the livers from the pan and place on a warm plate for later use.

Spray the skillet once more, then sauté the onion and garlic for 2 minutes, stirring constantly. Add the apples and continue to sauté for 4 more minutes. Deglaze the skillet with the Madeira wine until the drippings from the bottom of the pan are dissolved. Add the sugar, Tabasco® Sauce, and Worcestershire sauce; blend in well. Add the livers back into the skillet and stir them in well. Lower the heat to a simmer, and cook for 15 minutes. Serve hot over rice with plenty of the liquid and apple-vegetable mixture. Serves 6.

Lagniappe: Chicken livers get no respect! I happen to love them, and—believe it or not—they are not a bad choice of meat as far as fat is concerned. They are loaded with cholesterol, but are relatively low in fat. I think they are a good choice in moderation, such as the recipe above. This dish needs to be eaten right after it is cooked for the best taste and texture. The sweetness and tartness of the apples are a perfect marriage with the liver. Serving the dish over rice helps to increase the complex carbohydrates and adds tasty bulk to the meal.

Calories—417; Fat—4.8 g; Protein—23.3 g; Carbohydrates—68 g; Cholesterol—489 mg; Fiber—3.7 g; Sodium—711 mg
43 of the 417 calories are from fat.
10% of the calories come from fat.

Note: This recipe exceeds the American Heart Association guidelines for cholesterol (no more than 300 mg per day). The AHA does note that liver is rich in iron and vitamins and a small serving (no more than 3 ounces—which this recipe does meet) is okay about once a month. To meet the AHA guidelines don't serve this dish or any other organ-meat dish more than once a month.

CHICKEN SPAGHETTI

1 lb. chicken breasts, cut
   into small pieces
1 tsp. Cajun Spice Mix (see
   page 274)
Butter-flavored nonstick
   vegetable oil spray
1 large onion, finely
   chopped
4 cloves garlic, minced
1/2 cup minced celery
1 large bell pepper, finely
   chopped
8 large fresh mushrooms,
   sliced

2 tbsp. minced fresh basil
   (or 2 tsp. dried)
1 26 1/2-oz. can no-fat
   spaghetti sauce
2/3 cup Marsala wine
1 tsp. dried oregano
1/2 tsp. dried rosemary
2 large bay leaves
6 cups cooked hot spaghetti
2 tbsp. minced fresh
   parsley
6 tbsp. grated nonfat
   parmesan cheese

Season the chicken with the Cajun Spice Mix; set aside. Spray a large nonstick saucepan with the butter-flavored vegetable oil spray. Place the saucepan over medium-high heat until it is hot, then add the chicken and onions and sauté for 3 minutes, stirring often. Add the garlic, celery, and bell pepper and continue to sauté for 2 minutes. Add the mushrooms and basil and sauté for 2 more minutes. Add the spaghetti sauce, wine, oregano, rosemary, and bay leaves, cover, and reduce the heat to a simmer. Cook for 1 hour, stirring occasionally. Remove from the heat, add the parsley, and let the sauce stand for 2 minutes. Serve over cooked hot spaghetti with 1 tablespoon of nonfat parmesan on the side of each serving. Serves 6.

Lagniappe: This is a dish you can make completely in advance. You can store in the refrigerator for up to 4 days, or you can freeze it. To reheat, just defrost in the refrigerator and heat over low heat until the sauce is hot. Refrigerating seems to improve the flavor and help the sauce blend together. Making the spaghetti with breast meat significantly lowers the fat in the dish. Remember, chicken fat is no better for you than beef fat. Fat is fat! The difference is that chicken breast meat tends to be lower in fat than ground beef. If you make your own ground beef, you can make a meat that is lower in fat because you control the amount of fat in the grind.

Calories—338; Fat—3.5 g; Protein—27.7 g; Carbohydrates—52.4 g; Cholesterol—49 mg; Fiber—3.7 g; Sodium—637 mg

31 of the 338 calories are from fat.
9% of the calories come from fat.

CHICKEN ST. MARTINVILLE

2 breasts of chicken,
  boned, skinned, and split
  in half
1 1/2 tsp. Cajun Spice Mix
  (see page 274)
Butter-flavored nonstick
  vegetable oil spray
1 large onion, chopped

1 small red bell pepper, cut
  into strips
1 cup no-fat sour cream
1 tbsp. fresh lime juice
1/2 tsp. Tabasco® Sauce
1 cup green seedless grapes
4 cups cooked non-egg
  noodles

Season the chicken with the Cajun Spice Mix. Lightly spray a large skillet with the butter-flavored spray, then heat it over medium heat. When it is hot, add the chicken, onions, and bell pepper. Sauté, shaking the pan often, for 5 minutes on the first side, then turn the chicken over and cook on the other side for five more minutes. While the chicken is cooking, turn the onions and red bell pepper over and stir them around a few times.

Mix together the sour cream, lime juice, and Tabasco® Sauce in a small mixing bowl until well mixed. Stir in the grapes. When the chicken has cooked for 5 minutes on the second side, add the sour cream-grape mixture to the skillet and reduce the heat to a low simmer. Cook for 10 minutes, stirring often. Serve hot over cooked noodles. Serves 4.

Lagniappe: This is a rapid and surprising dish. I discovered cooking chicken with grapes a few cookbooks back, when I asked my one of my nieces what she would like in a dish named after her. She requested grapes; I chuckled, but I tried it. It worked, and it worked well, so here is another chicken and grape dish. This new no-fat sour cream is wonderful. It adds such dimension to a dish and holds up well in the cooking process. You can serve this over mashed potatoes if you like or over cooked white or brown rice. I've also served this over toast points, which is really elegant. Just top with a little fresh parsley and a sprinkle of paprika.

*Calories—416; Fat—4.6 g; Protein—41 g; Carbohydrates—62 g;
Cholesterol—73 mg; Fiber—1.7 g; Sodium—1003 mg*

41 of the 416 calories are from fat.
10% of the calories come from fat.

DIJON-GLAZED CHICKEN

2 tbsp. Dijon mustard
1 tbsp. brown sugar
1 tbsp. honey
1/2 tsp. Tabasco® Sauce
1 tsp. minced fresh ginger
Butter-flavored nonstick
  vegetable oil spray

4 4-oz. chicken breast
  halves, skinned and
  boned
2 tbsp. minced fresh
  parsley

Combine the first five ingredients in a small bowl; stir until well blended. Coat an outdoor grill rack with vegetable oil spray; then place on the grill over medium-hot coals. Place chicken on rack, brushing half of the glaze mixture over the chicken. Cook 5 minutes, turn the chicken, and brush with the remaining glaze. Cook for an additional 5 minutes, or until meat is cooked but juicy. Transfer chicken to a serving platter. Garnish with fresh parsley. Serve hot. Serves 4.

Lagniappe: This is an uncomplicated dish that tastes great. The smoky taste is heightened by the sweetness of the honey and sugar and the pungency of the mustard. Chicken breast that is cooked fast over hot coals will remain juicy. The basting sauce turns the chicken golden brown and fills it with delectable flavor. Serve with a crisp green salad and a potato, noodles, or rice. It is a sensational as well as balanced meal.

*Calories—227; Fat—4.5 g; Protein—35.9 g; Carbohydrates—8 g;
Cholesterol—97 mg; Fiber—trace; Sodium—120 mg*

41 of the 227 calories are from fat.
18% of the calories come from fat.

EASY BREAST OF CHICKEN SANDWICH

2 fresh English muffins
2 tbsp. nonfat mayonnaise
1 tbsp. Creole mustard
1/4 tsp. Tabasco® Sauce
1 recipe Pan-Seared
   Chicken Breast (see page
   203)

2 slices no-fat Swiss cheese
2 leaves iceberg lettuce
2 thin slices onion
2 thick slices tomato

Split the English muffins in half and lightly toast them. While the muffins are toasting, mix together the mayonnaise, Creole mustard, and Tabasco® Sauce until well blended. Remove the muffins from the toaster and generously spread the mayonnaise-mustard mix on both halves of the muffins. Place half a chicken breast on each of the English muffin bottoms. Put a slice of no-fat Swiss cheese on each piece of chicken. Top with onion, tomato, and the top half of the English muffin. Cut in half and serve. Serves 2.

Lagniappe: This is the recipe for two sandwiches. Of course, to make more, just double or triple the recipe. This is such an easy sandwich, but sometimes we forget about the easy things when we are looking for a low-fat dish. Sandwiches can be satisfying and full of goodness. You can use the chicken recipe hot or cold. It is good either way. This is a great, low-fat choice for lunch or a light evening meal. You can eat it with fat-free chips, puffs, or crackers to make your meal more like the old sandwiches and chips of the past.

Calories—452; Fat—5.4 g; Protein—50.5 g; Carbohydrates—44 g; Cholesterol—88 mg; Fiber—2.4 g; Sodium—2029 mg

49 of the 452 calories are from fat.
11% of the calories come from fat.

MANICOTTI

2/3 tsp. Cajun Spice Mix
(see page 274)
1/4 lb. chicken tenders or
chichen breasts (98% fat-
free)
1 gallon water
2 tsp. salt
1 8-oz. box manicotti
noodles (14 noodles per
box)
1 10-oz. pkg. frozen
spinach, defrosted and
well drained
1/4 cup fresh basil, finely
chopped

2/3 cup finely chopped
green onions
2 cups nonfat cottage
cheese
1 tbsp. finely chopped
celery
2 cloves garlic, minced
1/2 tsp. salt
1/2 tsp. Tabasco® Sauce
1/4 cup nonfat parmesan
cheese
1 26.5-oz. can no-fat
spaghetti sauce
1 cup no-fat mozzarella
cheese

Season the chicken tenders equally with the Cajun Spice Mix. Sear the chicken in a large nonstick skillet over high heat, cooking it for about 1 minute on each side. Remove from the pan and set aside to cool.

Place the water and salt in a large pot over high heat. When the water is boiling, add the noodles and cook them until they are al dente, about 5 minutes. Remove the noodles and let them cool. In a large mixing bowl, mix together the spinach, basil, green onions, cottage cheese, celery, garlic, salt, Tabasco® Sauce, and parmesan cheese. Finely chop the cooled chicken tenders, and mix them into the spinach mixture.

Spread a small amount of spaghetti sauce on the bottom of a large, 4 or 5-quart covered pan. Stuff the spinach-chicken mixture into the manicotti noodles and arrange the filled noodles side-by-side until all the noodles are filled and in the pan. There should be enough stuffing to fill all 14 noodles. Cover the noodles with the remaining sauce and sprinkle with the mozzarella cheese. Cover and bake at 350 degrees for 15 minutes. Remove the cover and bake for 5 more minutes. Remove and let the dish cool for 5 minutes, then serve. Serves 6.

Calories—333; Fat—1.9 g; Protein—30.8 g; Carbohydrates—49.4 g; Cholesterol—20 mg; Fiber—4.1 g; Sodium—1119 mg

17 of the 333 calories are from fat.
5% of the calories come from fat.

PAN-SEARED CHICKEN BREAST

**1 large chicken breast, skin
  and bones removed
1 tsp. Cajun Spice Mix (see
  page 274)**

**1/2 tsp. Old Hickory
  Smoked Salt**

Heat a nonstick skillet over medium heat until it is hot. Wash the chicken breast with cold water, then pat it dry with a plain white paper towel. Season with the Cajun Spice Mix and smoked salt. Cut the breast into two halves. Place both halves in the skillet, then sear for 2 minutes on the first side and for two more minutes on the other side. Turn over, lower the heat to low and cook for 3 more minutes on each side. Remove from the heat. Serves 2 or 4, depending on use.

Lagniappe: This is a varied dish. You can use it just as it is as a main dish meat, or you can chop it into small bite-sized pieces to use in other dishes, like Soft Chicken Tacos. You can also use it to make a tasty Easy Chicken Sandwich. See the recipe index for suggestions.

For one-half breast:
Calories—145; Fat—3.1 g; Protein—26.8 g; Carbohydrates—.6 g;
Cholesterol—73 mg; Fiber—trace; Sodium—450 mg

28 of the 145 calories are from fat.
19% of the calories come from fat.

PEACHY CHICKEN EUPHEMIE

2 whole chicken breasts
1 tsp. Cajun Spice Mix (see
page 274)
Butter-flavored nonstick
vegetable oil spray

2 cups Fresh Peach Sauce
(see pages 275-76)

Preheat the oven to 375 degrees. Remove the skin and bones, then cut off any excess fat on the chicken breasts. Split the breasts in half lengthwise, then season the breasts equally with the Cajun Spice Mix. Spray the bottom of a nonstick baking pan lightly with the butter-flavored vegetable oil spray. Cover the chicken with the Fresh Peach Sauce and place the chicken in the oven uncovered. Bake for 30 minutes at 375 degrees, basting the chicken several times during the baking. Serve hot with peach sauce. Serves 4.

Lagniappe: Be sure to cover the chicken with the peach sauce when you serve it. It is spectacular!

Calories—370; Fat—3.4 g; Protein—27 g; Carbohydrates—27.9 g; Cholesterol—73 mg; Fiber—.2 g; Sodium—433 mg

31 of the 370 calories are from fat.
8% of the calories come from fat.

PINEAPPLE CHICKEN

2 15 1/4-oz. chunk pineaple, with juice
3 tbsp. medium picante sauce
2 tbsp. soy sauce
1 tbsp. Worcestershire sauce
1/2 tsp. Tabasco® Sauce
3 cloves garlic, minced
1 medium onion, chopped
1 large red bell pepper, cut into strips
1 tbsp. grated fresh ginger
2 tbsp. minced fresh parsley
3 medium whole chicken breasts, split
2 tsp. Cajun Spice Mix (see page 274)
Nonstick vegetable oil spray

Mix together all but the last three ingredients until well blended. Season the chicken breasts with the Cajun Spice Mix. Spray the bottom of a shallow 9 x 12 x 2-inch baking dish with the vegetable oil spray. Place the chicken on the bottom of the dish. Cover the chicken with the pineapple-vegetable mixture. Cover with plastic wrap and refrigerate for at least 3 hours or overnight. When you are ready to bake, remove the plastic wrap and bake, uncovered, at 400 degrees for 45 minutes. Reduce the heat to 325 and bake for 15 more minutes. Serve one-half breast for each serving covered with plenty of the pineapple-vegetable mixture. Serve hot. Serves 6.

Lagniappe: This is a recipe that is best prepared the day before you want to serve it. The longer you are able to let the chicken sit in the pineapple-vegetable mixture (up to two days), the better it tastes. It only takes one hour to bake, and the flavors blend together delicately. I like to serve it over cooked white rice, but you can eat it as it is or with pasta. The sauce thickens and it has a nice savory sweet taste. If you don't mind a few more fat grams, you can use a whole chicken cut into serving pieces.

Calories—254; Fat—3.5 g; Protein—30 g; Carbohydrates—29 g; Cholesterol—73 mg; Fiber—1.7 g; Sodium—251 mg

31 of the 254 calories are from fat.
12% of the calories come from fat.

RASPBERRY CHICKEN MANUEL

2 whole chicken breasts
1 tsp. Cajun Spice Mix (see
  page 274)
Butter-flavored nonstick
  vegetable oil spray

1 cup Fresh Raspberry
  Salsa (see pages 276-77)

Preheat the oven to 375 degrees. Remove the skin and bones, then cut any excess fat from the chicken breasts. Split the breasts in half lengthwise, then season the breasts equally with the Cajun Spice Mix. Lightly spray the bottom of a nonstick baking pan with the butter-flavored vegetable oil spray. Cover the chicken with the Fresh Raspberry Salsa, then place the chicken in the oven uncovered. Bake for 30 minutes at 375 degrees, basting the chicken several times. Serve hot with raspberry salsa. Serves 4.

Lagniappe: Be sure to cover the chicken with the raspberry salsa when you serve. It is outstanding!

Calories—216; Fat—3.7 g; Protein—27.2 g; Carbohydrates—14.7 g; Cholesterol—73 mg; Fiber—1.6 g; Sodium—440 mg

33 of the 216 calories are from fat.
15% of the calories come from fat.

SOFT CHICKEN TACOS

8 medium white corn
tortillas (made without
any oil or fat)
1 recipe No-Fat Refried
Beans (see pages 228-29)
1 recipe Pan-Seared
Chicken Breast, chopped
into bite-size pieces (see
page 203)
1 1/2 cups shredded lettuce

1 large ripe tomato, diced
1 cup thinly sliced
cucumber
1/2 cup very thinly sliced
purple onion
1 cup no-fat sour cream
1/2 cup picante sauce
1 cup grated no-fat cheddar
or Swiss cheese

Preheat the oven to 175 degrees. Heat a nonstick skillet over medium-high heat until it is hot. Place a corn tortilla in the skillet, and heat it for about 25 seconds on each side. Remove from the pan and place on a plate, cover tightly with foil, then put into the 175-degree oven to hold for later use. Repeat the process until all eight tortillas are heated.

Arrange all the remaining ingredients on the table and put the warmed tortillas in the center so everyone can prepare their own tacos, or prepare them and serve as follows: Spread refried beans on a tortilla, then place a few pieces of seared chicken on top of the beans. Cover the chicken with lettuce, tomato, cucumber, and onion; then add the no-fat sour cream, picante sauce, and cheese as per recipe or to your taste. Fold the tacos in half and eat. Serves 4.

Lagniappe: Something has to be wrong! This tastes so good, it can't be good for you. Two tacos are plenty for most people, but you don't have to stop at two if you are still hungry. Have two more, you'll be eating hearty, but not loading up on fat. You can be creative with this recipe and substitute the toppings of your choice. Just be sure to choose nonfat toppings and eat to your heart's content!

Calories—468; Fat—5.6 g; Protein—41.9 g; Carbohydrates—67.6 g; Cholesterol—37 mg; Fiber—9.4 g; Sodium—2151 mg

50 of the 468 calories are from fat.
11% of the calories come from fat.

SPICY CHICKEN VAIL

2 8-oz. chicken breasts,
   skin and bones removed
1 tsp. Cajun Spice Mix (see
   page 274)
1/3 cup fat-free Catalina
   salad dressing

1 tbsp. Dijon mustard
1 tbsp. fresh lime juice
2 tsp. Worcestershire sauce
1/4 tsp. Tabasco® Sauce

Preheat the oven to 400 degrees. Cut each whole chicken breast into two pieces and wash with cold water. Cut off any visible signs of fat. Dry the chicken with a plain white paper towel. Season each breast piece equally with the Cajun Spice Mix and place the chicken in a shallow baking pan. Make a sauce by mixing together the remaining ingredients until well blended. Coat the chicken lightly with about 1/3 of the sauce, then bake uncovered at 400 degrees for 20 minutes, or until the chicken has turned white and is plump and juicy. Heat the remaining sauce over a low heat until the sauce begins to bubble and thicken somewhat. Serve the thickened sauce over the chicken. Serves 4.

Lagniappe: This dish is easy, tasty, and quite rich in appearance. Don't let the ease of preparation fool you, this is good eating. You can mix everything together in advance and allow the chicken to sit in the refrigerator until you are ready to cook it. Keep the remaining uncooked sauce covered in the refrigerator until you are ready to cook the chicken. I would not recommend freezing this dish, it is so simple to do, you can do it when you are ready to eat. The sauce doesn't hold up well in the freezer. You might like to serve this with a baked potato and a nice green vegetable; it will make a very low-fat meal that is worth eating and worth photographing. *Ça c'est bon!*

Calories—165; Fat—3.2 g; Protein—27 g; Carbohydrates—5.3 g; Cholesterol—73 mg; Fiber—trace; Sodium—475 mg

29 of the 165 calories are from fat.
18% of the calories come from fat.

Vegetables

BAKED POTATO FULLY DRESSED

4 medium white baking
potatoes
4 1/2-oz. packets Butter
Buds
1 cup minced green onions
4 tsp. Molly McButter
Natural Cheese Flavor
Sprinkles

Salt and fresh ground black
pepper to taste
12 tbsp. no-fat sour cream

Preheat the oven to 425 degrees. Scrub and wash potatoes thoroughly. Wrap them tightly in aluminum foil, then bake at 425 degrees for 30 minutes. Reduce the oven to 400 degrees for 30 more minutes or until the potatoes are done. Check by punching with a fork. If the fork goes through without any resistance, the potatoes are done. Remove the potatoes from the oven and let them stand for 5 minutes. With a towel around each potato, apply pressure with the palm of your hand while rolling the potato around to mash the insides somewhat. Make a slit through foil in the top of each potato. With a fork, separate the potato from the skin, then use the fork to fluff the insides of the potato.

Sprinkle each potato with one packet of Butter Buds and add 1/4 cup of green onions to each potato. Mix the Butter Buds and green onions well. Sprinkle with the cheese-flavored sprinkles, and season to taste with salt and fresh ground black pepper; taking care to mix the seasoning throughout. Spoon 3 tablespoons of the no-fat sour cream on top of each potato. Serve at once. Serves 4.

Lagniappe: This is the lunch food that sustains me. You can eat a large baked potato fixed this way and walk away full and without any guilt. This is a great side dish or a meal in itself. Hands down, I prefer a baked potato fixed this way to one using real butter and real sour cream. This is so rich and tasty that you won't believe it is fat-free. Sometimes I wonder if the no-fat sour cream people are really telling us the truth! It's hard to believe that it can be so good without any of the fat. Try it, you will be very surprised. If you eat a nonfat breakfast and a potato fixed this way for lunch, you can afford to eat a few more fat grams at your evening meal. I wish I could say I was suffering, but I'd be lying.

Calories—341; Fat—.3 g; Protein—11 g; Carbohydrates—106 g; Cholesterol—0 mg; Fiber—1.5 g; Sodium—850 mg

2 of the 341 calories are from fat.
Less than 1% of the calories come from fat.

BEETS CAROL

3 cups sliced beets
1/4 cup finely sliced onions
1/2 cup white vinegar
2 tbsp. sugar

1/2 tsp. Tabasco® Sauce
1 tsp. salt
1 tsp. black pepper
1/2 tsp. sweet basil

Mix all ingredients together well, then cover and refrigerate for 3 to 4 hours. Serve chilled. Serves 4.

Lagniappe: Make this dish up to 3 days ahead of time. Keep it stored in the refrigerator. It is only good cold. I like to eat this like a pickle or as a snack. Just a few slices help to really kill an appetite. This is a wonderful alternative to fat-loaded chips.

Calories—60; Fat—trace; Protein—1.2 g; Carbohydrates—16.9 g; Cholesterol—0 mg; Fiber—.7 g; Sodium—622 mg

1 of the 60 calories is from fat.
2% of the calories come from fat.

BEETS DON LOUIS

3 cups sliced beets
1/2 cup fat-free Catalina
  dressing
1 cup no-fat sour cream
1/2 tsp. Tabasco® Sauce

1/2 cup minced green
  onions
2 tbsp. finely minced fresh
  parsley

Heat the beets in their juice in a medium saucepan over medium heat until hot. Remove from the heat and add the Catalina dressing; blend together well. Add the remaining ingredients and stir until the sour cream is blended together. Serve warm. Serves 6.

Lagniappe: Beets are a great vegetable to serve with a number of dishes. The color is not typical for vegetables, so it offers you the possibility of adding a new hue to your plate and intensifying the drama of your presentation. The red color, when mixed with the white cream, creates a wonderful effect. You can make this dish in advance. However, do not freeze it. To bring the dish back to life, just reheat it over very low heat until warm.

Calories—99; Fat—.1 g; Protein—3.7 g; Carbohydrates—21 g; Cholesterol—0 mg; Fiber—.7 g; Sodium—589 mg

1 of the 99 calories is from fat.
1% of the calories come from fat.

BEETS GINGER

3 tbsp. light brown sugar
2 tbsp. sugar
2 tbsp. finely minced fresh
   gingerroot (or 1 1/2 tsp.
   ground ginger)
1/8 cup water
1/8 cup distilled white
   vinegar

1 1/2-oz. packet Butter
   Buds
1/2 tsp. Tabasco® Sauce
2 15-oz. cans whole beets,
   drained

In a medium saucepan over medium heat, combine the brown sugar and sugar and let the sugar melt. Add the ginger and continue cooking, stirring constantly, until the sugar begins to brown and caramelize. Add the water and vinegar; let the caramelized syrup dissolve in the water and vinegar, then add the Butter Buds, Tabasco® Sauce, and drained beets. Turn the heat down and simmer, covered for 10 minutes. Uncover and continue cooking over low heat, stirring constantly until most of the liquid evaporates and the beets have a nice glaze, about 4 minutes. Serve hot. Serves 6.

Lagniappe: This is a wonderful way to serve beets. You can make this in advance and refrigerate it until you are ready to serve. Just gently heat for about 4 minutes before serving. Do not freeze this dish; it just does not hold up after being frozen. The deep red color is a wonderful way to brighten up almost any plate.

Calories—69; Fat—.1 g; Protein—.8 g; Carbohydrates—18.9 g; Cholesterol—0 mg; Fiber—.2 g; Sodium—316 mg

1 of the 69 calories is from fat.
1% of the calories come from fat.

BROCCOLI PIMENTO

1 large broccoli head, cut
into florets
1/2 gal. water
2 tsp. salt
1 tsp. Cajun Spice Mix (see
page 274)

2 tbsp. Butter Buds
Juice of 1 medium lemon
1 4-oz. jar pimentos, in
strips
1 tbsp. finely minced green
onions

Wash the broccoli florets with cold water and trim them to bite-sized pieces. Place the water in a large saucepot over high heat, add the salt, and bring to a hard boil. Add the broccoli and let the water return to a hard boil. Cover the pot and cook for 2 minutes, then turn the heat off. Let the broccoli stand in the water for 3 to 4 more minutes, then drain in a colander and rinse the pot well. Season the broccoli with the Cajun Spice Mix.

In the same saucepot, combine the seasoned broccoli and all the remaining ingredients. Cover and cook over very low heat until the Butter Buds are dissolved, shaking the pan often to keep the florets from sticking to the pot. Serve at once. Serve hot. Serves 4.

Lagniappe: This is a fabulous green vegetable that will brighten up almost any plate. Broccoli is not only good for you, loaded with fiber, and filled with vitamins, it is also an attractive vegetable that adds to the ambience of your dinner. Don't make this in advance and refrigerate or freeze it. While broccoli does freeze well, it is never the same as freshly cooked broccoli. Broccoli, especially served as a low-fat dish, is healthy and beneficial in protecting your stomach and intestines from cancers. Eating broccoli once or twice a week can have very positive health benefits.

Calories—87; Fat—.5 g; Protein—3.4 g; Carbohydrates—17 g; Cholesterol—0 mg; Fiber—1.8 g; Sodium—580 mg

4.5 of the 87 calories are from fat.
5% of the calories come from fat.

BRUSSELS SPROUTS RICHARD

1 1/4 lb. Brussels sprouts
Butter-flavored vegetable oil
  spray
1/2 cup finely chopped
  green onions
1 clove garlic, minced
1/2 tsp. Cajun Spice Mix
  (see page 274)

2 tbsp. Butter Buds
1/4 cup dry white wine
1/2 tsp. Tabasco® Sauce
1 cup no-fat sour cream
1/4 cup minced fresh
  parsley

Trim the Brussels sprouts of all the excess leaves and stems, then place in a steamer and steam for about 12 minutes. While the sprouts are steaming, spray a nonstick medium skillet lightly with the butter-flavored vegetable oil spray and place it over medium heat. Sauté the onions and garlic for 3 minutes, stirring until the vegetables brown. Add the Brussels sprouts and sauté them for 2 more minutes. Season with the Cajun Spice Mix.

Mix the Butter Buds into the wine and add to the hot skillet with the sprouts. Season with Tabasco® Sauce, and cook until the Butter Buds dissolve. Lower the heat and add the sour cream and parsley. Simmer over low heat, stirring until well blended. Serve hot. Serves 4.

Lagniappe: Brussels sprouts are a wonderful vegetable. This dish really looks good on almost any plate. The sauce sets off the green sprouts. This recipe can be made in advance and refrigerated, but it loses too much when you try to freeze it. Completely cook the vegetables as directed, let them cool for a few minutes, then refrigerate for up to three days. Of course, as with any fresh vegetable, the pinnacle of flavor and freshness occurs right after the first cooking. My grandmother used to call Brussels sprouts *p'tit choux,* or "little cabbage." It was always fun to help her prepare the sprouts because they were so cute! I get Christine, my four-year-old, to eat them by calling them *cher p'tit choux.* It works every time—for now at least!

Calories—166; Fat—1.2 g; Protein—11 g; Carbohydrates—30.8 g; Cholesterol—0 mg; Fiber—2.7 g; Sodium—393 mg

11 of the 166 calories are from fat.
7% of the calories come from fat.

CAJUN FRIED RICE

1 tbsp. peanut oil
1/4 lb. very lean pork loin,
 cut into thin pieces
2 oz. shrimp, peeled,
 deveined, and finely
 chopped
1 tsp. Cajun Spice Mix (see
 page 274)
1/2 cup no-fat no-
 cholesterol egg substitute

2/3 cup finely chopped
 green onions
1/4 cup finely diced red bell
 pepper
3 cups cooked white long
 grain rice
2 tbsp. low-sodium soy
 sauce
1/4 tsp. Tabasco® Sauce

Heat a large skillet over medium-high heat until hot, then add the peanut oil and heat until it begins to smoke. Mix the pork and shrimp together and season with the Cajun Spice Mix. Add the seasoned meat to the skillet and sauté for 2 minutes, stirring constantly. Add the egg substitute, green onions, and bell pepper and cook for 2 more minutes, stirring constantly. Add the remaining ingredients and blend all together well. Lower the heat to low and cook until the rice is hot. Serve at once. Serves 6.

Lagniappe: This is a great rice side dish that you can substitute for any rice dish, as long as it doesn't need gravy.

Calories—193; Fat—3.6 g; Protein—11.2 g; Carbohydrates—27.7 g; Cholesterol—29 mg; Fiber—.3 g; Sodium—843 mg

32 of the 193 calories are from fat.
17% of the calories come from fat.

CARROT AND POTATO BAKE

1 lb. fresh carrots
2 lb. fresh red new potatoes
1 large onion, chopped
2 cloves garlic, minced
Butter-flavored nonstick
   vegetable oil spray
1 1/2 tsp. salt
1 1/2 tsp. fresh ground
   black pepper

1 1/2-oz. packet Butter
   Buds
2 tbsp. fresh rosemary (or 2
   tsp. dried)
1/4 cup finely minced green
   onions
2 tbsp. finely minced fresh
   parsley

Preheat the oven to 425 degrees. Wash and clean the carrots and potatoes. Cut the carrots into 1 1/2-inch pieces. Lightly spray the sides of a covered oven dish with the vegetable oil spray. Add the carrots, potatoes, onion, and garlic. Lightly spray the vegetables with the butter-flavored spray. Add the remaining ingredients and toss around until well mixed. Cover and bake at 425 degrees for 15 minutes. Remove the cover and stir well, then reduce the heat to 400 degrees and bake uncovered for 25 to 30 more minutes. Stir a few times during the remaining baking time. Serve hot as a vegetable or a side dish. Serves 6.

Lagniappe: This is an easy alternative to plain potatoes. It looks elegant and tastes like it's loaded with butter. The potatoes should be a golden brown, and the rosemary gives them an excellent aroma. You can substitute any other fresh herb you may have. Basil and thyme are also nice in this dish. This dish will help fill up your plate and your guests, but it won't fill them out!

Calories—154; Fat—.4 g; Protein—5.2 g; Carbohydrates—34.6 g; Cholesterol—0 mg; Fiber—2.1 g; Sodium—711 mg

4 of the 154 calories are from fat.
3% of the calories come from fat.

CAULIFLOWER ROSEMARY

3 cups water
1 tbsp. fresh rosemary (or 1
 tsp. dried)
4 cloves garlic, chopped
1 head cauliflower
1 tsp. salt

1/2 tsp. Tabasco® Sauce
Juice of 1 medium lemon
4 tbsp. nonfat parmesan
 cheese
1 tsp. minced fresh parsley

In a large saucepan over high heat, combine the water, rosemary, and cloves. Bring to a full boil, then cover. Reduce the heat to low and let it simmer for 10 minutes. While it is simmering, wash the cauliflower and cut it into florets. When the 10 minutes are up, add the florets, salt, and Tabasco® Sauce to the herbed water. Cover and simmer for 10 minutes. Remove from the heat and drain the cauliflower. Place in a serving dish and sprinkle with the lemon juice, cheese, and parsley. Serve at once. Serves 6.

Lagniappe: This dish is elementary, effortless, luscious, and speedy. Don't make it in advance and do not freeze it. You can get the cauliflower cleaned and trimmed in advance, which would make this a little faster to put together. You can use this vegetable with almost any dish, but it is particularly savory with tomato sauce. The flavors blend together well. The lemon and parmesan seem to enliven the flavor of cauliflower.

Calories—35; Fat—.2 g; Protein—2.5 g; Carbohydrates—7 g; Cholesterol—0 mg; Fiber—1.7 g; Sodium—446 mg

2 of the 35 calories are from fat.
5% of the calories come from fat.

EGGPLANT DRESSING

2 large eggplants
Cold water to cover
2 tsp. dry beef-flavored
  instant bouillon
1 large onion, chopped
1 large bell pepper,
  chopped
3 cloves garlic, minced
3 tbsp. minced celery

1 tsp. Cajun Spice Mix (see
  page 274)
5 cups cooked white long
  grain rice
1/2 cup minced green
  onions
2 tbsp. minced fresh
  parsley

Select smooth-skinned, bright, and shiny eggplants. Cut the eggplants into quarters. Leave the skin on if the eggplant is smooth. Cut off any bad spots. Place the eggplant into a large saucepot and cover with cold water. Place the water over high heat and bring it to a boil; let the eggplant boil for one minute. Reduce the heat to medium, and cook for 5 minutes. Drain the eggplant and set aside; do not try to squeeze all the water from the eggplant. It should be quite juicy. Heat a large non-stick skillet over medium heat until it is hot. Add the eggplant, beef-flavored bouillon, onions, bell pepper, garlic, and celery. Cook, stirring constantly, for 5 minutes. Add the remaining ingredients and stir in well. Reduce the heat to low, and cook for 15 minutes, stirring often. Serve at once. Serves 6.

Lagniappe: This is a great dish that has the garden fresh flavor of eggplant without any oils. You get to taste the wonderful flavor of eggplant. This makes a nice vegetable or a side dish. Eggplant is a vegetable that finds its way into the produce market throughout most of the year. I especially like this dish in the summer when the eggplants are picked fresh from the gardens of my dad or my father-in-law. I used to plant a garden, but I got tired of having the largest selection of weeds in North America. It's much easier to pick the vegetables from someone's nicely weeded grounds.

Calories—239; Fat—.7 g; Protein—5.7 g; Carbohydrates—52 g; Cholesterol—.2 mg; Fiber—2.1 g; Sodium—1080 mg

6.2 of the 239 calories are from fat.
3% of the calories come from fat.

EGGPLANT FRED LAWRENCE

1 large eggplant
1/2 gal. water
2 tbsp. salt
1/2 gal. water
1 tbsp. salt
Butter-flavored nonstick
  vegetable oil spray
1 large onion, chopped
1 medium bell pepper,
  chopped

1 stalk celery, finely
  chopped
1/2 cup chicken broth
1/2 tsp. Tabasco® Sauce
2 1/2-oz. packets Butter
  Buds
1 tsp. Cajun Spice Mix (see
  page 274)

Wash the eggplant and cut it into large blocks. Put the eggplant into a large bowl and cover with the first half gallon of water. Add the 2 tablespoons. of salt. Let it soak for 15 minutes to remove the bitterness. Drain the eggplant well and place into a large saucepan and cover with the remaining half gallon and add the one tablespoon of salt. Place over medium high heat and boil for 8 minutes. Drain the eggplant in a colander and rinse with hot water. Spray a large nonstick surface skillet with the butter-flavored vegetable oil spray; place the skillet over medium high heat and heat until the skillet is hot. Add the onions, bell pepper and celery and sauté for 3 minutes, stirring constantly. Add the chicken broth and Tabasco® Sauce and bring to a boil, then reduce to a simmer and braise the vegetables for 3 more minutes. Add the eggplant, Butter Buds and Cajun Spice Mix and mix in well. Continue to braise over medium heat, stirring often for about 15 minutes. Serve hot. Serves 4.

Lagniappe: This is the eggplant dish for those who like eggplant or for those who hate it. It is practically just eggplant, so those who like the taste of eggplant will love it. It is so good, that those who didn't think they'd like eggplant will. The only problem: you'll never again be able to say you don't like eggplant! This recipe shows the difference between a sauté and a braise. To sauté you have to "fry" in an oil; it can be a very little bit of oil, but it has to be an oil. A braise is cooking in a liquid, like the chicken broth in this recipe. They are both ways of cooking vegetables or meats for that matter, both are good cooking techniques.

Don't confuse the two. I also want to let you know that soaking the eggplant really does reduce the bitterness. The salt in the water creates an electrolyte solution that causes a chemical reaction to take place and the bitterness basically falls out as a precipitate. Grandma didn't know a thing about chemistry, but she knew to soak eggplant in salt water to remove the bitterness!

Calories—66; Fat—.9 g; Protein—2 g; Carbohydrates—13.2 g; Cholesterol—.2 mg; Fiber—1.5 g; Sodium—1500 mg
8 of the 66 calories are from fat.
12 % of the calories come from fat.

EGGPLANT THOMAS

2 medium eggplants
1 gal. water
1 1/2 tbsp. salt
Butter-flavored vegetable oil
  spray
1 large onion, chopped
1 medium bell pepper,
  chopped

2 cloves garlic, minced
2 tbsp. celery, minced
1 1/2-oz. packet Butter
  Buds
1 tsp. Cajun Spice Mix (see
  page 274)

If the eggplant is nice and smooth, just cut it into large blocks. If it has a few bruises on it, cut the bad spots off, then cut it into large blocks. Put the blocks into a large bowl, and add 1 tablespoon of the salt and 1/2 gallon of the water. Let the eggplant soak for 15 minutes to help remove the bitterness. Drain and rinse well.

Place the eggplant in a large pot, add the remaining 1/2 tablespoon of salt, and the other 1/2 gallon of water. Bring to a boil. Boil for about 7 minutes. Drain in a colander, and rinse with hot tap water. Spray a large nonstick skillet with one spray of the butter-flavored oil. Place on medium-high heat and, when the skillet is hot, add the onions, bell pepper, garlic, and celery. Sauté for 4 minutes. Add the eggplant, Cajun Spice Mix, and Butter Buds, then sauté for 5 more minutes, stirring often. Serve at once. Serves 6.

Lagniappe: This is a great eggplant recipe for those who love eggplant; it is also a great recipe for those who hate eggplant (because it is so good). It will forever change the way you feel about eggplant. It is simple and it tastes wonderful. Remember to soak the eggplant to remove the bitterness; it really works. I really like this recipe, and I hope you will too.

Calories—105; Fat—.5 g; Protein—1.8 g; Carbohydrates—10 g; Cholesterol—0 mg; Fiber—1.6 g; Sodium—450 mg

4 of the 105 calories are from fat.
4% of the calories come from fat.

FRESH TURNIPS BOREL

2 lb. fresh young turnips
Water to cover
2 tsp. salt
1 1/2-oz. packet Butter
  Buds
1/3 cup boiling water
1/4 cup finely chopped
  onions

1/2 tsp. salt
2/3 tsp. fresh ground black
  pepper
1/2 tsp. Tabasco® Sauce
1 tbsp. minced fresh
  parsley

Clean and wash the turnips well. Cut off the tops and the root bottoms. Place in a large saucepan and cover with water. Add the 2 teaspoons of salt and bring to a boil over high heat. Boil the turnips until they are tender, about 25 minutes, depending on the size. Check for doneness with a fork; when the fork is easily inserted all the way through the center of the turnips, they are done. Remove from the heat and drain. Allow the turnips to cool.

Mix together the Butter Buds and 1/3 cup of boiling water, then pour into a large skillet. Place the skillet over medium heat and bring to a simmer. Add the onions and braise them in the Butter Buds for 5 minutes.

While the onions are braising, slice the turnips into circles, then add the turnips to the skillet with the onions. Season with salt, fresh ground black pepper, Tabasco® Sauce, and fresh parsley. Allow the seasonings to simmer with the turnips for 3 minutes, then serve. Serves 6.

Lagniappe: This is the turnip recipe for those who really like turnips, because it is basically just turnips. This recipe allows the wonderful sweetness of the turnip to shine. Fresh turnips are available six to eight months out of the year, but they are especially sweet in the late fall and early winter and very early spring. Don't look for giant turnips; the small, tender ones are the best. They are milder in flavor and higher in sugar. I said this is the recipe for those who like turnips, but also give it a try with those who say they don't; I think they will be surprised!

Calories—40; Fat—.2 g; Protein—1.4 g; Carbohydrates—9.7 g; Cholesterol—0 mg; Fiber—.6 g; Sodium—575 mg

2 of the 40 calories are from fat.
5% of the calories come from fat.

MACQUE CHOUX

8 large ears of corn
1 tbsp. peanut oil
2 tsp. unsalted butter
1 large onion, chopped
1 large green bell pepper, cored, seeded, and chopped

2 cloves garlic, minced
2 large ripe tomatoes, seeded and chopped
1 tsp. Cajun Spice Mix (see page 274)
Salt to taste

Cut kernels from corn cobs. Heat a large skillet over medium heat. Add peanut oil and heat until it just starts to smoke. Add butter, onions, bell pepper, and garlic; sauté until the onion is translucent, 1 to 2 minutes. Add corn and cook for 5 minutes, stirring often. Stir in tomatoes and Cajun Spice Mix, reduce heat to low, and simmer, stirring often, until the corn is tender, about 10 minutes. If the corn becomes too dry, add a little water. Season to taste with salt and serve hot. Serves 8.

Lagniappe: Pronounced "mock shoe," this dish could be translated as "smothered corn." Macque Choux is one of my all-time favorite vegetables. I remember when I was young, we'd get corn from my grandfather's farm. We'd shuck corn all day, then cut it. Momma would make big batches of Macque Choux, then she would put most of it in the freezer to eat at a later date. She would leave an amount for us to eat for maybe a day or two. My brothers and I all liked it so much that we were limited to how much we could have at dinner time. Momma would keep the rest stored in the refrigerator for the next meal. Well, at night, we would take turns sneaking into the kitchen and getting a spoon to eat cold. Boy, was that good (*ça c'est beaucoup bon*)! Momma always used to wonder why the corn would shrink so at night. To this day, she doesn't know why. After she reads this, the mystery of the shrinking Macque Choux will be forever solved!

I have noticed that when I make Macque Choux at my house, it has a tendency to shrink as well. I've also noticed all those dirty spoons in the sink in the morning! I wonder if Debbie, Nicole, or Christine is to blame? Maybe it's all of them! This recipe can be made in advance, covered, and refrigerated for two days. It also freezes well. Just thaw in the refrigerator until you are ready to cook, then heat in a saucepan or skillet until it is hot.

Calories—125; Fat—4 g; Protein—3 g; Carbohydrates—23 g; Cholesterol—3 mg; Fiber—1.7 g; Sodium—115 mg

35 of the 125 calories are from fat.
28% of the calories come from fat.

MEATLESS TACOS

8 medium white corn
    tortillas (made without
    any oil or fat)
1 recipe No-Fat Refried
    Beans (see pages 228-29)
1 cup no-fat cheddar or
    Swiss cheese
1 1/2 cups shredded lettuce

1 large ripe tomato, diced
1 cup very thinly sliced
    cucumber
1/2 cup very thinly sliced
    purple onion
1 cup no-fat sour cream
1/2 cup picante sauce, hot
    or mild

Preheat the oven to 175 degrees. Heat a nonstick skillet over medium-high heat until it is hot. Place a corn tortilla in the skillet and heat it for about 25 seconds on each side. Remove from the pan and place on a plate, then cover tightly with foil and put into the oven to hold for later use. Repeat the process until all eight tortillas are heated.

Spread refried beans on a warmed tortilla, then top the beans with the remaining ingredients. Fold the taco in half and eat as you would any soft taco. Or, arrange all the ingredients and the warmed tortillas on the table and your guests make their own tacos. Serves 4.

Lagniappe: For a nonfat delight, this is the meal. The beans with the cheese and all that wonderful no-fat sour cream make you feel like you are really eating high on the hog! You are really just eating healthy, but enjoying it. This recipe really proves that good eating isn't tied to fat. Serve this as an entree for dinner or lunch, or it makes a great between-meal snack. You can also use this a salad if you like; it looks like a salad to the untrained eye!

Calories—358; Fat—2.5 g; Protein—27.3 g; Carbohydrates—67 g; Cholesterol—8 mg; Fiber—9.6 g; Sodium—1842 mg

23 of the 358 calories are from fat.
6% of the calories come from fat.

MUSHROOMS MARIE LEBLANC

Juice of 1 medium lemon
1 qt. cold water
1 lb. large mushrooms,
  sliced
Nonstick butter-flavored
  vegetable oil spray
1 tbsp. minced shallots
1 tbsp. finely chopped fresh
  basil (or 1 tsp. dried)

1/4 cup beef stock or
  bouillon
1/2 cup dry white wine
2 tbsp. Butter Buds
1/2 tsp. Tabasco® Sauce
1/2 tsp. salt
1/4 tsp. white pepper
2/3 cup no-fat sour cream

Put the lemon juice, water, and mushrooms into a large glass bowl and let the mushrooms soak for 5 minutes. Drain well. Spray a large nonstick skillet with the butter-flavored spray, and place the skillet over medium heat until hot. Add the shallots and sauté for 1 minute, then add the mushrooms and basil and sauté for 4 minutes, stirring often. Mix together the beef stock, wine, Butter Buds, and Tabasco® Sauce; then add this mixture to the skillet. Cook until the mixture comes to a boil, then season with salt and white pepper. Blend in the sour cream until it is smooth and the sauce has thickened. Serve hot. Serves 4.

Lagniappe: You'll swear you are eating a rich and creamy sauce! Guess what, you are, but it isn't loaded with fat. This recipe really highlights the type of gourmet eating you can do without fats. This can either be served as a vegetable or it can be used as a wonderful sauce to top a piece of broiled meat, like chicken or fish. It will make you feel that you are eating the *crème de la crème.*

Do not make this in advance. I don't like the texture or looks after refrigeration. You might wonder why I washed the mushrooms in lemon water. This process will keep the mushrooms white even after cooking. Because the sauce is so white, I didn't want the mushrooms to turn dark and destroy the beauty of the sauce.

Calories—89; Fat—1.1 g; Protein—5.3 g; Carbohydrates—15.3 g; Cholesterol—0 mg; Fiber—2.6 g; Sodium—573 mg

10 of the 89 calories are from fat.
11% of the calories come from fat.

NO-FAT CAJUN FRENCH "FRIES"

4 medium white potatoes
Cold water to cover
Butter-flavored nonstick
  vegetable oil spray

1 tsp. Cajun Spice Mix (see
  page 274)
Salt to taste

Preheat the oven to 450 degrees. Cut the potatoes like you would cut regular French fries. Place them in a large bowl and cover them with cold water. Let them soak for 3 minutes. Wrap a baking tray with tin foil, then spray it lightly with the butter-flavored vegetable oil spray. Remove the potatoes and let them drain on white paper towels. Sprinkle the Cajun Spice Mix on them and place them on the baking sheet. Bake for 25 to 30 minutes at 450 degrees. Remove and season to taste with extra salt. Serve hot. Serves 4.

Lagniappe: This is absolutely one of the best recipes in this book. It is so easy, and it will kill your desire for fried potatoes. I eat lots of them! In fact, at lunch I can just eat a double or triple order of these fries and I'm full on a fat-free meal. I've served these to friends and not told them that they were not deep-fried in oil. No one noticed. When I told them they were eating fat-free fries, they didn't believe me. Try them; you'll be truly astonished.

If by some chance you don't eat them all, you can refrigerate them, then reheat these "fries" in the oven at 400 degrees until they are hot. That makes them a real plus over the deep-fried variety.

Calories—90; Fat—.4 g; Protein—2.4 g; Carbohydrates—20.4 g; Cholesterol—0 mg; Fiber—2 g; Sodium—200 mg

4 of the 90 calories are from fat.
4% of the calories come from fat.

NO-FAT REFRIED BEANS

1 16-oz. can no-fat refried
  beans
1/4 cup minced onions
2 tbsp. finely minced bell
  pepper
1/2 tsp. salt

1 tsp. onion powder
1/2 tsp. Tabasco® Sauce
1 tbsp. Worcestershire
  sauce
3 tbsp. hot picante sauce

Heat a nonstick saucepan or skillet over medium heat. When the pot is hot, add all the ingredients and heat, stirring often, until the beans are just beginning to bubble. Use as you would refried beans. Serve hot. Serves 4.

Lagniappe: This is a nonfat version of refried beans that tastes as good as the real thing. You can use this as a bean dip or as side dish or as an ingredient in other recipes. One such recipe is Soft Chicken Tacos. You can also make No-Meat Soft Tacos that are outstanding. See the index for both recipes.

Calories—104; Fat—.5 g; Protein—7.2 g; Carbohydrates—19.9 g; Cholesterol—0 mg; Fiber—6.4 g; Sodium—814 mg

5 of the 104 calories are from fat.
5% of the calories come from fat.

NO-MEAT CHILI

Nonstick vegetable oil spray
1 large onion, finely
    chopped
1 large green bell pepper,
    chopped
1 large red bell pepper,
    chopped
1 cup minced carrots
1/2 cup minced celery
4 cloves garlic, minced
1 14 1/2-oz. can beef broth
2 14 1/2-oz. cans Cajun-
    style or regular stewed
    tomatoes
1 8-oz. can nonfat tomato
    sauce
5 tbsp. chili powder

3 tbsp. Worcestershire
    sauce
2 tbsp. sugar
2 tsp. cumin powder
1 tsp. onion powder
1 tsp. garlic powder
1 tsp. salt
1/2 tsp. cayenne pepper
1/2 tsp. Tabasco® Sauce
2 15-oz. cans no-fat kidney
    beans
2 15-oz. cans no-fat pinto
    beans
2 15-oz. cans corn
1 15-oz. can no-fat black
    beans

Lightly spray a large sauce pot, preferably with a nonstick surface, with the vegetable oil spray, then place on medium-high heat. Add the onions, green and red bell peppers, carrots, celery, and garlic; sauté, stirring often, until the vegetables are limp, about 3 to 5 minutes. Add the beef broth, cover, and simmer for 5 minutes. Add the stewed tomatoes and tomato sauce, and blend together well. Cover and simmer for 5 more minutes. Add the remaining ingredients, raise the temperature to high, and bring the mixture to a boil, stirring often. Reduce the heat to a simmer, cover, and cook for 20 more minutes. Serve hot with fat-free crackers or chips. Serves 8.

Lagniappe: You won't miss the meat in this chili. It has so much depth that you'll love the taste. Don't let the long list of ingredients scare you. This is simple and easy. It is almost just a matter of opening the cans and dumping them out. Remember that you use seasonings and spices to give variety and excitement to a dish. You only get the tastes you put in! The main reason for the high sodium count is the use of canned vegetables. If you want to reduce the sodium, you can use dried beans where possible, leaving out the salt when you cook them. You can also try to find and use the low-sodium varieties of canned vegetables.

Calories—362; Fat—1.7 g; Protein—19.7 g; Carbohydrates—74.5 g; Cholesterol—0 mg; Fiber—10.6 g; Sodium—1696 mg

15 of the 362 calories are from fat.
4% of the calories come from fat.

PAW PAW'S CAJUN CUSHAW

1 large (about 10 cups cubed) cushaw
6 cups water
1/2 tsp. salt
1/4 tsp. dried lemon peel spice

1 1/2 cups sugar
2 1/2-oz. packets Butter Buds
3/4 tsp. cinnamon
1/2 tsp. nutmeg
1 tsp. vanilla extract

In a large saucepot over high heat, combine the cushaw, water, salt, and lemon peel spice. Cook over high heat until the water comes to a hard boil. Stir, cover, and cook for 5 minutes. Reduce the heat to medium, stir the cushaw, and cook until all the cubed cushaw meat has the consistency of applesauce (about 30 minutes to 1 hour, depending on the tenderness and age of the cushaw meat). Stir, then add the sugar and Butter Buds. Cover and cook until most of the liquid has evaporated and the mixture again has the consistency of very thick applesauce. Add the cinnamon, nutmeg, and vanilla extract. Stir until the seasonings are well blended. Remove from the heat, allow the cushaw to stand for about 5 minutes, then serve. Makes 8 large servings.

Lagniappe: This is an old recipe from my younger days. My grandfather Theriot was a truck farmer, and he used to raise the biggest and best cushaws around. He would literally have thousands in the field. We would pick them with him and load them into his old pickup, then ride to town to sell them at a local grocery store chain. He used to get fifty cents a cushaw, and the store used to sell them for twenty-five to thirty-five cents per pound. They usually weighed five to seven pounds each. It was one of my earliest lessons in economics. I saw that the people who did all the work raising food really got the least for it. Regardless, we always had all the cushaw we wanted, and the whole family really loved it.

The recipe above is the same genuine taste of cushaw, minus the loads of real butter we used to use. This recipe gives you the same consistency and the same rich taste. It is as creamy as the original version with fewer calories and no fat. Cushaw from the late summer tends to be very tender. As the calendar moves toward October, the meat thickens and is more dense. It takes longer to cook, but the end product still has the same taste. You can make Paw Paw's Cajun White Squash by substituting cubed white summer squash for the cushaw in the recipe. Keep all the same ingredients and measurements. The squash will cook slightly faster than the cushaw, so the dish will usually be ready in 30 minutes or less.

Calories—248; Fat—1.5 g; Protein—2.3 g; Carbohydrates—60.2 g; Cholesterol—0 mg; Fiber—3 g; Sodium—316 mg
14 of the 248 calories are from fat.
6% of the calories come from fat.

SAUTEED FRESH MUSHROOMS

1 tbsp. light butter (5.5
grams fat per tbsp.)
1 tbsp. finely chopped
shallots
3 cloves garlic, finely
minced
1 lb. fresh mushrooms,
sliced
1/2 tsp. Tabasco® Sauce
1 tsp. white wine
Worcestershire sauce

1/2 tsp. salt
1/2 tsp. fresh ground black
pepper
1 tsp. onion powder
1/2 tsp. garlic powder
1/2 tsp. dried basil
1/4 tsp. dried oregano
1/8 tsp. dried thyme
1 1/2-oz. packet Butter
Buds
1/3 cup warm water

Melt the butter in a large nonstick skillet over medium heat until it begins to smoke, then quickly add the shallots and garlic. Sauté for 3 minutes, stirring constantly, then add the mushrooms and sauté them for 3 minutes, stirring often. Add the remaining ingredients, and stir until well blended. Reduce the heat to low and simmer until about half of the liquid has evaporated. Serve hot on top of seafood or meat, or serve as a side dish. Serves 4.

Lagniappe: This is more of a topping for other dishes than a dish by itself, that is, unless you are like my wife, who just likes to eat it from the skillet with a fork. She loves mushrooms. This is really a wonderful dish for people who enjoy mushrooms. My wife spreads the mushrooms over a slice of French bread to make an open-faced mushroom sandwich. I happen to like my sautéed mushrooms over a chicken breast or a nice fillet of fish. However you choose to serve them, you will enjoy this recipe if you like mushrooms.

I encourage you to use ripe mushrooms, not the tight white mushrooms that are first put out in the market. A mushroom is just like a fruit, it ripens. As it ripens, it opens up from the tight ball that you'll find initially put out by the grocer. I enjoy choosing those mushrooms that the store has decided to mark down because they are darker in color (and at their peak of flavor). They think the consumer won't buy them. After you sauté them for a few minutes, no one will be able to tell you got the marked down mushrooms, and yours will taste better and cost less.

Calories—67; Fat—1.9 g; Protein—2.7 g; Carbohydrates—10.3 g; Cholesterol—8 mg; Fiber—.7 g; Sodium—495 mg

17 of the 67 calories are from fat.
25% of the calories come from fat.

SMOTHERED POTATOES

2 large onions, thinly sliced
2 1/4 lb. red potatoes,
   peeled and cut into bite-
   sized pieces
2 cloves garlic, minced
1 tbsp. minced bell
   peppers

1 1/2-oz. packet Butter
   Buds
1/2 cup warm water
1 1/2 tsp. salt
1 tsp. fresh ground black
   pepper
1/2 tsp. Tabasco® Sauce

Preheat the oven to 350 degrees. Put all ingredients into a nonstick oven pan that has a lid and place into the 350-degree oven for 30 minutes. Remove from the oven and cook for 3 to 5 minutes on top of the stove, stirring often to prevent the potatoes from darkening too much. Serve as a side dish or as the main dish for a meatless meal. Serve hot. Serves 6.

Lagniappe: This is a very old Cajun evening dish. On the Fridays that fish was not available, this was the meal. Of course, this is a fat-free version of what used to be made with loads of lard. The potatoes and onions provide all the liquid and luscious flavor needed to make this a real winner.

    This dish cannot be frozen because the onions will lose too much of their taste and the potatoes begin to break apart. Although it is best to serve this dish right after cooking it, you can refrigerate it for up to 3 days if it is kept covered and cold.

Calories—163; Fat—.7 g; Protein—4.3 g; Carbohydrates—36.4 g; Cholesterol—0 mg; Fiber—.8 g; Sodium—706 mg

6 of the 163 calories are from fat.
4% of the calories come from fat.

SNOW PEAS AGNES

1 tbsp. olive oil
1 1/2 lb. fresh snow pea
  pods, cleaned and
  trimmed
1/2 cup finely chopped
  green onions
2 tbsp. minced celery

1/3 cup chicken broth
2 tsp. soy sauce
1/2 tsp. salt
1/4 tsp. Tabasco® Sauce
1/4 tsp. white pepper
1 tbsp. minced fresh
  parsley

Heat a nonstick skillet over medium heat until hot, then add the olive oil. When the oil starts to smoke, add the snow peas, green onions, and celery. Sauté for 4 minutes, stirring often. Add the broth, soy sauce, salt, Tabasco® Sauce, and white pepper; mix well. Let the liquid come to a boil, then reduce the heat to a low simmer and cover. Simmer for 3 minutes. Add the parsley and serve. Serves 6.

Lagniappe: This is a quick recipe. Do not make it in advance. The peas will wilt too much and lose their crispness when refrigerated. This is a colorful dish that will add to the looks of any entree. Snow peas are delicate and so luscious. This is also a quick recipe.

Calories—122; Fat—2.8 g; Protein—6.6 g; Carbohydrates—18.5 g; Cholesterol—.1 mg; Fiber—4.2 g; Sodium—386 mg

25 of the 122 calories are from fat.
21% of the calories come from fat.

STUFFED TURNIPS ABBEVILLE

16 large turnips (about
    4 lb.)
Water to cover
2 tsp. salt
1 recipe Turnip Jambalaya
    (see pages 172-73)
1 16.5-oz. can cream-style
    corn

1 tsp. onion powder
1/4 tsp. Tabasco® Sauce
1 tbsp. sugar
1/4 cup seasoned bread
    crumbs
Butter-flavored nonstick
    vegetable oil spray

Clean and wash the turnips. Trim the top and bottom off and place them in a large pot. Cover with water, add the salt, then bring the pot to a boil. Boil for 15 minutes, then remove from the heat and drain.

Prepare the Turnip Jambalaya according to the recipe. In a small pot, add the cream-style corn, onion powder, Tabasco® Sauce, and sugar. Place over medium heat and cook, stirring often, for 5 minutes. Pour the cream-style corn into the Turnip Jambalaya, and mix it in well. Return to the 16 large turnips that should be cool. Scoop out the center, leaving enough on the sides and bottom for the turnip to hold firm.

Preheat the oven to 400 degrees. Spoon the jambalaya-corn mixture into each of the turnips, and sprinkle with seasoned bread crumbs. Spray lightly with butter-flavored nonstick vegetable oil spray and bake uncovered for 25 minutes at 400 degrees. Serve two turnips to each person as an entree or one turnip as a side vegetable dish. Serves 8.

Lagniappe: It's beautiful and the taste will wow you. I really like to serve food in the food itself. It cuts down on dishes! Seriously, when you use the natural food as a container it adds to the ambience of the meal. It kind of brings man back to his roots (no pun intended).

This dish can be made completely in advance and refrigerated or frozen for later use. Just let them thaw in the refrigerator, then cover and bake them at 350 degrees for about 12 minutes. I could eat a half dozen of these, and it wouldn't really be that bad as far as fat grams are concerned. This is a good recipe to use whenever you find large turnips in the store or in your garden.

Calories—330; Fat—5.3 g; Protein—20.6 g; Carbohydrates—55 g; Cholesterol—36 mg; Fiber—2.9 g; Sodium—1255 mg

47 of the 330 calories are from fat.
14% of the calories come from fat.

SWEET PEAS ASHLEY

Butter-flavored nonstick
  vegetable oil spray
1 small onion, finely
  chopped
1 clove garlic, minced
1 tbsp. minced carrot
2 tbsp. minced celery
1 tsp. all-purpose flour
1 15-oz. can small sweet
  peas

1 tbsp. sugar
1 tbsp. Butter Buds
1/4 tsp. Tabasco® Sauce
1 tsp. white Worcestershire
  sauce
1/2 cup no-fat sour cream
2 tbsp. minced fresh
  parsley

Spray a medium-sized nonstick saucepan with the butter-flavored spray, then place it over medium heat. Heat until it is hot, then add the onion, garlic, carrot, and celery and sauté the vegetables for 3 minutes. Add the flour and cook for 3 minutes over low heat, stirring often. Add the peas and their liquid, sugar, Butter Buds, Tabasco® Sauce, and Worcestershire sauce. Mix in well. Cook until the sauce begins to thicken somewhat. Add the no-fat sour cream and blend in well. Cook over low heat for 1 minute, then add the parsley. Serve hot. Serves 4.

Lagniappe: Don't make this in advance. It is easy, and it is considerably better just after it is cooked. I like to eat these peas with mashed potatoes (see index for recipe) and a small piece of fish or chicken.

Calories—106; Fat—.3 g; Protein—6.1 g; Carbohydrates—22 g; Cholesterol—0 mg; Fiber—3.7 g; Sodium—488 mg

2.5 of the 106 calories are from fat.
2% of the calories come from fat.

NO-FAT YAM "FRIES"

4 medium yams
Cold water to cover
Butter-flavored nonstick
vegetable oil spray

2 tsp. sugar
1/4 tsp. cinnamon

Preheat the oven to 450 degrees. Cut the yams like you would cut French fries. Place them in a large bowl and cover them with cold water. Let them soak for 3 minutes. Line a baking tray with tin foil, then spray it lightly with the butter-flavored vegetable oil spray. Remove the yams and let them drain on white paper towels. Place the yams on the baking sheet, then bake for 25 to 30 minutes at 450 degrees.

In a small mixing bowl, combine the sugar and cinnamon until blended. Remove the yam "fries" from the oven and sprinkle with the cinnamon-sugar mixture. Serve at once. Serves 4.

Lagniappe: This is one of those accidental recipes I created when I was really trying to make something else. I was going to make my oven fries, but I was out of potatoes. I had some yams, so I decided to give it a try. Guess what? I loved them. You can use sweet potatoes in the place of yams. There is no difference in the cooking time or preparation, so use whichever you have. If you don't want the cinnamon and sugar taste, the "fries" are also good with a light dusting of salt. The salt will bring out the natural sweetness of the yams.

Calories—127; Fat—.4 g; Protein—2 g; Carbohydrates—29.8 g; Cholesterol—0 mg; Fiber—2.1 g; Sodium—12 mg

4 of the 127 calories are from fat.
3% of the calories come from fat.

ZUCCHINI BAYOU LAFOUCHE

Butter-flavored nonstick
   vegetable oil spray
2 cloves garlic, mashed and
   finely minced
2 tbsp. finely chopped
   shallots
1 tbsp. minced celery
4 medium fresh zucchini,
   julienned

1/2 cup dry white wine
1/2 tsp. cayenne pepper
2/3 tsp. salt
1/4 tsp. black pepper
3 tbsp. nonfat parmesan
   cheese
2 tbsp. parsley

Spray a large nonstick skillet with the butter-flavored vegetable oil. Heat the skillet over medium-high heat. When it begins to smoke, add the garlic, shallots, and celery. Sauté for 2 minutes, then add the zucchini. Sauté for 4 minutes, then add the white wine. Bring it to a boil, then reduce the heat to low and continue stirring. Add the cayenne, salt, and black pepper; mix in well. Cook for 3 more minutes over low heat, then top with the parmesan cheese and parsley just before you are ready to serve. Serve hot. Serves 4.

Lagniappe: This recipe shows just how extraordinary vegetables can be. For years, I thought vegetables required loads of fat to taste good. What I've discovered is the real taste of the vegetables themselves. A nonstick skillet is the real key to low-fat cooking. The surface allows for a colossal reduction in oil. It also allows the real taste of the vegetables to blossom.

   A word about garlic: Notice the directions call for crushing the garlic, then mincing. This is a custom for me. In this way, you are able to get the complete flavor of garlic. You have to crush it then chop it, or you'll lose one of the two main components of the flavor we know as garlic.

Calories—59; Fat—.4 g; Protein—2.3 g; Carbohydrates—7.9 g; Cholesterol—0 mg; Fiber—.5 g; Sodium—441 mg

4 of the 59 calories are from fat.
7% of the calories come from fat.

Desserts

APPLE CAKE

3 large apples, cored and
  thinly sliced
1/4 cup sugar
2 tbsp. light brown sugar
1 tbsp. cinnamon
1 tsp. nutmeg
3 cups all-purpose flour
2 cups sugar
1 tbsp. baking powder
1/2 tsp. salt

1 tsp. cornstarch
1 cup no-fat no-cholesterol
  egg substitute
1 1/4 cups unsweetened
  applesauce
1/4 cup orange juice
2 tsp. vanilla extract
Vegetable oil and flour
  spray
1/4 cup powdered sugar

Preheat the oven to 350 degrees. In a small mixing bowl, combine the apples, sugar, brown sugar, cinnamon, and nutmeg; mix well and set aside for later use. In a large mixing bowl, combine the flour, sugar, baking powder, salt, and cornstarch until well mixed. Add the egg substitute, applesauce, orange juice, and vanilla to the flour; blend together well. Pour one-third of the batter into a heavy metal bundt cake pan that has been sprayed with a vegetable oil and flour spray. Cover the batter with half of the apples, then cover the apples with another third of the batter. Repeat the process by adding the remaining apples and pouring the remaining batter on top of the apples. Bake the apple cake at 350 degrees for about 75 minutes, or until a toothpick comes out clean when stuck into the middle of the cake. Remove the cake from the oven and allow it to cook for 10 minutes. Sprinkle with powdered sugar and serve. Serve cool or warm. Serves 10.

Lagniappe: This is, for all practical purposes, a completely fat-free cake. It is best just after it is baked, but it is good even after it cools. Now a word about fat-free cakes: They will not compete with cakes that have oil and whole eggs in them. They are heavier and lack the overall quality of a "real" cake. However, it is a wonderful alternative to the oil and fat of a regular cake. This is a case sort of having your cake and eating it too.

When I was testing this recipe to decide if I needed to do anything different, I ate about half the cake each time Debbie or I made it. Debbie finally made a crack about it being a good thing that it wasn't the real cake or I would have had two months' worth of fat grams in a few minutes.

When you are looking for a fat-free dessert, Apple Cake is a wonderful choice. The applesauce is used to replace the oil and, because it is an apple cake, the change in the cake is more subtle than in other baked goods. I like it because I can eat a lot of it. I say it will serve ten, but not if you eat very large pieces. When you are counting fat grams and not calories, you can afford the luxury of pigging out on this cake (or you can just say you are testing it).

Calories—380; Fat—.4 g; Protein—5.7 g; Carbohydrates—85 g; Cholesterol—0 mg; Fiber—1.6 g; Sodium—280 mg

4 of the 380 calories are from fat.
1% of the calories come from fat.

BANANA CREAM PIE

2 1.3-oz. packets Dream Whip
1/4 cup no-fat sour cream
1 tsp. vanilla extract
2 1/2 cups cold skim milk
2 3.4-oz. pkg. instant banana cream pudding and pie filling

2 medium bananas, cut into 1/4-inch slices
1 recipe Graham Cracker Crust (see page 255)

In a large mixing bowl, combine the Dream Whip, sour cream, and vanilla with 1 cup of the cold skim milk. Beat at high speed for about 5 minutes, or until peaks form. Add the pudding mix and the rest of the milk; beat at low speed until blended. When blended, beat at high speed for about two minutes. Place the banana slices around the edge and bottom of the pie shell. Pour the banana pudding mix over the bananas, heaping it high. Refrigerate for at least four hours. Serve chilled. Serves 8.

Lagniappe: What a super pie! It is simple and swift to put together, but the taste is grand. You can make this pie in advance and refrigerate it for up to three days. You can change the filling to any other flavor you like. Remember, as long as you use skim milk, the instant pie filling has no fat in it.

Calories—293; Fat—1.7 g; Protein—4.4 g; Carbohydrates—62.7 g; Cholesterol—9 mg; Fiber—.7 g; Sodium—594 mg

15 of the 293 calories are from fat.
5% of the calories come from fat.

BANANA CREPES

2 large bananas
Butter-flavored nonstick
  vegetable oil spray
2 tbsp. brandy

1/4 tsp. cinnamon
2 tbsp. sugar
1 recipe Crêpes (see pages
  96-97)

Peel the bananas and cut them into thin slices. Lightly spray a medium nonstick skillet with the butter-flavored spray, then sauté the bananas over low-medium heat, turning a few times to ensure that they heat up and begin to soften. Remove from the heat, add the brandy, then return to the heat and flambé by lighting the brandy carefully with a match. Do not do anything but slightly shake the pan until the flame dies. Remove the skillet from the heat.

Mix together the cinnamon and sugar until well blended. Arrange about four slices of banana onto each crêpe, sprinkle equally with the cinnamon sugar and roll the crêpes. Serve two crêpes to each person. Serves 4.

Lagniappe: This is a wonderfully light and fat-free dessert or an excellent breakfast. It hints of Bananas Foster, but is less work, fewer calories, and none of the fat. You can top these crêpes with a nonfat whipped topping or nonfat frozen yogurt if you would like to make a more filling dessert. This is flashy and mouth-watering dessert. Don't do anything in advance for this dessert. It is so quick and easy that you won't need to plan anything but getting the ingredients together. Don't forget the matches!

Calories—162; Fat—1 g; Protein—5.6 g; Carbohydrates—29.7 g; Cholesterol—1 mg; Fiber—.8 g; Sodium—133 mg

9 of the 162 calories are from fat.
6% of the calories come from fat.

BLUEBERRY CHEESECAKE TARTS

2 8-oz. pkg. fat-free cream
cheese
1 cup sugar
2/3 cup no-fat no-
cholesterol egg substitute
2 tbsp. fresh lemon juice

1 tsp. vanilla extract
1/4 tsp. nutmeg
1/8 tsp. lemon zest
12 individual vanilla wafers
3/4 cup light blueberry pie
filling

Preheat the oven to 400 degrees. In a large mixing bowl, beat the fat-free cream cheese until smooth and creamy. Slowly add the sugar, beating until the mixture is light and fluffy. Pour in the egg substitute gradually while beating. Beat in the lemon juice, vanilla, nutmeg, and lemon zest until well blended. Place a vanilla wafer in the bottom of each of twelve paper muffin cups. Spoon the cream cheese mixture equally into each muffin cup. Bake at 400 degrees for 10 minutes, then reduce the heat to 350 degrees and bake for 15 minutes. Remove and allow the tarts to cool. Refrigerate overnight in the muffin pans. When you are ready to serve, remove the paper and top with 1 tablespoon pie filling on each of the tarts. Makes 12 tarts.

Lagniappe: This is a great sweet tooth cure. It is really hard to tell the difference between this recipe and one made with regular cream cheese. If it's hard to tell which is regular and which is low-fat, you've got a great product. Set them out and don't tell anyone they are low in fat! This is a case of having your tart and eating it as well!

Per tart:
Calories—131; Fat—.6 g; Protein—6.7 g; Carbohydrates—23.6 g;
Cholesterol—67 mg; Fiber—.2 g; Sodium—253 mg

5 of the 131 calories are from fat.
4% of the calories come from fat.

BREAD PUDDING

3 cups French bread, torn
  into pieces
1 1/2 cups evaporated skim
  milk
1 cup sugar
1 cup no-fat no-cholesterol
  egg substitute
1/2 cup raisins
1 medium apple, cut into
  small pieces

1 large peach, cut into
  small pieces
1 tbsp. pecan pieces
1 tsp. ground nutmeg
1 tsp. cinnamon
1/2 tsp. allspice
2 tsp. vanilla extract

Place the bread and the milk into a large mixing bowl and let the bread soak for 5 minutes. Add the sugar and egg substitute and mix together well. Add the raisins, apple, peach, and pecans and fold it in. Add the spices and vanilla and blend in well. Lightly spray the bottom of a 2 1/2-quart shallow casserole with the butter-flavored vegetable oil. Pour the pudding into the casserole, then bake at 375 degrees for 1 hour, or until the center of the pudding is set. Check by sticking a clean knife into the center of the pudding. If the knife comes out clean, the pudding is ready. Serve warm with Brandy-Butter Sauce. Serves 8.

Lagniappe: You can make this pudding ahead of time and reheat it in the oven or microwave. Serve with generous amounts of the Brandy-Butter Sauce. Although it may sound like it has a lot of fat, it doesn't. You can freeze this pudding, but it will cause little liquid to form on the outside of the pudding when you defrost it. The taste will still be great, but you will lose a little of the texture.

Calories—232; Fat—1.4 g; Protein—6.7 g; Carbohydrates—49.5 g; Cholesterol—1 mg; Fiber—1 g; Sodium—192 mg

13 of the 232 calories are from fat.
6% of the calories come from fat.

CHERRIES SHALON

1/4 cup sugar
2 tbsp. light brown sugar
1/2 cup cherry or grape
 juice
1/4 tsp. ground allspice
1/8 tsp. ground cinnamon
2 cups fresh cherries, pits
 removed
1 tsp. fresh grated orange
 peel or orange zest

1/3 cup Grand Marnier
 liqueur
2/3 cup cognac
1 1/2-oz. packet Butter
 Buds
4 cups nonfat vanilla frozen
 yogurt

Heat a large nonstick skillet or flambé pan over medium heat until it is hot. When the pan is hot, add the sugar and light brown sugar. Try to spread it out across the pan. As the sugars begin to melt, use a spoon to swirl the unmelted sugar into the melted sugar. When the sugar turns a golden brown, quickly blend in the cherry juice. Do not wait too long, or the sugar will turn dark brown or even black.

Add the allspice and cinnamon and stir in well. Add the cherries and fresh grated orange peel and heat over medium heat for 4 minutes, then add the Grand Marnier. Stir the liqueur in well and let the dish simmer for about 3 more minutes, stirring often. Carefully add the cognac and, as soon as it has heated up a little, light the pan with a match. Flambé until the flame burns out. Do not try anything fancy, just stir lightly with a spoon. Add the Butter Buds and stir in until they have dissolved. The sauce should thicken somewhat and begin to bubble. Spoon generous amounts of the sauce and cherries over vanilla nonfat frozen yogurt. Serve at once. Serves 8.

Lagniappe: This is almost a nonfat Cherries Jubilee. If you can't get fresh cherries, just use canned dark sweet cherries. Do not use pie filling cherries, or you will really have a mess. If you want to get closer to the regular recipe for Cherries Jubilee, you can substitute Kirsch liqueur for the Grand Marnier. Kirsch liqueur is a little hard to find, but it is out there. You almost always have to special order it from your liqueur store. I like the flavor of Grand Marnier in this recipe; if the truth be known, I like the flavor of Grand Marnier right from a spoon! Try this flambé, especially when you can get fresh cherries. You'll like it.

Calories—279; Fat—.7 g; Protein—3.9 g; Carbohydrates—48.7 g; Cholesterol—5 mg; Fiber—1.1 g; Sodium—1251 mg

6 of the 279 calories are from fat.
2% of the calories come from fat.

CHOCOLATE DREAM CAKE

9 large egg whites
1/2 tsp. cream of tartar
1/2 cup boiling water
1 1/2-oz. packet Butter
  Buds
1/2 cup unsweetened cocoa
1/2 cup evaporated skim
  milk
2 cups cake flour
1 3/4 cups sugar

2 tsp. baking soda
1/8 tsp. nutmeg
1/2 tsp. salt
1 cup no-fat no-cholesterol
  egg substitute
2 tsp. vanilla extract
Vegetable oil and flour
  baking spray
1 recipe Fluffy White Frosting (see page 251)

Preheat the oven to 350 degrees. In a large mixing bowl, sprinkle the cream of tartar on top of the egg whites. Let them set for a few minutes at room temperature. In a small mixing bowl, combine the boiling water, Butter Buds, and cocoa and stir until the cocoa is well blended. Stir in the milk. Set the chocolate aside.

In another large mixing bowl, combine the flour, sugar, baking soda, nutmeg, and salt. Using a wire whisk, stir until well blended. Add the egg substitute, vanilla extract and the cocoa mixture. Beat at medium speed with an electric mixer until smooth. Set aside while you beat the egg whites until they are stiff. Use a large spoon or a spatula to spoon the cocoa-flour batter over the beaten egg whites. Fold in until well blended, but try not to deflate the egg whites. Pour into a 10-inch tube pan that has been lightly sprayed with vegetable oil and flour baking spray. Bake at 350 degrees for one hour and 10 minutes, or until a toothpick inserted into the center of the cake comes out clean. Remove from the pan and frost with the Fluffy White Frosting. Serves 10.

Lagniappe: This is a marvelous cake. When frosted, it is exquisite. I especially like it during the holiday season. I usually drop additional decorations like red and green sprinkles on the cake to make it look festive. The cake is great plain as a coffee cake, and you can also cut it in half and put frosting in the middle, making it a nice layer cake.

Calories—431; Fat—.9 g; Protein—10.4 g; Carbohydrates—98.7 g; Cholesterol—.5 mg; Fiber—.1 g; Sodium—420 mg

8 of the 431 calories are from fat.
2% of the calories come from fat.

CHOCOLATE TRIPLE TREAT

12 individual fat-free devil's
food cookies
1 cup no-fat sour cream
1/2 cup fat-free cream
cheese
1 tbsp. fresh lemon juice

1 1/2 tsp. vanilla extract
2 3.4-oz. boxes instant
chocolate pudding
4 1/2 cups cold skim milk
1 1.3-oz. packet Dream
Whip

Chop the cookies finely or put them into a food processor and chop them. Sprinkle the chopped cookies into the bottom of a nice 2-quart dessert dish. Put the sour cream, cream cheese, lemon juice, and 1 teaspoon of vanilla in a small mixing bowl and beat with an electric mixer until smooth. Spoon the sour cream mixture on top of the cookies. Cover with plastic wrap, and refrigerate for later use. In another mixing bowl, add the chocolate pudding and four cups of the skim milk. Beat with a wire whisk or an electric mixer until well blended, about 2 minutes. Remove the plastic wrap, and pour the pudding on top of the sour cream mixture. In another bowl, mix the packet of Dream Whip, the remaining 1/2 cup of skim milk, and the remaining 1/2 teaspoon of vanilla; beat at high speed with an electric mixer until the topping thickens and forms peaks, about 4 minutes. Cover the pudding with the Dream Whip. Refrigerate for 30 minutes or longer, and serve cold. Serves 8.

Lagniappe: This recipe uses two of my favorite foods. First is no-fat sour cream. This product has been most influential in convincing me that I can eat well and stay on a low-fat diet. It is so versatile and delicious. I like it as well as I like the real thing. In fact, I always substitute the nonfat variety for the real thing, even when I am cooking for fat lovers! It holds up well, has a great consistency, and looks like the real thing.

The second great food in this recipe is the nonfat devil's food cookies. I could eat an entire box! The great taste and lack of fat does my heart good—literally. These cookies are great by themselves, so I just had to do a recipe (or perhaps two) with them. You can make this dessert the day before you want to serve it and keep it refrigerated (as long as you can keep the family out of it). Don't go looking for nonfat instant pudding; the regular stuff is fat-free! The fat in instant pudding isn't in the mix, it's in milk. So we use skim milk and the product remains fat-free.

Calories—355; Fat—.2 g; Protein—9.5 g; Carbohydrates—62 g; Cholesterol—2.3 mg; Fiber—.4 g; Sodium—650 mg

2 of the 355 calories are from fat.
Much less than 1% of the calories come from fat.

FLUFFY CARAMEL FROSTING

1 cup dark brown sugar
1 cup light brown sugar
2/3 cup water
3 tbsp. dark corn syrup

4 large egg whites
1/2 tsp. cream of tartar
1 tsp. vanilla extract

In a medium saucepan over medium-high heat, combine the sugars and stir constantly until the sugar begins to melt and begins to turn brown (caramelize). Add the water and corn syrup; bring to a boil. Continue to cook until the mixture comes to the hard-ball stage. That stage is reached when a little of the syrup mixture forms a hard (almost rock hard) ball when dropped into cold water.

While the syrup is cooking, beat the egg whites, cream of tartar, and vanilla extract to the stiff-peak stage. When the sugar mixture is ready, slowly pour the sugar mixture into the stiff egg whites while the mixer is on. Take care not to pour the hot mixture onto the electric beaters because it will splatter the hot syrup. The frosting should be fluffy and thick. This is enough frosting to frost one large cake. When it is on the cake, it will serve 8.

Lagniappe: This is my regular Fluffy Carmel Frosting. I didn't have to do anything to it to make it fat-free. Don't forget that sugar has no fat. If you eat enough of it, it might make you fat, but sugar itself doesn't have a gram of fat. It does have calories. This makes a wonderful frosting for chocolate, yellow, or white cakes.

Calories—239; Fat—trace; Protein—1.7 g; Carbohydrates—59.7 g; Cholesterol—0 mg; Fiber—0 g; Sodium—86 mg

Less than 1 of the 239 calories is from fat.
Much less than 1% of the calories come from fat.

FLUFFY WHITE FROSTING

2 cups sugar
2/3 cup water
3 tbsp. light corn syrup

4 large egg whites
1/2 tsp. cream of tartar
1 tsp. vanilla extract

In a medium saucepan over medium-high heat, combine the sugar, water, and corn syrup; bring to a boil. Continue to cook until the mixture comes to the hard-ball stage. That stage is reached when the syrup mixture forms a hard ball when dropped into cold water.

While the syrup is cooking, beat the egg whites, cream of tartar, and vanilla extract to the stiff-peak stage. When the sugar mixture is ready, slowly pour the sugar mixture into the stiff egg whites while the mixer is on. Do not pour the hot mixture onto the electric beaters, or it will splatter the hot syrup. The frosting should be fluffy and thick and resemble marshmallow frosting. This is enough frosting to frost one large cake. When it is on the cake, it will serve 8.

Lagniappe: This is my regular white frosting. I didn't have to do anything to it to make it fat-free. Very often, I find people that mistake sugar for fat. Sugar has calories but no fat. This makes a wonderful frosting for almost any cake. Enjoy.

Calories—214; Fat—trace; Protein—1.7 g; Carbohydrates—53.7 g; Cholesterol—0 mg; Fiber—0 g; Sodium—74 mg

Less than 1 of the 325 calories is from fat.
Much less than 1% of the calories come from fat.

FRESH BLACKBERRY CREPES NICHOLAS

3 tbsp. sugar
1/4 cup water
6 oz. fresh or frozen black-
    berries (a little more than
    a cup)

2 1/2 tsp. cornstarch
1/4 cup cold water
1 recipe Crêpes (see pages
    96-97)

In a saucepan over medium heat, let the sugar melt and begin to caramelize to a light brown color. Quickly add the first 1/4 cup of water and 10 of the blackberries. Stir until the sugar has dissolved in the water and the mixture comes to a hard boil. Cook for 3 minutes at boiling, stirring constantly. Add the remaining berries and gently stir them in. Mix together the cornstarch and the remaining 1/4 cup of cold water until all the cornstarch is dissolved.

The berries should return to a boil; when they do, stir in the cornstarch mixture. Cook, stirring constantly, until the mixture thickens nicely. Remove from the heat and let the sauce stand for 2 minutes. Place two crêpes on each of 4 plates, and spoon generous amounts of the berries and sauce into the center of each crêpe. Roll the crêpes, placing the two edges under the bottom. Spoon a little sauce on top of each crêpe. Serve at once. Serves 4.

Lagniappe: Simply marvelous! You can't ask for an easier or more versatile recipe. The sauce is out of this world. You can serve it hot or cold. I like to use it cold on toast, right from the refrigerator. You can also use it to top a nice slice of angel food cake or on top of nonfat vanilla or blackberry frozen yogurt. If you want, you can top the crêpes with a nice helping of nonfat whipped topping. The puff of white looks great against the dark berries. When you eat desserts like this one, you will wonder how you are eating like this and still losing weight! The secret is in the lack of fat!

Calories—128; Fat—.6 g; Protein—5.2 g; Carbohydrates—25.8 g; Cholesterol—1 mg; Fiber—1.6 g; Sodium—132 mg

5 of the 128 calories are from fat.
4% of the calories come from fat.

FROSTED FLAKE TREATS

1/2 cup light corn syrup
1/2 cup sugar
1 tsp. light brown sugar
1/4 cup applesauce
1/4 cup unsweetened cocoa
2 tbsp. water

1 1/2-oz. packet Butter Buds
1 tsp. vanilla extract
4 cups Frosted Flakes cereal

Mix together all the ingredients but the vanilla and cereal. Bring to a boil. Let the mixture boil for 2 minutes, stirring constantly. Remove from the heat and add the vanilla; stir in well. Put the cereal in a large bowl and pour the sugar mixture over it. Carefully toss the flakes until they are coated with the sugar mixture. Drop the coated flakes by tablespoonfuls onto waxed paper, then let the cookies harden. Serve after the cookies have cooled. Makes about 60 cookies.

Lagniappe: This is a great cookie recipe to make with children. They like Frosted Flakes, and they like spooning the coated flakes onto the waxed paper. It is also a good way to get children to eat a sweet that is not that bad for them. Again, the fat count on this recipe is great; it is also a great-tasting sweet. You can also make this recipe with Rice Krispies or Corn Flakes as well.

Per Cookie:
Calories—28; Fat—.07 g; Protein—.2 g; Carbohydrates—6.7 g; Cholesterol—0 mg; Fiber—trace; Sodium—34 mg

.6 of the 28 calories are from fat.
2% of the calories come from fat.

FRUIT CAKE

2 cups graham cracker
  crumbs
2 cups vanilla wafer crumbs
1 1/2 cups candied mixed
  fruits, chopped
1 cup golden raisins
1 cup chopped dates

1 can sweetened condensed
  milk
1/4 tsp. nutmeg
1 tsp. vanilla extract
2 tbsp. finely chopped
  pecans

In a large mixing bowl, mix together all the ingredients. Press the mixture into a log mold or a ring mold. Cover with plastic wrap and refrigerate overnight. Serve as you would any fruit cake. Serves 12.

Lagniappe: During the holiday season it's hard not to be able to eat fruit cake, so I wanted to make a fruit cake that tastes like the real thing but is short on fat. This will give you the real taste of fruit cake without all the fat. Try it. It is easy and will fill your yearly craving for fruit cake.

If you want, you can spoon a bit of brandy or cognac on top while it is in the refrigerator or spoon some on just before serving.

Calories—185; Fat—1.5 g; Protein—8 g; Carbohydrates—37.6 g; Cholesterol—8 mg; Fiber—.3 g; Sodium—585 mg

14 of the 185 calories are from fat.
7% of the calories come from fat.

GRAHAM CRACKER CRUST

2 cups graham cracker
crumbs (about 11 whole
crackers per cup)
1/4 cup sugar
1 1/2-oz. packet Butter
Buds

2 tbsp. no-fat sour cream
2 tbsp. hot water
Butter-flavored nonstick
vegetable oil spray

Preheat the oven to 350 degrees. Put all the ingredients into a large bowl and blend together well. Press the crumb mixture into the bottom of a pie pan, baking dish, or springform pan that has been sprayed lightly with butter-flavored vegetable oil. Bake at 350 degrees for 12 minutes, or until nicely browned. Cool and use as a crust for any pie that needs a graham cracker crust. Makes one crust. Serves 8.

Lagniappe: This crust is so close to the real thing that you won't be able to tell the difference. You can make the crust in advance and freeze it if you like. There are three ways to get the graham cracker crumbs. First, you can buy the crumbs already crushed from the store. This is the easiest method, but it is also the most expensive. A second method would be to use whole crackers (about 11 per cup), break them into a food processor, and pulse into large pieces. Your third option is to just crush the crackers with the end of a meat cleaver in a large bowl or place the crackers out on a tray and crush them with a rolling pin. Be careful not to over crush. This crust is a great way to lower the fat content for your favorite tart or pie.

Calories—102; Fat—1.4 g; Protein—1.5 g; Carbohydrates—21.5 g; Cholesterol—0 mg; Fiber—.3 g; Sodium—203 mg

12 of the 102 calories are from fat.
12% of the calories come from fat.

GRAND MARNIER-CHOCOLATE CHEESECAKE

12 Snack Well's chocolate
cream sandwich cookies
2 8-oz. pkg. fat-free cream
cheese
1 cup sugar
1 cup nonfat cottage cheese
1/3 cup unsweetened cocoa
1/4 cup all-purpose flour
1/4 cup Grand Marnier
liqueur

1 tsp. vanilla extract
1/4 tsp. salt
1 large egg
1/2 cup no-fat no-
cholesterol egg substitute
2 tbsp. Baker's semi-sweet
chocolate chips

Preheat the oven to 350 degrees. Place the chocolate cream sand-wich cookies between two sheets of plastic wrap and crush the cookies with a rolling pin, or chop the cookies finely in a food processor. Spread the chocolate cookies on the bottom of a 7-inch springform cake pan, and lightly press them with your fingers. Bake the crust for 5 minutes at 300 degrees then remove and allow the crust to cool. Set it aside for later use.

In a heavy mixing bowl with an electric mixer (or in a large food processor), cream the cream cheese with the sugar until smooth, then add the cottage cheese, cocoa, flour, Grand Marnier, vanilla, and salt. Process or blend until all is mixed together well and the batter is smooth. Add the egg and egg substitute and blend until it is smooth. Fold in the chocolate chips. Slowly pour the mixture over the cookie crust in the springform pan. Bake at 300 degrees for 70 minutes, or until the cake is set. Let it cool in the pan on a wire rack. Cover the cake and chill in the refrigerator for at least 8 hours.

Remove the sides from the cake pan and slide the cake onto a serv-ing platter. Slice and serve. Serves 12.

Lagniappe: Orange and chocolate go together well, and this cake is a tribute to this marriage. You can use another chocolate cookie that is 1 gram of fat per cookie, but I find that Snack Well's is a great tasting and quality product. The cream in the cookie helps to set the crust of the cheesecake. Do not overcook the crust, it will burn. All in all, you will find that this a scrumptious cheesecake that will please any palate. The nonfat products used in this recipe have advanced to the point that they taste quite good.

Calories—213; Fat—2.4 g; Protein—15 g; Carbohydrates—34.5 g; Cholesterol—30 mg; Fiber—.1 g; Sodium—521 mg

22 of the 213 calories are from fat.
10% of the calories come from fat.

HOT FRESH PEACH SUNDAE

2 cups nonfat vanilla frozen yogurt
1 cup Fresh Peach Sauce (see pages 275-76)

4 tbsp. light Cool Whip

Place a cup of nonfat vanilla yogurt in each of two bowls and cover with 1/2 cup of warm Fresh Peach Sauce. Add 2 tablespoons of light Cool Whip on top of each. Serve at once. Serves 2.

Lagniappe: Simple, easy, and oh so good! You can make the peach sauce in advance, and just keep it refrigerated until you are ready to use it. I like to heat the sauce up in the microwave. The recipe calls for large sundaes, but you can cut everything in half. That might work for most people, but when I want something really sweet and rich, this is the recipe for me. You can eat it to your heart's content because of the low fat count. Assemble and enjoy!

Calories—489; Fat—less than 1 g; Protein—6.5 g; Carbohydrates—75.5 g; Cholesterol—10 mg; Fiber—.2 g; Sodium—320 mg

9 of the 489 calories are from fat.
2% of the calories come from fat.

INSTANT CHEESECAKE

1 3.4-oz. package instant
   lemon pudding and pie
   filling
2 cups cold skim milk
2 tbsp. no-fat sour cream

1 8-oz. pkg. fat-free cream
   cheese, softened
1 recipe Graham Cracker
   Crust (see page 255)

In a large mixing bowl, beat together the instant pudding mix, the cold skim milk, and the sour cream until the pudding becomes thick. Cut the cream cheese into chunks and add them to the lemon pudding. Continue to beat with an electric mixer until smooth. Pour into the graham cracker crust and refrigerate for a couple of hours. Serve chilled. Serves 8.

Lagniappe: Instant is the best word to describe this dessert. It is quick and easy and very low fat. This is one of those dishes that tastes like it is the real thing. You can cover it with canned pie filling cherries or blueberries for a special treat. In fact, we'll call it Instant Cherry Cheesecake or Instant Blueberry Cheesecake by just pouring one 20-ounce can of cherry or blueberry pie filling on top of the cheesecake. It makes for a great finish—without much effort!

Calories—185; Fat—1.5 g; Protein—8 g; Carbohydrates—37.6 g; Cholesterol—8 mg; Fiber—.3 g; Sodium—585 mg

14 of the 185 calories are from fat.
7% of the calories come from fat.

MOLASSES SPICE COOKIES

1/2 cup unsweetened
    applesauce
1/4 cup firmly packed light
    brown sugar
1 cup molasses
1 tsp. vanilla extract
2 cups all-purpose white
    flour
1 cup whole wheat flour
1 1/2-oz. packet Butter
    Buds

1 tsp. allspice
1 tsp. ground ginger
1 tsp. nutmeg
1/4 tsp. ground cloves
1 tsp. baking powder
1 tsp. baking soda
1/4 tsp. salt
1/3 cup sugar

In a medium mixing bowl, cream together the applesauce, brown sugar, molasses, and vanilla until light and velvety. In a large mixing bowl, combine the remaining ingredients except for the 1/3 cup of sugar. Slowly add the liquid mixture into the dry mixture to make a stiff dough. Roll the dough into a large ball and chill it overnight.

Mold the dough into 1-inch round balls and roll the balls in the 1/3 cup of sugar. Place the balls on a nonstick baking sheet, then bake in a preheated 300-degree oven for about 12 to 15 minutes, or until the cookies are somewhat crisp. Cool completely, then serve. Makes about 54 cookies.

Lagniappe: These are wonderful old-time cookies. They are like the cookies my grandmother used to make years ago. Of course, she would use lots of fresh butter. The Butter Buds do give some hint of the butter taste, but these cookies are nonfat, so you can't help but love this substitute. Having cookies around that offer you a low-fat alternative to other sweets that are high in fat gives you the ability to snack on something sweet. Basically, you don't have to suffer, just eat a couple of cookies when you get the urge!

Calories—47; Fat—.1 g; Protein—.7 g; Carbohydrates—11 g; Cholesterol—0 mg; Fiber—.1 g; Sodium—42 mg

Less than 1 of the 47 calories is from fat.
Less than 2% of the calories come from fat.

NO-BAKE DATE-NUT BALLS

4 cups miniature
  marshmallows
2 cups graham cracker
  crumbs
1 1/2 cups chopped dates

2 tbsp. finely chopped
  pecans
1 14-oz. can sweetened
  condensed milk
1/2 tsp. vanilla extract

Combine all the ingredients together in a large mixing bowl. Using your hands, roll the mixture into small balls. Place on waxed paper and refrigerate for at least 3 hours. Store in the refrigerator. Makes about 50 balls.

Lagniappe: This is a quick and easy cookie. To reduce the fat, the only thing I did was cut down on the pecans. If you were not watching fat grams, this recipe would have a cup of pecans. I like to make this recipe with children. They really like getting their hands all sticky and rolling balls of this tasty mixture. Just try to keep their hands out of their mouths until they are through. Oh yes, also be sure to wash their hands before they leave the kitchen, or you will have a sticky house for weeks to come. These cookies need to stay in the refrigerator and chilled. They are somewhat sticky to the touch, but they are so scrumptious, it's worth a little stickiness.

Per Cookie:
Calories—62; Fat—1.5 g; Protein—1 g; Carbohydrates—11.6 g; Cholesterol—4 mg; Fiber—.5 g; Sodium—40 mg

14 of the 62 calories are from fat.
22% of the calories come from fat.

OLD-FASHIONED CHEESECAKE

12 whole Snack Well's
   cream sandwich cookies
2 8-oz. pkg. fat-free cream
   cheese
1 cup sugar
1 cup nonfat cottage cheese
1/4 cup fresh lemon juice
1/4 cup all-purpose flour

3 tsp. vanilla extract
1/4 tsp. salt
1/2 tsp. nutmeg
1/8 tsp. cinnamon
2 large eggs
1 cup no-fat no-cholesterol
   egg substitute

Preheat the oven to 350 degrees. Place the cream sandwich cookies between two sheets of plastic wrap and crush the cookies with a
rolling pin, or chop the cookies finely in a food processor. Spread the
crushed cookies on the bottom of a 7-inch springform cake pan and
lightly press into the bottom and slightly up the side of the pan. Bake
the crust for 5 minutes at 300 degrees, then remove and allow the crust
to cool. Set it aside for later use.

In a heavy mixing bowl with an electric mixer or in a large food
processor, cream the cream cheese with the sugar until smooth, then
add the cottage cheese, lemon juice, flour, vanilla, salt, nutmeg, and cinnamon. Process or blend until all is mixed together well and the batter
is smooth. Add the eggs and egg substitute and blend until it is smooth.

Slowly pour the mixture over the cookie crust in the springform
pan. Bake at 300 degrees for 70 minutes, or until the cheesecake is set.
Let it cool in the pan on a wire rack. Cover the cake and chill in the
refrigerator for at least 8 hours. Remove the sides from the cake pan,
then slide the cake onto a serving platter. Slice and serve. Serves 12.

Lagniappe: Cheesecake is always a favorite. This low-fat version will
please you like you wouldn't believe possible. The cream in the cookies helps to set the crust of the cheesecake. You can cover the cake with
blueberry or cherry pie filling if you like, or top it with fresh sliced strawberries. I like it just like it is. Low-fat food doesn't have to fit in the old
molds we set for them in our minds. Enjoy!

*Calories—182; Fat—2.1 g; Protein—15.1 g; Carbohydrates—30.6 g;
Cholesterol—52 mg; Fiber—.1 g; Sodium—530 mg*

19 of the 182 calories are from fat.
10% of the calories come from fat.

PEACH FLAMBE NICOLE

1/4 cup sugar
2 tbsp. light brown sugar
1/4 cup fresh orange juice
1/8 tsp. ground cloves
2 cups fresh sliced peaches,
  peeled
1 tsp. fresh grated orange
  peel or orange zest

1/3 cup Triple Sec liqueur
2/3 cup brandy
1 1/2-oz. packet Butter
  Buds
4 cups nonfat vanilla
  yogurt

Heat a large nonstick skillet or flambé pan over medium heat. When the pan is hot, add the sugar and light brown sugar. Try to spread it out across the pan. As the sugars begin to melt, use a spoon to swirl the unmelted sugar into the melted sugar. When the sugar turns a golden brown, quickly blend in the orange juice. Do not wait too long, or the sugar will turn dark brown or even black. Add the cloves and stir in well.

Add the peaches and fresh grated orange and heat over medium heat until the peaches become limp, about 3 minutes, then add the Triple Sec. Stir the liqueur in well and let the dish simmer for about 3 more minutes, stirring often. Carefully add the brandy and, as soon as it has heated up a little, light the pan with a match. Flambé until the flame burns out. Do not try anything fancy; just stir lightly with a spoon. Add the Butter Buds and stir in until they have dissolved. The sauce should thicken somewhat and begin to bubble. Spoon generous amounts of the sauce and peaches over vanilla nonfat yogurt. Serve at once. Serves 8.

Lagniappe: This is a simple, easy, yet tasty flambé. I love to entertain with flambés. They are always a show stopper. When we work so hard to plan a great meal, we need to have something easy and fun to finish off the meal in grand style. A flambé does just that for you.

Calories—245; Fat—.1 g; Protein—3.4 g; Carbohydrates—41 g; Cholesterol—5 mg; Fiber—.3 g; Sodium—122 mg

1 of the 245 calories is from fat.
Much less than 1% of the calories come from fat.

PINEAPPLE FLAMBE CHRISTINE

1/3 cup sugar
3 tbsp. light brown sugar
1/4 cup pineapple juice
1/4 tsp. ground mace
1/8 tsp. ground nutmeg
3 cups fresh pineapple, cut
   into cubes

1 tsp. fresh grated lime peel
   or lime zest
1/3 cup Cointreau liqueur
2/3 cup dark rum
1 1/2-oz. packet Butter
   Buds
4 cups nonfat vanilla yogurt

Heat a large nonstick skillet or flambé pan over medium heat until it is hot. When the pan is hot, add the sugar and light brown sugar. Try to spread it out across the pan. As the sugars begin to melt, use a spoon to swirl the unmelted sugar into the melted sugar. When the sugar turns a golden brown, quickly blend in the pineapple juice. Do not wait too long, or the sugar will turn dark brown or even black. Add the mace and nutmeg and stir in well.

Add the fresh pineapple cubes and fresh grated lime. Heat over medium heat until the pineapple gives up some of its liquid and reduces in size, about 5 minutes, then add the Cointreau. Stir the liqueur in well and let the dish simmer for about 3 more minutes, stirring often. Carefully add the rum. As soon as it has heated up a little, light the pan with a match. Flambé until the flame burns out. Do not try anything fancy, just stir lightly with a spoon. Add the Butter Buds and stir in until they have dissolved. The sauce should thicken somewhat and begin to bubble. Spoon generous amounts of the sauce and pineapple pieces over vanilla nonfat frozen yogurt. Serve at once. Serves 8.

Lagniappe: Flambés are wonderful to work with and a highlight of any meal. I really like them because they are showy and allow you to spend your preparation time on other dishes. You can cut the pineapple in advance and refrigerate it until you are ready to start. You can also use this leftover sauce to top pancakes the morning after. One large pineapple should yield around 3 cups of cubes.

Calories—267; Fat—.3 g; Protein—3.3 g; Carbohydrates—46.8 g; Cholesterol—5 mg; Fiber—1 g; Sodium—123 mg

3 of the 267 calories are from fat.
1% of the calories come from fat.

POPPY SEED CAKE

CAKE:

2/3 cup sugar
1 tbsp. dark brown sugar
1/4 cup sweetened
  applesauce
1/2 cup no-fat no-
  cholesterol egg substitute
1 1/2 cups all-purpose flour
1 1/2-oz. packet Butter
  Buds

2 tsp. baking powder
1 tsp. baking soda
1/8 tsp. salt
1 tbsp. poppy seeds
1 cup no-fat sour cream
2 tsp. vanilla extract
Vegetable oil and flour
  baking spray

GLAZE:

1 1/2 cups powdered sugar
1 tsp. vanilla extract

2 tsp. no-fat sour cream

Preheat the oven to 350 degrees. In a large bowl, cream together the sugars, applesauce, and egg substitute with an electric mixer until well mixed. In another bowl, combine the flour, Butter Buds, baking powder, baking soda, salt, and poppy seeds until well blended. A little at a time, add the flour mixture into the creamed sugar mixture, blending well after each addition of the flour mixture. Add in the sour cream and vanilla and blend it in well.

Spray a 9-inch square pan with the vegetable oil and flour spray, then pour the batter into the pan. Bake for 30 to 35 minutes at 350 degrees, or until a wooden toothpick comes out clean when inserted into the center of the cake.

To make the glaze, mix the three ingredients together well. When the cake is ready, remove it from the oven and immediately spread the glaze on top of the hot cake. Allow the cake to cool on a wire rack for 10 minutes, then serve. Serves 9.

Lagniappe: Have your cake and eat it on a low-fat diet. This cake is delicious and easy to make. Remember cakes made with applesauce do have a tendency to get moldy when left unrefrigerated. If you don't eat all the cake, store it in the refrigerator. I like to eat a nice piece of cake to help cut my craving for sweets. It is so low in fat that you can enjoy it with no guilt.

Calories—318; Fat—.5 g; Protein—6.2 g; Carbohydrates—73 g; Cholesterol—0 mg; Fiber—.1 g; Sodium—323 mg

5 of the 318 calories are from fat.
2% of the calories come from fat.

PECAN PRALINES

1 cup light brown sugar, packed
1/2 cup dark brown sugar, packed

1/2 cup white sugar
1/4 cup water
1 cup (4 oz.) pecan pieces

Line two baking sheets with wax paper. In a medium-sized, heavy saucepan, combine sugars with 1/4 cup of water. Simmer over medium heat, stirring occasionally. Cook, without stirring, until the syrup registers 248 degrees and is at the hard-ball stage (when a bit of the syrup dropped into ice water forms a firm ball), 5 to 7 minutes. Remove from the heat and stir in the pecans. Working quickly, drop the mixture by the heaping tablespoonfuls onto the prepared baking sheets. If the mixture hardens in the pan, return the pan to low heat and stir until smooth. Let the pralines stand, uncovered, at room temperature until firm, about 30 minutes. Carefully lift the pralines from the wax paper. Makes about 24 pralines.

Lagniappe: You can make the pralines and store them in an airtight container with layers separated by wax paper, at room temperature for up to 1 week. That is, if you hide them! If found, they won't last one day! This is an old-style praline, not the milky creamy type found in New Orleans. The only fat in this comes from the pecans themselves; there is no milk or butter in them. This is excellent with a strong cup of good Cajun coffee. We have two types of coffee in Cajun Country, strong and weak. Weak coffee is coffee you stir and the spoon stands straight up when you let go. Strong coffee is the kind of coffee that dissolves the spoon as soon as you put it in (just a little Cajun humor to go with the sweets)!

Calories—96; Fat—3 g; Protein—0 g; Carbohydrates—18 g; Cholesterol—0 mg; Fiber—.1 g; Sodium—0 mg

26 of the 96 calories are from fat.
27% of the calories come from fat.

RASPBERRY CREPES AMANDA

1/4 cup sugar
1/4 tsp. nutmeg
1 tbsp. fresh orange zest
  (or peel)
2/3 cup fresh or frozen
  raspberries

1/4 cup brandy
1/4 cup orange juice
1 recipe Crêpes (see pages
  96-97)

Heat a medium nonstick skillet over medium heat until it is hot. Add the sugar, then let it melt and begin to caramelize. Just as it turns a light golden brown, add the nutmeg, orange zest, and raspberries. Constantly stir, and cook for 2 minutes. Remove the skillet from the heat and add the brandy. Carefully return the skillet to the heat. Strike a match and move the match near the skillet to ignite the pan. Flambé, gently shaking the skillet until the flame goes out. Do not try to do anything fancy, just lightly shake the pan. When the flame is out, add the orange juice and let the liquid reduce by half. Fill the crêpes, one at a time and roll them over. Continue the process until all eight crêpes are folded. Serve at once, two crêpes per serving. Serves 4.

Lagniappe: This is a marvelous dessert. It is exquisite, flashy and full of fabulous gusto. It only takes minutes to fix, and it looks so sumptuous. Any time you flambé, you will wow your guests. It is distinctive enough for company, but simple enough for everyday dining. You can make the crêpes up to two or three days ahead of time. This means you don't have to spend a lot of time on your dessert. It is hard to believe something this good is virtually nonfat. I honestly used to believe that a dish like this couldn't be made without butter. What we get is the full flavor of the raspberry.

The reason we make the light caramel is to balance the acridity of the raspberry with the bitterness of the caramel. Interestingly enough, this is a case of two bitters making something taste mellow and luscious, yet not too sweet. You can top this with a nonfat whipped topping if you like; I don't think it is necessary, but the wisp of white would look nice against the deep red of the raspberry sauce.

A word of caution: Be careful with the flambé. Do not do anything but gently shake the pan until the flame is completely out. This is a hot skillet, and a brandy fire does get very hot. The flame will not last that long; the alcohol will burn out quickly. What a treat!

Calories—130; Fat—.6 g; Protein—5.3 g; Carbohydrates—26.7 g; Cholesterol—.8 mg; Fiber—1.1 g; Sodium—131 mg

5 of the 130 calories are from fat.
4% of the calories come from fat.

STRAWBERRY-BANANA TART

1 cup sifted cake flour
2 tbsp. sugar
2 tbsp. cold unsalted butter, cut into slices
2 tbsp. ice water
1 8-oz. pkg. fat-free cream cheese
1 cup lemon-flavored nonfat yogurt

3 tbsp. powdered sugar
1 large banana, peeled and sliced
1 tbsp. lemon juice
1 1/3 cups strawberries, cut in half
2 tbsp. apple jelly, melted

Combine flour and sugar in a large bowl; cut in the butter with a fork or pastry blender until the mixture is a coarse meal. Sprinkle with ice water (1 tablespoon at a time); stir with a fork just until moistened. Roll dough into a 10-inch circle on an ungreased baking sheet; fold edges under and flute. Prick bottom with a fork, cover, and refrigerate for 20 minutes. Bake at 400 degrees for 10 to 15 minutes, or until lightly browned. Cool completely on a baking sheet. Transfer the tart shell to a serving plate.

In a small bowl, beat the cream cheese at medium speed with an electric mixer until quite smooth. Beat in the yogurt and powdered sugar. Gently spread the cheese mixture in the bottom of the tart shell. Combine the banana slices and lemon juice in a small bowl; stir gently until every piece of banana is coated with lemon juice.

Arrange banana slices and strawberries evenly over the cheese mixture. Brush the fruit evenly with jelly; then refrigerate for 1 hour. Serve chilled. Serves 8.

Lagniappe: This is a real dessert! You will eat it and think that someone made a mistake! This can't be so good and yet still good for you.
Guess again! It is both. Don't limit yourself to just bananas and strawberries. I also like this tart with bananas and fresh blueberries. Use 1 1/2
cups of blueberries and the large bananas to make a Blueberry-Banana
Tart. I also like to use slices of fresh peaches. Use 2 1/2 cups of fresh
sliced peaches instead of the bananas and strawberries for a wonderful
Peach Tart. This is a great desert and a wonderful way to end an elegant dinner.

*Calories—220; Fat—3.4 g; Protein—4.8 g; Carbohydrates—128 g;
Cholesterol—25 mg; Fiber—.7 g; Sodium—188 mg*

*31 of the 220 calories are from fat.
14% of the calories come from fat.*

Miscellaneous

BRANDY-BUTTER SAUCE

1 cup sugar
2 1/2 tbsp. cornstarch
1/4 tsp. salt
1 1/2 cups boiling water

2/3 cup brandy
2 1/2-oz. packets Butter
Buds
1 tsp. vanilla extract

Mix the sugar, cornstarch, and salt in a medium saucepan over medium heat. Stir the sugar mixture constantly until some of the sugar begins to melt. It should start to caramelize, or turn a light brown. Slowly add the boiling water until it is all used, then reduce the heat and carefully add the brandy and Butter Buds. Be careful if you are cooking over a gas burner; the brandy could burst into flames. Cook, stirring often, over low heat for about 6 minutes or until the sauce is thick and smooth. Remove from the heat, add the vanilla, and blend it in. This sauce is excellent over bread pudding, cakes, or nonfat yogurt. Makes about 2 cups of sauce.

Lagniappe: This is a wonderful fat-free sauce! You will think you are eating the richest butter sauce possible. This is superb over bread pudding. You don't have to be stingy. You can make this sauce in advance and refrigerate it for later use. It will keep for about a week, refrigerated. To use, just heat up over low heat, stirring until the sauce is warm.

Per tablespoon:
Calories—42; Fat—0 g; Protein—0 g; Carbohydrates—7 g; Cholesterol—0 MG; Fiber—0 g; Sodium—43 mg
None of the 42 calories are from fat.

BUTTER SAUCE

2 1/2-oz. packets Butter
  Buds
1/2 cup low-sodium and
  low-fat chicken broth
2 tbsp. fresh lime juice
2 tsp. cornstarch

1/2 tsp. Tabasco® Sauce
1/4 tsp. salt
1 tsp. white wine
  Worcestershire sauce
1/4 tsp. white pepper

Mix all the ingredients together in a medium saucepan, then stir until well blended. Place over medium heat and let the mixture come just to the boiling point, stirring often. Use as a butter sauce over seafood or over vegetables. Makes about 1/2 cup of butter sauce. Serve warm.

Lagniappe: You'll love the taste of this sauce and swear it is real butter. It is nonfat and it is delicious. You can make the sauce in advance and refrigerate it until you are ready to serve. To use, just heat over low heat until the sauce is hot.

Per tablespoon:
Calories—17; Fat—.1 g; Protein—.2 g; Carbohydrates—3.1 g; Cholesterol—.1 mg; Fiber—0 g; Sodium—280 mg
1 of the 17 calories is from fat.

6% of the calories come from fat

CAJUN NIBBLES

2 1/2 cups Cheerios cereal
2 cups Corn Chex cereal
1 1/3 cups Wheat Chex
  cereal
2 1/4 cups Rice Chex cereal
1 cup mini shredded wheat
3 cups mini nonfat pretzels
1 tsp. Cajun Spice Mix (see
  page 274)
1/2 tsp. Tabasco® Sauce
1 tsp. garlic salt

1 tsp. onion powder
2 tbsp. dried parsley flakes
1 tsp. dried sweet basil
1/4 tsp. dried oregano
  leaves
1/4 cup grated nonfat
  parmesan cheese
1 tbsp. grated romano
  cheese
2 1/2-oz. packets Butter
  Buds

Mix together all ingredients in a large crock pot. Be sure to stir well. Cover and cook on low for 4 hours, stirring about once an hour. Uncover and continue to cook on low for 30 more minutes. Remove and allow to cool to room temperature. Store in an airtight container or zip-lock bags. Use as a low-fat snack or as a snack with sandwiches at lunch. Makes about 3 quarts of nibbles.

Lagniappe: One thing that I really needed on a very low-fat diet was snack food that looked like the snack foods of old. This is a simple recipe that will give you lots of high fiber, low-fat, and low-calorie snack food. I like to have it bagged in zip-lock bags. It kind of looks like the trash foods I used to love to snack on. Feel free to substitute your favorite cereal types in the place of any cereal above; just look for nonfat or low-fat cereal. I really like to use this to kill that urge to eat when I'm starving—like when I come home from work. Enjoy!

Per 1/2 cup serving:
Calories—65; Fat—.4 g; Protein—1.7 g; Carbohydrates—13.4 g; Cholesterol—.4 mg; Fiber—1 g; Sodium—300 mg

4 of the 65 calories are from fat.
6% of the calories come from fat

CAJUN SPICE MIX

1/4 cup salt	1 tbsp. white pepper
2 tbsp. cayenne pepper	2 tsp. dried basil
2 tbsp. paprika	1 tsp. chili powder
1 1/2 tbsp. onion powder	1/4 tsp. dried thyme
1 tbsp. garlic powder	1/4 tsp. ground mustard
1 tbsp. fresh ground black pepper	1/8 tsp. ground cloves

In a mixing bowl, combine all the ingredients. Place in a small jar or spice bottle. Use to season any item as you would use table salt. Makes about 6 ounces.

Lagniappe: This spice mix can be stored in a tightly covered glass jar or a nice spice jar in a cool, dry place out of direct light for up to 4 months. I always like to date the bottle, so I know just how fresh the mixture is. This is a great personal Christmas gift. Just mix it, package it in a nice bottle with a few Cajun recipes that use it, and you've got a nice little gift that reminds the person of you every time they reach for the spice mixture!

Per teaspoon:
Calories—5; Fat—0 g; Protein—.2 g; Carbohydrates—1.1 g; Cholesterol—0 mg; Fiber—tr; Sodium—767 mg
None of the 5 calories are from fat.

CHRISTMAS PUNCH

1/2 gallon cranberry juice	1 large orange
1/2 gallon pineapple juice	2 tsp. almond extract
Juice of	1 1/4 cups sugar
1 large lemon	1/2 gallon ginger ale
Juice of	Ice

In a large punch bowl, mix together all the ingredients except for the ginger ale. Stir well until the sugar is completely dissolved. Add the ginger ale and enough ice to fill the punch bowl to 1 inch from the top. Serve at once. Serves 20 as a party punch.

Lagniappe: This is a wonderful holiday punch. The tartness of the cranberry blends wonderfully with the pineapple juice. You'll have your guests asking for the recipe!

Calories—196; Fat—.1 g; Protein—.4 g; Carbohydrates—50 g; Cholesterol—0 mg; Fiber—.2 g; Sodium—12 mg

1 of the 196 calories is from fat.
Much less than 1% of the calories come from fat

FRESH PEACH SAUCE

3 tbsp. light brown sugar
1/4 cup sugar
4 large fresh peaches, cut
   into thin slices
1 tbsp. fresh lemon juice
1/4 cup brandy

1/2 tsp. ground cinnamon
1/4 tsp. allspice
1/2 cup water
1 1/2-oz. packet Butter
   Buds

Heat a medium nonstick skillet over medium heat. When it is hot, add light brown sugar. Try to spread it across the skillet. As the sugar begins to melt, use a wooden spoon to swirl the solid sugar into the melted sugar. When the brown sugar turns golden brown, quickly add the regular sugar, fresh peach slices, and lemon juice. Do not wait too long after the golden color is reached, or the sugar will turn dark brown or even black. Cook for 3 minutes, stirring constantly, then add the brandy, cinnamon, and allspice. Be careful, so the brandy does not ignite.

Add the water and butter buds, then cook over medium heat, stirring constantly for about 5 minutes. Remove from the heat and use the sauce over meats or over nonfat frozen yogurt. Makes about 2 cups of sauce.

Lagniappe: This sauce can be used as a basting sauce for meats like chicken or pork, or it can be used as a warm sauce over vanilla nonfat yogurt. Either way, it is delicious. Fresh peaches are so nice to cook with. Be sure to choose peaches that are fresh, sweet smelling, and just give a bit when you push on them with your finger. If the peach has no smell of fresh peach to it, pass it by. Also be careful not to pick a peach that is so soft that your finger punches right into it or one that has the smell of alcohol, which tells you it has over ripened.

Per 1/4 cup:
Calories—113; Fat—.1 g; Protein—.1 g; Carbohydrates—13.8 g;
Cholesterol—0 mg; Fiber—.1 g; Sodium—89 mg

1 of the 113 calories is from fat.
Less than 1% of the calories come from fat

FRESH RASPBERRY SALSA

3 tbsp. sugar
2 tbsp. light brown sugar
3 tbsp. fresh orange juice
1 tsp. fresh orange zest
2 cups fresh raspberries (or
  10 oz. frozen)

1/4 cup Grand Marnier
  liqueur
1/2 cup hot picante sauce
1 1/2-oz. packet Butter
  Buds

Heat a medium nonstick skillet over medium heat. When it is hot, add the sugar and light brown sugar. Try to spread it across the skillet. As the sugars begin to melt, use a wooden spoon to swirl the unmelted sugar into the melted sugar. When the sugar turns golden brown, quickly add the orange juice and orange zest. Do not wait too long after the golden color is reached, or the sugar will turn dark brown or even black. Add about half the raspberries to the pan and crush them. Stir them well, then add the Grand Marnier, picante sauce, and Butter Buds.

Cook over medium heat, stirring constantly for about 5 minutes. Add the rest of the berries and cook for 2 more minutes, stirring carefully. Remove from the heat and use the sauce over meats. Makes about 2 cups of sauce.

Lagniappe: This is a great salsa that can be used in any way regular salsa can be used. I like it over chicken or pork tenderloin. The fresh raspberry taste is enhanced by the bitterness and pungency of the caramel. Two bitter tastes combine to form a sweet taste. I also like to use this salsa alone with corn tortillas that have been heated on a non-stick grill or skillet. It makes the perfect low-fat snack.

Per tablespoon:
Calories—18; Fat—.1 g; Protein—.1 g; Carbohydrates—3.6 g; Cholesterol—0 mg; Fiber—.4 g; Sodium—46 mg

1 of the 18 calories is from fat.
6% of the calories come from fat

GRILLED NONFAT CHEESE SANDWICH

2 slices bread
2 slices no-fat American cheese

Butter-flavored vegetable oil spray

Arrange the two slices of cheese between the bread slices so all the bread is covered. Heat a nonstick skillet over medium heat, then spray one side of the bread with the butter-flavored spray and place it down on the skillet. Heat for about 1 minute on the first side, then spray the other side of the sandwich with the butter-flavored spray and heat that side for about one minute. Continue to heat and flip until both sides of the bread are golden brown and the cheese melted. Serve at once. Serves 1.

Lagniappe: Who says you have to give up grilled cheese to eat a low-fat diet? Well you don't. You get the great taste of a real cheese sandwich without the fat. The key is finding a good no-fat cheese. I happen to like Kraft Fat-Free American Singles. You can use the cheddar or Swiss if you like, or a combination. These are fairly close to the real taste and flavor of the fat laden products. Enjoy!

Calories—215; Fat—3 g; Protein—16 g; Carbohydrates—34 g; Cholesterol—10 mg; Fiber—1 g; Sodium—1030 mg

27 of the 215 calories are from fat.
13% of the calories come from fat

PECAN-WHISKEY SAUCE

1 cup sugar
2 1/2 tbsp. cornstarch
1/4 tsp. salt
1 1/2 cups boiling water
2/3 cup whiskey

2 1/2-oz. packets Butter
Buds
2 tbsp. chopped pecans
1 tsp. vanilla extract

Mix the sugar, cornstarch, and salt in a medium saucepan over medium heat. Stir the sugar mixture constantly until some of the sugar begins to melt. It should start to caramelize or turn a light brown. Slowly add the boiling water until it is all used, then reduce the heat and carefully add the whiskey and Butter Buds. Be careful if you are cooking over a gas burner; the whiskey could burst into flames. Cook, stirring often, over low heat for about 6 minutes, or until the sauce is thick and smooth. Remove from the heat, add the pecans and vanilla, and blend it in. This sauce is excellent over bread pudding, angel food cake, or nonfat yogurt. Makes about 2 cups of sauce.

Lagniappe: This is a wonderful low-fat sauce! You will think you are eating an excessively rich butter sauce. This sauce is marvelous over bread pudding. Have as much as you like! You can make this sauce in advance and refrigerate it for later use. It will keep for about a week, refrigerated. To use, just heat up over low heat, stirring until the sauce is warm. *Ça c'est bon!*

Per tbsp. of sauce:
Calories—44; Fat—.2 g; Protein—trace; Carbohydrates—7.1 g; Cholesterol—0 mg; Fiber—0 g; Sodium—43 mg

2 of the 44 calories are from fat.
5% of the calories come from fat

PIMIENTO CHEESE SANDWICHES

3 1-oz. slices no-fat Swiss-
flavored cheese
3 1-oz. slices no-fat
cheddar-flavored cheese
1 2-oz. jar diced pimientos
2 tbsp. finely diced green
bell pepper
1 tbsp. finely chopped
green onion

1 tbsp. picante sauce, hot
or mild
1/2 tsp. yellow prepared
mustard
1/3 cup nonfat mayonnaise
1/4 tsp. fresh ground black
pepper
4 slices fat-free bread

Finely chop the cheeses and add them to a medium-sized mixing bowl. Add all the remaining ingredients, except for the bread. Stir together until well blended. Spread half the mixture on each of two slices of bread and top with the other two slices of bread. Serve at once. Serves 2.

Lagniappe: This recipe first happened on Ash Wednesday at lunch time. We couldn't have meat, and our pantry was fairly bare for our house. What to do? I got the great idea to make pimiento cheese sandwiches, which was one of my favorite sandwiches when I did not care about eating loads of fat. Basically, I had given them up. Well they are back, but in a low-fat version that sure tastes good. All I could think while I was eating this delicious sandwich was, "So this is penance!" It had to be divine inspiration because it tastes heavenly!

Calories—225; Fat—1.1 g; Protein—18.3 g; Carbohydrates—35.8 g; Cholesterol—12 mg; Fiber—4.7 g; Sodium—1480 mg

10 of the 225 calories are from fat.
4% of the calories come from fat

RUM SAUCE

1 cup sugar
1 cup all-purpose flour
2 1/2-oz. packets Butter
Buds

1/2 cup dark rum
1 tsp. vanilla extract

Put all the ingredients in the top of a double boiler that has water in the bottom section and cook over medium heat, stirring until the sauce is light and fluffy. This is a wonderful sauce to use over a bread pudding. Serve hot. Makes about 2 cups of sauce.

Lagniappe: This is nonfat and so luscious it will confound you! You will think you are eating the most extravagant sauce possible. This is splendid over bread pudding or any dessert that is enhanced by a sauce. You can make this sauce in advance and refrigerate it for later use. It will keep for about a week in the refrigerator. To use, just warm up over low heat, stirring until the sauce is warm.

Per tablespoon:
Calories—49; Fat—trace; Protein—.4 g; Carbohydrates—9.1 g; Cholesterol—0 mg; Fiber—trace; Sodium—43 mg

Less than 1 of the 49 calories is from fat.
Less than 1% of the calories come from fat

STRAWBERRY ECSTASY PUNCH

6 cups cranberry-strawberry drink, chilled
1/2 gallon strawberry non-fat frozen yogurt, softened

2 cups frozen sliced sweetened strawberries, partially thawed
1 2-liter bottle Seven-Up, chilled

Combine the cranberry-strawberry drink, yogurt, and strawberries in a large punch bowl. Use a wire whisk or electric beater to mix together until the punch is creamy. Pour in the Seven-Up just before you are ready to serve. Serves 20 as a party punch.

Lagniappe: Nonfat frozen yogurt is sinfully delectable. Adding this yogurt to our punch brings it alive and creates a creamy scrumptious treat. Punches are always a focal point at a party, and this one won't let you down. Don't tell your guests that they are drinking a nonfat punch, or at least wait until after they tell you how good it is.

Calories—189; Fat—.1 g; Protein—2.6 g; Carbohydrates—45.7 g; Cholesterol—4 mg; Fiber—.4 g; Sodium—65 mg

Less than 1 of the 189 calories is from fat.
Less than 1% of the calories come from fat

CREAMY CRAB SPREAD

1 lb. fresh lump crabmeat
2/3 cup finely chopped
  green onions
1 tbsp. minced celery
2 tbsp. diced red bell
  pepper
1 tbsp. fresh lemon juice

1 tsp. Cajun Spice Mix (see
  page 274)
2 tbsp. fat-free mayonnaise
2 tbsp. no-fat sour cream
1 tbsp. fresh parsley,
  minced
1/2 tsp. Tabasco® Sauce

Look through the lump crabmeat and pick out any obvious shells that might have been overlooked by the pickers. In a large mixing bowl, mix together all the remaining ingredients until well blended. Gently blend in the crabmeat. Take care not to tear the delicate pieces of lump meat, but make sure everything is coated well with the sauce. Chill for at least 2 hours or overnight. Serve as a spread on nonfat crackers, chips, or fresh French bread. Makes about 3 cups of spread. Serves 10 people as a spread.

Lagniappe: This is simple, easy, and scrumptious! Not only does this make an excellent spread, but you can use this spread to make other dishes like Crabmeat Stuffed Tomatoes or Chilled Crabmeat Crêpes St. Martinville. The nice thing about lump crabmeat is that it is almost impossible to mess up a recipe with it. It is so delicate, rich, and filling, but surprisingly low in fat (although it is high in cholesterol).

When you buy a pound of lump crabmeat, it may seem expensive, but it goes far and you are buying pure meat—no fillers. It is also ready to eat right from the carton, so all you have to do is mix it into your dish. Often we make the mistake of thinking that we have to sauté it in loads of butter for any taste to come of it. Try this recipe and you can be the judge. You can make this spread completely the day before and refrigerate it until you serve it. How easy can you get?

Calories—49; Fat—.5 g; Protein—8.6 g; Carbohydrates—2.3 g; Cholesterol—35 mg; Fiber—.1 g; Sodium—134 mg

4 of the 49 calories are from fat.
8% of the calories come from fat.

Index